Machiavelli and the Orders of Violence

Niccolò Machiavelli is the most prominent and notorious theorist of violence in the history of European political thought – prominent because he is the first to candidly discuss the role of violence in politics, and notorious because he treats violence as virtue rather than as vice. In this original interpretation, Yves Winter reconstructs Machiavelli's theory of violence and shows how it challenges moral and metaphysical ideas. Winter attributes two central theses to Machiavelli. First, violence is not a generic technology of government but a strategy that tends to correlate with inequality and class conflict. Second, violence is best understood not in terms of conventional notions of law enforcement, coercion, or the proverbial "last resort," but as performance. Most political violence is effective not because it physically compels another agent who is thus coerced; rather, it produces political effects by appealing to an audience. As such, this book shows how in Machiavelli's world violence is designed to be perceived, experienced, remembered, and narrated.

YVES WINTER is assistant professor of political science at McGill University. His research is concerned with critical and historical approaches to violence and with conceptions of political order. His work has been published in *Political Theory, Contemporary Political Theory, Constellations, International Theory, Social Research*, and *New Political Science*.

Machiavelli and the Orders of Violence

YVES WINTER

McGill University

CAMBRIDGE
UNIVERSITY PRESS

CAMBRIDGE
UNIVERSITY PRESS

University Printing House, Cambridge CB2 8BS, United Kingdom

One Liberty Plaza, 20th Floor, New York, NY 10006, USA

477 Williamstown Road, Port Melbourne, VIC 3207, Australia

314–321, 3rd Floor, Plot 3, Splendor Forum, Jasola District Centre, New Delhi – 110025, India

79 Anson Road, #06–04/06, Singapore 079906

Cambridge University Press is part of the University of Cambridge.

It furthers the University's mission by disseminating knowledge in the pursuit of education, learning, and research at the highest international levels of excellence.

www.cambridge.org
Information on this title: www.cambridge.org/9781108426701
DOI: 10.1017/9781108635578

First published 2018

Printed in the United States of America by Sheridan Books, Inc.

A catalogue record for this publication is available from the British Library.

Library of Congress Cataloging-in-Publication Data
NAMES: Winter, Yves, author.
TITLE: Machiavelli and the orders of violence / Yves Winter.
DESCRIPTION: First edition. | Cambridge ; New York : Cambridge University Press, 2018. | Includes bibliographical references.
IDENTIFIERS: LCCN 2018010097| ISBN 9781108426701 (hardback) | ISBN 9781108445443 (pbk.)
SUBJECTS: LCSH: Machiavelli, Niccolò, 1469-1527–Criticism and interpretation. | Political violence. | Violence.
CLASSIFICATION: LCC JC143.M4 W56 2018 | DDC 303.601–dc23
LC record available at https://lccn.loc.gov/2018010097

ISBN 978-1-108-42670-1 Hardback
ISBN 978-1-108-44544-3 Paperback

Contents

Acknowledgments   *page* vii

Note on Texts Cited   xi

    Introduction   1

1 Spectacle   34

2 Force   66

3 Cruelty   89

4 Beginnings   111

5 Institutions   141

6 Tumults   167

    Conclusion   192

Bibliography   201

Index   221

Acknowledgments

I have written the bulk of this book since moving to McGill in 2013, yet the ideas that animate it have been gestating for a long time before transpiring in their current form. The life of the mind is supposed to be solitary, but I am not very good at working in isolation. Hence, over the years, I have incurred a great number of debts to people and institutions who have supported my work along the way.

This book has benefited from two terrific manuscript workshops, one in New York, organized by Antonio Vázquez-Arroyo, and one at McGill, with the Montreal Groupe de Recherche Interuniversitaire en Philosophie Politique, organized by Jacob Levy and Saleema Nawaz Webster and chaired by Hasana Sharp. I owe a special debt to the commentators for their thorough and detailed suggestions: in New York, Robyn Marasco, Antonio Vázquez-Arroyo, Nick Xenos, and Jennifer Duprey; and in Montreal, Jason Frank, Karuna Mantena, Peter Stacey, Paula Clarke, Christian Nadeau, and Matthias Fritsch. I am also grateful to all who read and discussed the manuscript, including Arash Abizadeh, Aberdeen Berry, Cameron Cotton-O'Brien, Kieran Jimenez, Eliot Litalien, Catherine Lu, Briana McGinnis, Will Roberts, Derval Ryan, Travis Smith, and Muhammad Velji.

Over the years, a number of people have commented on parts of the manuscript, and I wish I could acknowledge them all. My principal interlocutors in writing this book have been Antonio Vázquez-Arroyo, Will Roberts, Robyn Marasco, and Hasana Sharp. Each of them raised pivotal questions and offered insightful comments. They have made the book more robust, more assertive, and more precise than I could have otherwise. Among the Machiavellisti, John McCormick, Filippo Del

Lucchese, and Miguel Vatter have offered important feedback. They each conveyed incisive observations and criticisms of the project and of various chapters that have greatly improved the argument.

Gretchen Bakke read an early version of the entire manuscript and was instrumental in helping me conceive of the book as a whole. Earlier versions of several chapters were presented at the annual meetings of the American Political Science Association, the Association for Political Theory, the European Consortium for Political Research, and the Western Political Science Association, as well as at conferences, workshops, and invited lectures at Brunel University, McGill University, University of Chicago, University of Minnesota, and Université de Montréal. I thank the participants and the organizers of these events, especially (in addition to the people already named) Yann Allard-Tremblay, Ivan Ascher, Banu Bargu, Sonali Chakravarti, Michelle Clarke, Patrick Coby, Mary Dietz, Andrew Dilts, Jérémie Duhamel, Fabio Frosini, Dustin Howes, Jack Jackson, Mark Jurdjevic, Victoria Kahn, Demetra Kasimis, Alex Livingston, Amanda Maher, James Martel, Melissa Matthes, Lida Maxwell, Keally McBride, Alison McQueen, Mihaela Mihai, Cynthia Milton, Jeanne Morefield, Vittorio Morfino, Rose Owen, David Owen, Gabriele Pedullà, Tania Rispoli, Robert Sparling, Mathias Thaler, and Will Wittels.

Most of what I know about performance theory I learnt from Joshua Chambers-Letson. At critical junctures, he and Sonali Chakravarti provided encouragement and advice. Sometime last year, they persuaded me to finally let go of the manuscript.

My colleagues at McGill University have enthusiastically engaged with my work. I owe particular thanks to Arash Abizadeh, Jacob Levy, Catherine Lu, Victor Muñiz-Fraticelli, Will Roberts, Hasana Sharp, Christa Scholtz, Mark Antaki, Evan Fox-Decent, and Gavin Walker. Among my former colleagues at Minnesota, I would like to thank Nancy Luxon, Joan Tronto, Dara Strolovitch, Regina Kunzel, and Bud Duvall for creating an invigorating intellectual environment. Dara has been a formidable mentor to me.

My interests in Machiavelli and in theories of violence date to my graduate studies. At Berkeley, I had the privilege of working with Wendy Brown, whose theoretical imagination and pedagogy continue to be a model. I am grateful to Étienne Balibar and Judith Butler for introducing me to a conceptual language for thinking about violence. My thinking about violence has been shaped by countless conversations with Hagar Kotef, whose intellect has left traces all over this book. The intellectual community at Berkeley was formidable, and it is difficult to convey how much I benefited from many conversations with Michael Allan, Diana Anders, Libby Anker, Ivan Ascher, Nima Bassiri, David Bates, Jimmy Casas Klausen, Pheng Cheah, George Ciccariello-Maher, Michelle Dizon, Jack Jackson, Katherine Lemons, Saba Mahmood, Peter Skafish, Sharon Stanley, Paul Thomas, Andrew Weiner, Susanne Wengle, Ben Wurgaft, Ben Yost, and Ben Young. Katrin Meyer spent many hours discussing Machiavelli with me and Gabriel Rockhill and I had endless conversations about methods. I learnt a lot from these exchanges. The friendship and intellectual camaraderie of Patricia Purtschert and Yannik Thiem have been cornerstones of my life in more ways than I can express.

My editor at Cambridge University Press, Robert Dreesen, has been enthusiastic about this project from its early stages. I would also like to thank Joshua Penney, Kevin Hughes, and Sindhu Ayyappan for copy-editing and production. Chriscinda Henry steered me to the cover image by the Florentine painter Andrea del Sarto. For their research assistance, I would like to thank Helen Baker, Oliver Chan, and especially Kelsey Brady.

An earlier version of Chapter 6 was published in *Political Theory* ("Plebeian Politics: Machiavelli and the Ciompi Uprising." *Political Theory* 40, no. 6 [2012]: 736–66). Mary Dietz, the journal's editor at the time, sent me six pages of single-spaced comments on the original article manuscript. I am yet to recover from this act of gratuitous benevolence.

Work on this project was funded by a research grant from the Fonds de recherche du Québec – Société et culture (FRQSC). At McGill, I also received financial and institutional assistance from the Department of Political Science, the Arts Research Internship Award, and the Yan P. Lin Centre's Research Groups on Constitutional Studies and on Global Justice. At the University of Minnesota, the Department of Political Science and the Imagine Fund provided support. Postdoctoral fellowships offer convenient opportunities for revising a dissertation, though I used mine to begin new research projects. Still, my thanks go to Wesleyan University's Center for the Humanities, the Andrew W. Mellon Foundation, and the Swiss National Science Foundation.

I am grateful to my family for their love and support. Thank you to Ada Winter-Rabeau, André and Karin Winter, Jaron Winter, and Daniel and Mary Lemons. Katherine Lemons has had to live with Machiavelli for more than a decade. Her perceptiveness, insight, energy, and love have sparked more flames in my life and work than I can account for. My debt and gratitude to her know no bounds. Anouk Noa Lemons-Winter and Nasim Élias Lemons-Winter were both born during the writing of this book. They have brought love, curiosity, and wonder into the world.

Note on Texts Cited

Unless otherwise indicated, I have relied on the following editions and translations:

CW   *Machiavelli: The Chief Works and Others*, trans. Allan Gilbert, 3 vols. (Durham: Duke University Press, 1989).

D   *Discorsi sopra la prima deca di Tito Livio*. In *Opere I*, ed. Corrado Vivanti (Turin: Einaudi Gallimard, 1997).
Discourses on Livy, trans. Harvey C. Mansfield and Nathan Tarcov (Chicago: University of Chicago Press, 1996).

EN   *Edizione Nazionale delle Opere di Niccolò Machiavelli*, ed. Jean-Jacques Marchand, Mario Martelli, Francesco Bausi et al. (Rome: Salerno, 2001–17).

FH   *Istorie Fiorentine*. In *Opere III*, ed. Corrado Vivanti (Turin: Einaudi, 2005).
Florentine Histories, trans. Laura F. Banfield and Harvey C. Mansfield (Princeton, NJ: Princeton University Press, 1988).

OP   *Machiavelli: Opere*, ed. Corrado Vivanti, 3 vols. (Turin: Einaudi, 1997–2005).

P   *Il Principe*, ed. Giorgio Inglese (Turin: Einaudi, 2013–14).
The Prince, trans. Harvey C. Mansfield, second edition (Chicago: University of Chicago Press, 1998).

Introduction

Violence has always been the *ultima ratio* in political action.
— Hannah Arendt, *The Origins of Totalitarianism*

It has been and remains one of the abiding concerns of the Western political theorist to weave ingenious veils of euphemism to conceal the ugly fact of violence.
— Sheldon Wolin, *Politics and Vision*

A POLITICAL THEORY OF VIOLENCE

Violence is sometimes depicted as a symptom of political disorder, of chaos, and even as an antonym of order. Hence the proscription of unsanctioned violence is often cited as one of the structural imperatives and historical successes of modern liberal states. On the flip side of the coin, maintaining a space in which violence is outlawed depends conceptually and empirically on the state's capacity and periodic deployment of overwhelming forms of repressive violence.[1] Thus the very order that is threatened by violence relies on it, both as a means by which it is instituted and as a mechanism of its reproduction. Violence, in other words, is both subject to orders and constitutive of them. The expression "orders of violence" is mine rather than Machiavelli's, but the word

---

[1] On this antinomy, see Étienne Balibar, *Violence and Civility: On the Limits of Political Philosophy*, trans. G. M. Goshgarian (New York: Columbia University Press, 2015), 1–24.

"orders" [*ordini*] figures prominently in the Machiavellian lexicon. It sometimes denotes rules or institutions and sometimes formations or ways of doing something. To think of formations of violence in terms of "orders" thus addresses not only violence's constitutive implication in political order but also the ways in which it is organized, sequenced, and coordinated.

Political violence is not a uniform phenomenon. Some formations of violence seek to reproduce the status quo, others seek to transform it; some are ostentatiously exhibited, others are out of sight. To address these formations in a way that goes beyond platitudes requires a grasp of how, in each case, violence functions, what its internal logics and mechanisms are, whether violence is concealed or displayed, actual or latent, escalating or suspended. These diverse forms pose a challenge to political theorists. They suggest that attempts to theorize violence by subsuming its forms under a single conceptual umbrella are likely to disappoint. To treat violence in an undifferentiated way, whether as an evil to be proscribed from the political world or an all-purpose instrument stored in the cliché-ridden political toolbox, cannot account for the heterogeneity of its forms. Political violence is best understood as historically specific effects of strategies and tactics deployed against the background of a given balance of forces. This is what Machiavelli argued five centuries ago, and it remains true today. Rather than treating violence as an evil, Machiavelli demystifies it and views it as a political tactic. Proposing an embodied and materialist analysis of how violence operates, what its causes and effects, phenomenal forms, targets, mechanisms, and circuits are, he makes political violence thinkable. In doing so, he puts forward a historical and political perspective that deflates, depersonalizes, and de-moralizes violence in politics, three moves that are crucial for a political reckoning with questions of violence.

Machiavelli is an analyst, advocate, and critic of violence. As an analyst, he probes the causes, dynamics, and functions of violence in the formation and reproduction of states. As an advocate, he defends particular modes of violence – especially anti-oligarchic ones – as politically justified while denouncing gratuitous bloodshed. And as a critic, he offers an abiding challenge to moral and ontological approaches to political violence. A Machiavellian perspective calls into question a number of presuppositions that inform modern liberal and democratic political discourses. It challenges the idea that political violence is an index of social disintegration and political disorder. It calls into question the liberal vision of political modernity as an epochal effort to contain violence.

It disputes the identification of violence with tyranny and authoritarian government, just as it queries the romantic aspiration to evacuate violence from political life altogether. It casts doubt on the idea that violence can be conclusively separated from speech; that cruelty is an archaic and politically defunct mode of violence; and that violence marks the natural prehistory and founding rationale of the modern state, yet is overcome by the very form of that state. But it also questions the modern realist's conviction that violence represents a pre-political instrument of nature and as such, an inescapable last resort.

Everyone knows that violence can be used to kill and to maim and that the threat of physical violence compels people to do things they would otherwise refuse. But beyond these truisms, what do we know about the mechanics by which violence produces political effects? Political theorists and philosophers have frequently debated when and under what conditions violence is legitimate. They have sometimes, less frequently, asked what violence is. But they have rarely ventured into describing and analyzing the mechanisms of its production, circulation, and consumption. As a result, political theorists know a fair amount about the *when* of violence but little about the *what* and the *how*.

The debate about violence in contemporary political theory and philosophy is characterized by a peculiar conjunction: an explosion of discourse about violence coupled with a series of disavowals. While academic debates proliferate, violence is routinely *depoliticized*. That is to say, violence is relegated outside the domain of politics or treated as an unpolitical implement within. Let me briefly sketch four ways in which this depoliticization tends to take place: (1) marginalization, (2) technicization, (3) moralization, and (4) ontologization.

Marginalization. The most obvious manner in which violence is depoliticized is by representing it as alien or peripheral to the political sphere.[2] Theorists who regard discourse or persuasion as the characteristic medium of politics often depict violence as anomalous, exceptional, or pathological, as a mode of conduct at odds with the conventions of

---

[2] One version of such marginalization frames democracy as a fundamental opposite of violence. In Barrington Moore's words, "One quite strongly held opinion about the connection between violence and democracy holds that modern Western democracy is both an improved substitute for violence and altogether incompatible with any form of violence. Ballots are better than bullets, so the saying goes, and fortunate is the country that has learned to substitute free discussion for violence from either the right or the left." Barrington Moore, Jr. "Thoughts on Violence and Democracy" *Proceedings of the Academy of Political Science* 29, no. 1 (1968), 1.

political life.[3] The natural law tradition conventionally characterized the transition from the state of nature to society as a renunciation of natural violence. Thus violence is figured as an uncivilized or premodern relic, left behind or transformed at the proverbial threshold of the political world. Frequently represented as naked, crude, and mute, violence is considered as a product of pre-political nature. Sometimes, such naturalizations take the form of essentialist claims about human nature, for instance the idea that aggression is an immutable feature of human psychology; sometimes they take the opposite tack, depicting violence as fundamentally unnatural and inhuman; and at other times, they represent violence as an all-too human weakness, a sort of character vice that demands therapy in the form of moral education.[4] What unites these approaches is that they imagine violence as a pre-political vestige that needs to be channeled, diverted, or reworked.

Technicization. The type of philosophical liberalism that marginalizes violence along such lines is frequently ridiculed as naïve by authors who describe themselves as realists. Realist political discourse typically concedes – as a matter of course – that violence plays an important role in political life.[5] In fact, many realists regard violence as such an obvious instrument in politics that they consider the entire debate about violence trivial.[6] Yet by deeming violence banal and transparent, such authors also proceed to depoliticize it. When violence is treated as a "last resort" or

---

[3] Habermas's theory of communicative power which seeks to "strip ... power of its violent substance by rationalizing it" is a perfect example. See Jürgen Habermas, *Between Facts and Norms: Contributions to a Discourse Theory of Law,* trans. William Rehg (Cambridge: Polity, 1996), 188, see also 151, 182.

[4] For some classic formulations of authors who derive violence from philosophical anthropologies, see René Girard, "Mimesis and Violence: Perspectives in Cultural Criticism," *Berkshire Review* 14 (1979); Konrad Lorenz, *On Aggression,* trans. Marjorie Kerr Wilson (New York: Harcourt Brace Jovanovich, 1974). The idea that violence is a disruption of the natural order of things goes back to Aristotle. See Aristotle, *Physics,* trans. R. P. Hardie, and R. K. Gaye (Princeton, NJ: Princeton University Press, 1984), 230a29–b9, 253b33–255b35. For violence as a character vice with moral education as its antidote, see Richard Rorty, *Contingency, Irony, and Solidarity* (Cambridge: Cambridge University Press, 1989), 141.

[5] Kenneth Waltz writes: "In politics force is said to be the ultima ratio." Kenneth N. Waltz, *Theory of International Politics* (Reading, MA: Addison-Wesley, 1979), 113.

[6] Richard Tuck notes: "Of course, when the Roman texts were accorded overwhelming respect, as began to happen in fifteenth century Italy, Roman ideas about the need for a city to use relatively unscrupulous violence in the pursuit of liberty and glory naturally resurfaced in a strong form – most famously and distinctively in the case of Machiavelli. As we can now see, however, in this area he simply put very clearly indeed something which had always been present in the Roman texts, the character of which does not need further repeating."

as the "ultima ratio" of politics, the implicit premise is that violence is tantamount to enforcement. It imposes a political will by coercing other actors to perform or desist from particular acts. Violence is thus regarded as a mechanistic cause; its various instantiations are presumed to be isomorphic, translatable into gradated expressions of potency and impact.[7] Accordingly, violence poses primarily operational problems, and insofar as it is just a tool, there is little that is theoretically profound about it. In Hannah Arendt's well-known words, violence is "incapable of speech," which is why "political theory has little to say about the phenomenon of violence and must leave its discussion to the technicians."[8]

Moralization. Violence is routinely represented as an evil. As such, moral and political philosophers have subjected it to endless debates about the conditions under which its use is permissible. From just war theory through the dirty hands problem, to the torture and ticking bomb controversies, there are entire genres of moralistic discourse that approach violence exclusively as a problem of justification.[9] One of the characteristics of these debates is that they are astonishingly abstract and replete with esoteric thought experiments.[10] Such abstraction triggers a third kind of depoliticization, because it obscures the contexts of power and domination in which violence is actually deployed, sanitizing the moral considerations of any contamination by political reality. In doing so, they typically bracket considerations of causes, dynamics, and implications. Often implied is a conception of violence as an apolitical or antipolitical acid that eats away

---

Tuck's argument that Machiavelli is merely an echo chamber for the Roman adage that politics relies on violence is undercut by his obsessive invocation of a rhetoric of evidence. The rhetorical appeal to self-evidence ("of course,"..."naturally,"..."as we can now see,"..."simply,"..."very clearly indeed") raises a question: If it is so obvious that unscrupulous violence is the natural means for liberty and glory, then why does this self-evident truth need an armada of adverbial amplifiers? See Richard Tuck, *The Rights of War and Peace: Political Thought and International Order from Grotius to Kant* (Oxford: Oxford University Press, 1999), 2.

[7] See Dustin E. Howes, *Toward a Credible Pacifism: Violence and the Possibilities of Politics* (Albany: State University of New York Press, 2009), 2.

[8] Hannah Arendt, *On Revolution* (London: Penguin, 1990), 19.

[9] Here I have in mind not the classic restatement of Just War theory by Michael Walzer, which deserves credit for its attempt to think through historical cases but rather recent work by revisionist authors. See, for example, Jeff McMahan, "Innocence, Self-Defense and Killing in War," *Journal of Political Philosophy* 2, no. 3 (1994); David Rodin, *War and Self-Defense* (Oxford: Clarendon Press, 2002).

[10] See for instance Frances Kamm, "Terrorism and Severe Moral Distinctions," *Legal Theory* 12, no. 1 (2006); Jeff McMahan, "Torture in Principle and in Practice," *Public Affairs Quarterly* 22, no. 2 (2008).

at the normative foundations of social and political life. On this view, violence is an exogenous threat to moral life yet nonetheless susceptible to evaluation by the ledgers of moral philosophy.

Ontologization. Historically, the ontology of violence has frequently been framed in terms of a panoply of metaphysical binaries that oppose violence to nature, culture, representation, language, and logos. These metaphysical schemas depoliticize violence by definitional *fiat*, along the same lines as the marginalization discussed earlier. A philosophically more sophisticated version of ontologizing violence is advanced by Jacques Derrida (and favored by some strands of radical democratic theory) who regards violence as a condition of signification and of thought as such. Violence, on this reading, refers not to injury of a body or to any phenomena that supervene on preexisting nonviolent situations. Rather, violence is understood as originary, as isomorphic with the act of naming, classifying, and differentiating that is instituted through language.[11] Although this transcendental violence is sometimes distinguished from empirical instances, the equivocation suggests an ambiguity between the two that tends to dematerialize and mystify empirical violence. Historical formations of violence are emptied of political content and treated not as effects of concrete historical struggles but as derivative of a more profound originary violence.

Whether it is by dismissing, trivializing, moralizing, or dematerializing violence, these four faces of depoliticization have contributed to the current impasse in contemporary political theory: the proliferation of discourse about violence coupled with a peculiar disavowal. Machiavelli, I argue, offers a much-needed corrective of such views. He advances a materialist conception of political violence that eschews both liberal moralism and realist technicism without succumbing to ontologization. He contests the idea of violence as natural, naked, or crude and instead advances a conception of political violence that is constitutively entangled

---

[11] Empirical manifestations of violence are derivative of this primary violence, insofar as they presuppose moral categories that are inaugurated by the originary violence of language. See Jacques Derrida, *Of Grammatology*, trans. Gayatri Chakravorty Spivak (Baltimore: Johns Hopkins University Press, 1976), 106, 112; Jacques Derrida, *Writing and Difference*, trans. Alan Bass (London: Routledge, 1978), 79–153. See also Rodolphe Gasché, *Deconstruction: Its Force, Its Violence* (Albany: State University of New York Press, 2016); Elizabeth Grosz, "The Time of Violence: Deconstruction and Value," *Cultural Values* 2, no. 2/3 (1998); Hent de Vries, *Religion and Violence: Philosophical Perspectives from Kant to Derrida* (Baltimore: Johns Hopkins University Press, 2001), xv–xvii, 1; Elizabeth Frazer and Kimberly Hutchings, "Avowing Violence: Foucault and Derrida on Politics, Discourse and Meaning," *Philosophy & Social Criticism* 37, no. 1 (2011).

with symbolic supports, rituals, and dispositions. Political violence, Machiavelli insists, always involves mediation. While violence is always bodily, it is never immediate. These symbolic aspects are central to the ways in which violence produces political effects. Hence Machiavelli treats violence not as a natural residue but as variegated tactics that are subject to specific protocols, logics, and constraints.

TRAJECTORIES OF MACHIAVELLIAN VIOLENCE

This book is both about political violence and about Machiavelli. Machiavelli's preoccupation with violence is widely acknowledged but poorly understood by commentators. In a brief but important section of *Politics and Vision* (originally published in 1960), Sheldon Wolin high-lights the originality of Machiavelli's thinking about violence. Noting Machiavelli's preoccupation with applying violence in a controlled way and dosing it appropriately, Wolin contends that he devised an "economy of violence, a science of the controlled application of force."[12] This idea of an *economy of violence* is central both to my argument about violence and to my interpretation of Machiavelli. Wolin's suggestive but overly condensed pages invite a more sustained and detailed investigation of the topic, yet so far, the Machiavelli scholarship has not delivered the goods. Over the course of the past five decades, some aspects of Machiavellian violence have been treated extensively in the literature: the concepts of the citizen-soldier, social conflict, spectacular executions, and key violent figures such as Romulus, Hannibal, Agathocles, and Cesare Borgia.[13] While studies of these issues have shed light on various dimensions of

---

[12] Sheldon Wolin, *Politics and Vision* (Princeton, NJ: Princeton University Press, 2004), 198. The task of a progressive politics, Merleau-Ponty wrote a decade prior, is to find a violence that subsides over time. On Wolin's reading, Machiavelli may well have been the first author in the history of political thought to articulate this idea. See Maurice Merleau-Ponty, *Humanism and Terror: The Communist Problem*, trans. John O'Neill (Boston: Beacon Press, 1969). On the formulation of an "economy of violence," see also Ettore Janni, *Machiavelli*, trans. Marion Enthoven (London: George G. Harrap, 1930), 282.

[13] On the citizen-soldier, see J. G. A. Pocock, *The Machiavellian Moment: Florentine Political Thought and the Atlantic Republican Tradition* (Princeton, NJ: Princeton University Press, 1975); Timothy J. Lukes, "Martialing Machiavelli: Reassessing the Military Reflections," *The Journal of Politics* 66, no. 4 (2004); Ezio Raimondi, "Machiavelli and the Rhetoric of the Warrior," *MLN* 92, no. 1 (1977); Barbara Spackman, "Politics on the Warpath: Machiavelli's Art of War," in *Machiavelli and the Discourse of Literature*, ed. Albert Russell Ascoli and Victoria Kahn (Ithaca, NY: Cornell University Press, 1993). On class conflict and tumults, see Filippo Del Lucchese, *Conflict, Power, and Multitude in*

Machiavellian violence, they are remarkably discontinuous with one another. In particular, the military studies tend to treat questions of war and military organization as separate from the scenes of cruelty from *The Prince*. J.G.A. Pocock's groundbreaking argument concerning Machiavelli's revival of republicanism stresses the importance of the citizen-soldier yet considers political violence solely as a question of who should bear arms.[14] Similarly, most of the work on Machiavelli's militia project and his *Art of War* treats violence as unpolitical, as if the problem of military organization could be separated from the concerns with force and cruelty developed in the political works.[15] The same goes for recent

Machiavelli and Spinoza (London: Continuum, 2009); John P. McCormick, *Machiavellian Democracy* (Cambridge: Cambridge University Press, 2011); Gabriele Pedullà, *Machiavelli in tumulto: Conquista, cittadinanza e conflitto nei 'Discorsi sopra la prima deca di Tito Livio'* (Rome: Bulzoni, 2011). On executions, see Wayne A. Rebhorn, *Foxes and Lions: Machiavelli's Confidence Men* (Ithaca, NY: Cornell University Press, 1988), 86–134. On Romulus, see Gennaro Sasso, "Machiavelli e Romolo," in *Machiavelli e gli antichi e altri saggi* (Milan and Naples: Ricciardi, 1986–1997), vol. 1. On Hannibal, see Robert Fredona, "*Liberate Diuturna Cura Italiam*: Hannibal in the Thought of Niccolò Machiavelli," in *Florence and Beyond: Culture, Society and Politics in Renaissance Italy: Essays in Honour of John M. Najemy*, ed. David S. Peterson and Daniel E. Bornstein (Toronto: Centre for Reformation and Renaissance Studies, 2008); Jean-Jacques Marchand, "Da Livio a Machiavelli. Annibale e Scipione in *Principe*, XVII," *Parole Rubate: Rivista Internazionale di Studi sulla Citazione* 7, no. 13 (2016). On Agathocles, see Victoria Kahn, *Machiavellian Rhetoric: From the Counter-Reformation to Milton* (Princeton, NJ: Princeton University Press, 1994), 18–43; Victoria Kahn, "Revisiting Agathocles," *The Review of Politics* 75, no. 4 (2013); John P. McCormick, "Machiavelli's Agathocles: From Criminal Example to Princely Exemplum," in *Exemplarity and Singularity: Thinking Through Particulars in Philosophy, Literature, and Law*, ed. Michèle Lowrie and Susanne Lüdemann (London: Routledge, 2015); John P. McCormick, "Machiavelli's Inglorious Tyrants: On Agathocles, Scipio and Unmerited Glory," *History of Political Thought* 36, no. 1 (2015). On Cesare Borgia, see Gennaro Sasso, *Machiavelli e Cesare Borgia: Storia di un giudizio* (Rome: Edizioni dell'Ateneo, 1966); Gennaro Sasso, "Ancora su Machiavelli e Cesare Borgia," *La Cultura* 7, no. 1 (1969); Jean-Jacques Marchand, "L'évolution de la figure de César Borgia dans la pensée de Machiavel," *Schweizerische Zeitschrift für Geschichte / Revue suisse d'histoire* 19, no. 2 (1969).
14 Pocock, *The Machiavellian Moment*.
15 See for instance Marcia L. Colish, "Machiavelli's Art of War: A Reconsideration," *Renaissance Quarterly* 51, no. 4 (1998); Felix Gilbert, "Machiavelli: The Renaissance of the Art of War," in *Makers of Modern Strategy. From Machiavelli to the Nuclear Age*, ed. Peter Paret (Princeton, NJ: Princeton University Press, 1986); Michael Mallet, "The Theory and Practice of Warfare in Machiavelli's Republic," in *Machiavelli and Republicanism*, ed. Gisela Bock, Quentin Skinner, and Maurizio Viroli (Cambridge: Cambridge University Press, 1990); Mikael Hörnqvist, "Perché non si usa allegare i Romani: Machiavelli and the Florentine Militia of 1506," *Renaissance Quarterly* 55, no. 1 (2002); Mikael Hörnqvist, "Machiavelli's Military Project and the Art of War," in *The Cambridge Companion to Machiavelli*, ed. John M. Najemy (Cambridge: Cambridge

studies about empire that have offered important correctives to the conventional and peaceful view of republicanism.[16] As much as these interpretations highlight the imperialist character of Machiavelli's republicanism, they treat the issue of warfare apart from other formations of violence. What is missing from this scholarship is a systematic treatment of political violence, including its various formations and "orders," something this book seeks to offer.

It is not that scholars haven't recognized the weight of violence in Machiavelli's work. But patterns of depoliticization similar to those I identified in the broader literature – marginalization, technicization, moralization, and ontologization – are replicated in the Machiavelli scholarship. On one end of the spectrum are readers who marginalize Machiavelli's preoccupation with violence by confining violence entirely to *The Prince*, thus presenting a sanitized picture of the *Discourses* and the *Florentine Histories*. In this way, violence is associated with one regime type – tyranny – and cordoned off from Machiavelli's theory of republican politics.[17] On the other end of the spectrum is the anti-Machiavellian tradition that ranges from Elizabethan attacks on the evil "Machiavel" to contemporary moralists. Sixteenth-century critics tended to worry about Machiavelli's heresies and his instrumental conception of virtue, whereas today he is reproached for glorifying violence and war.[18]

University Press, 2010). For interpretations of the military writings that pay more attention to the politics of violence, see Raimondi, "Machiavelli and the Rhetoric of the Warrior"; Spackman, "Politics on the Warpath"; Yves Winter, "The Prince and His Art of War: Machiavelli's Military Populism," *Social Research* 81, no. 1 (2014).

[16] Mark Hulliung, *Citizen Machiavelli* (Princeton, NJ: Princeton University Press, 1983); Mikael Hörnqvist, "The Two Myths of Civic Humanism," in *Renaissance Civic Humanism*, ed. James Hankins (Cambridge: Cambridge University Press, 2000); Mikael Hörnqvist, *Machiavelli and Empire* (Cambridge: Cambridge University Press, 2004).

[17] Hans Baron, "Machiavelli: The Republican Citizen and the Author of 'the Prince'," *English Historical Review* 76 (1961); John M. Najemy, "Society, Class, and State in the *Discourses on Livy*," in *The Cambridge Companion to Machiavelli*, ed. John M. Najemy (Cambridge: Cambridge University Press, 2010), 101–2.

[18] On the sixteenth-century critics, see Sydney Anglo, *Machiavelli – The First Century: Studies in Enthusiasm, Hostility, and Irrelevance* (Oxford: Oxford University Press, 2005); Victoria Kahn, "Machiavelli's Reputation to the Eighteenth Century," in *The Cambridge Companion to Machiavelli*, ed. John M. Najemy (Cambridge: Cambridge University Press, 2010). For the contemporary criticisms, see Gerhard Ritter, *Die Dämonie der Macht: Betrachtungen über Geschichte und Wesen des Machtproblems im politischen Denken der Neuzeit* (Stuttgart: H.F.C. Hannsmann, 1947); Neal Wood, "Machiavelli's Concept of *virtù* Reconsidered," *Political Studies* 15, no. 2 (1967); Markus Fischer, "Machiavelli's Rapacious Republicanism," in *Machiavelli's Liberal Republican Legacy*, ed. Paul A. Rahe (Cambridge: Cambridge University Press, 2006);

By attributing to him a noninstrumental conception of violence (a valorization of violence as an end in itself), these traditional moralists condemn Machiavelli as a promoter of evil. By contrast, Leo Strauss and some of his followers read him as a teacher of evil precisely because of his instrumental conception of violence and the attendant subversion of the classical connection between politics and ethics.[19]

To ascribe to Machiavelli an inversion of the conventional moral stance on violence, i.e. a defense of violence for its own sake, is to misunderstand his political project. This is evident, as Gennaro Sasso notes, when Machiavelli is compared to the classic figures in European political thought that stand for such an inversion of values: Thrasymachus in Plato's *Republic* and Callicles in the *Gorgias*. Both Thrasymachus and Callicles defend the view that states are founded on violence and that justice is nothing other than the advantage of the stronger. But this vision is a far cry from Machiavelli's. In Machiavelli's work, there is no evidence of Thrasymachus's insistence that injustice pays, that the unjust are happy, and that the just are unhappy.[20]

Most modern scholars attribute to Machiavelli – rightly in my view – an *instrumental* conception of violence, but there is considerable disagreement about the nature of this instrument. Narrow views of instrumentality are advanced by readers who ascribe to Machiavelli a proto-scientific analysis of politics.[21] This perspective, common in the postwar period,

Jacques Maritain, "The End of Machiavellianism," in *The Range of Reason* (New York: Scribner, 1952).

[19] Leo Strauss, *Thoughts on Machiavelli* (Chicago: University of Chicago Press, 1958), 232–33; Harvey C. Mansfield, *Machiavelli's Virtue* (Chicago: University of Chicago Press, 1996), 6–28.

[20] Gennaro Sasso, "Introduzione," in *Il principe e altri scritti* (Florence: La nuova Italia, 1963), xxx. A more persuasive version of the view that Machiavelli glorifies violence comes from readers who emphasize Machiavelli's gendered vision of the world and attribute his fascination with violence to his celebration of virility. Yet, while Machiavelli's deeply gendered perspective may account for his preoccupation with violence, it does not get at his theorization and analysis thereof. See Hanna F. Pitkin, *Fortune Is a Woman: Gender and Politics in the Thought of Niccolò Machiavelli* (Berkeley: University of California Press, 1999); Wendy Brown, *Manhood and Politics: A Feminist Reading in Political Theory* (Totowa, NJ: Rowman & Littlefield, 1988); Cary J. Nederman and Martin Morris, "Rhetoric, Violence, and Gender in Machiavelli," in *Feminist Interpretations of Machiavelli*, ed. Maria J. Falco (University Park: Pennsylvania State University Press, 2004).

[21] Herbert Butterfield, *The Statecraft of Machiavelli* (London: G. Bell and Sons Ltd., 1940); Ernst Cassirer, *The Myth of the State* (New Haven, CT: Yale University Press, 1946), 116–62; Leonardo Olschki, *Machiavelli the Scientist* (Berkeley, CA: Gillick Press, 1945); Augustin Renaudet, *Machiavel: Étude d'histoire des doctrines politiques* (Paris: Gallimard, 1942); Luigi Russo, *Machiavelli* (Bari: Laterza, 1949).

regards Machiavelli as an unemotional engineer with a mechanistic notion of violence. While these interpretations have been largely discredited, some of their postulates – that Machiavelli regards violence as a sufficient means and its wielders as capable of controlling and calibrating violence's effects – continue to flourish in recent scholarship.

The abstract conception of violence inherited from this literature has shaped the deadlocked debate about whether Machiavelli's teachings are moral, immoral, or amoral. Much of this debate has centered on Benedetto Croce's claim that Machiavelli separates politics and ethics and develops an anguished conception of the "autonomy of politics."[22] The interminable metanormative controversy about violence's justifications is probably a symptom of our times, reflecting the apprehensions of a political liberalism that condones violence under exceptional conditions yet anxiously chews over possible justifications. Yet whether Machiavelli was an anguished soul who reconciled himself to the occasional use of wicked means to save the state or whether he in fact relished the use of cruelty is beside the point. As in the broader discourse of political theory, these disputes over the morality of violence have diverted attention from Machiavelli's principal focus: rendering violence an object of critical reflection. The quest for moral lucidity is a distraction, because it tempts interpreters either to rescue Machiavelli from the seemingly evil things he says or to blame him for them. In the process, violence is normalized as the prosaic instrument of political order or treated as an exceptional response to conditions of necessity.

Two reasons are often advanced for Machiavelli's preoccupation with violence. The first identifies violence as the indispensable means to govern people who do not spontaneously obey. While they can eventually be lured into docility, force is unavoidable to ensure compliance.[23] The second considers violence to be the outcome of a hopelessly partisan and partial conception of political reality. Violence, on this interpretation,

---

[22] Benedetto Croce, *Politics and Morals*, trans. Salvatore J. Castiglione (New York: Philosophical Library, 1945), 59. For a defense, see Federico Chabod, *Machiavelli and the Renaissance*, trans. David Moore (New York: Harper & Row, 1958), 184. For important critiques, see Isaiah Berlin, "The Originality of Machiavelli," in *Against the Current: Essays in the History of Ideas* (London: Pimlico, 1979); Mansfield, *Machiavelli's Virtue*, 6–52. For an overview, see Eric W. Cochrane, "Machiavelli: 1940–1960," *The Journal of Modern History* 33, no. 2 (1961), 115.

[23] See for instance Skinner's claim that Machiavelli is "an almost Hobbesian skeptic about the possibility of inducing men to behave well except by cajolery or force." Quentin Skinner, *The Foundations of Modern Political Thought* (Cambridge: Cambridge University Press, 1978), 1:185.

results from the incessant conflict in a political world without a neutral and disinterested vantage point.[24] These two ideas – that force is necessary to ensure compliance and that politics is irremediably conflictual – are, I agree, central Machiavellian tenets. Nonetheless, they do not explain the sundry formations of violence Machiavelli observes and discusses in the life of states. Contrary to the opinions often attributed to him, Machiavelli does not offer a set of platitudes about the inescapability of violence in politics. Violence, for Machiavelli, is not the inevitable result of human nature.[25] Neither does it derive from a technical understanding of politics, from a belief that the state is an end in itself, or from an abstract notion of "the political."[26] This puts him in an uneasy relation to the tradition that often claims him as its forebear: political realism.

MACHIAVELLI'S POPULAR REALISM

Machiavelli's criticism of moral and metaphysical ideas has earned him the reputation of being the "first important political realist."[27] And

---

[24] See, for example, Chantal Mouffe, *On the Political* (London: Routledge, 2005), 7. Some of the interpreters who have most strongly emphasized the conflictual character of Machiavelli's conception of politics have been reticent to address violence conceptually. See Claude Lefort, *Machiavelli in the Making*, trans. Michael B. Smith (Evanston, IL: Northwestern University Press, 2012); Antonio Negri, *Insurgencies: Constituent Power and the Modern State*, trans. Maurizia Boscagli (Minneapolis: University of Minnesota Press, 1999); Miguel E. Vatter, *Between Form and Event: Machiavelli's Theory of Political Freedom* (Dordrecht; Boston, MA: Kluwer, 2000).

[25] Contra Strauss, *Thoughts on Machiavelli*, 279; Felix Gilbert, *Machiavelli and Guicciardini: Politics and History in Sixteenth-Century Florence* (Princeton, NJ: Princeton University Press, 1965), 156–57; Berlin, "The Originality of Machiavelli," 41. As Lefort points out, Machiavelli seems quite indifferent to the idea of a pre-political human nature. Lefort, *Machiavelli in the Making*, 225. See also Yves Winter, "Necessity and Fortune: Machiavelli's Politics of Nature," in *Second Nature: Rethinking the Natural through Politics*, ed. Crina Archer, Laura Ephraim, and Lida Maxwell (New York: Fordham University Press, 2013), 27–29.

[26] Machiavelli's considerations have little in common with the abstract and schematic account of the political offered by Carl Schmitt (for whom violence is at once the instrument, effect, and manifestation of the logic of enmity that structures the political). See Carl Schmitt, *The Concept of the Political*, trans. George Schwab (Chicago: University of Chicago Press, 1996).

[27] E. H. Carr, *The Twenty Years' Crisis 1919–1939* (London: Macmillan, 1958), 63. See also Fischer, "Machiavelli's Rapacious Republicanism," 36; Steven Forde, "Varieties of Realism: Thucydides and Machiavelli," *The Journal of Politics* (1992), 373, 387, 389; Grant B. Mindle, "Machiavelli's Realism," *The Review of Politics* 47, no. 2 (1985); Richard Bellamy, "Dirty Hands and Clean Gloves: Liberal Ideals and Real Politics," *European Journal of Political Theory* 9, no. 4 (2010); Daniel R. Sabia, "Machiavelli's Soderini and the Problem of Necessity," *The Social Science Journal* 38(2001); Jonathan

indeed, if one were to seek a political tradition that challenges the depoliticization of violence diagnosed in the previous section, the tradition of political realism would seem an obvious choice. After all, Machiavelli shares some of the basic tenets of most realists: the preference for reality over wishful thinking, the emphasis on motivations and actions, and the recognition that political life is fundamentally conflictual.[28] Thus, international relations theorists such as E. H. Carr, Raymond Aron, and Reinhold Niebuhr pay tribute to Machiavelli as an important source for the realist tradition.[29]

Political realists typically argue that politics – or a part thereof, such as international relations – falls outside the scope of morality. Echoing Carl Schmitt, Hans Morgenthau writes that "the political realist defends the autonomy of the political sphere, as the economist, the lawyer, the moralist maintain theirs."[30] In Carr's words, realists "hold that relations between states are governed solely by power and that morality plays no part in them."[31] While not all realists subscribe to Morgenthau's or Carr's views, many accept a version of the claim that politics is special and hence not subject to ordinary moral constraints. A special case can be made for "dirty hands theorists," who defend the comprehensive scope of morality but concede that moral demands may be trumped by other considerations.[32]

Haslam, *No Virtue Like Necessity: Realist Thought in International Relations since Machiavelli* (New Haven, CT: Yale University Press, 2002).

[28] See for instance Bernard Williams, *In the Beginning Was the Deed: Realism and Moralism in Political Argument* (Princeton, NJ: Princeton University Press, 2005), 2; Raymond Geuss, *Philosophy and Real Politics* (Princeton, NJ: Princeton University Press, 2008), 9–13.

[29] Carr, *The Twenty Years' Crisis*, 63; Robert McAfee Brown, ed. *The Essential Reinhold Niebuhr: Selected Essays and Addresses* (New Haven, CT: Yale University Press, 1987), 123; Raymond Aron, *Machiavel et les tyrannies modernes* (Paris: Editions de Fallois, 1993). This is not the case for Morgenthau, who regards Machiavelli as a utopian. Hans J. Morgenthau, "The Machiavellian Utopia," *Ethics* 55, no. 2 (1945).

[30] Hans J. Morgenthau, *Politics among Nations: The Struggle for Power and Peace* (New York: Knopf, 1954), 13, see also 15–16.

[31] According to Carr, "The realist view that no ethical standards are applicable to relations between states can be traced from Machiavelli through Spinoza and Hobbes to Hegel." Carr, *The Twenty Years' Crisis*, 153.

[32] For the classic statement, see Michael Walzer, "Political Action: The Problem of Dirty Hands," *Philosophy & Public Affairs* 2, no. 2 (1973). On the relation between dirty hands theorists and realists, see C. A. J. Coady, "The Problem of Dirty Hands." *The Stanford Encyclopedia of Philosophy* Spring 2014 Edition: https://plato.stanford.edu/archives/spr2014/entries/dirty-hands/.

My view is that Machiavelli's relation to the realist tradition is more complicated than commonly recognized. Machiavelli, I argue, defends a particular and nonconventional form of realism. Against the tendencies of some realists to be ahistorical in their analyses, conservative in their prescriptions, and elitist in their orientations, Machiavelli offers a *historicist*, *radical*, and *popular* realism.

Historicism. Many realist thinkers acknowledge the historicity of politics; nevertheless, most treat violence as a universal and ubiquitous mechanism of coercion and insist on its inescapability in politics. IR realists routinely refer to violence (or "force" as is the preferred nomenclature) as a self-evident and universal instrument of foreign policy.[33] That violence or the threat thereof is an "intrinsic element of politics" seems to be a matter of consensus;[34] yet that the historical diversity of forms and logics of violence makes such claims rather dubious has not received much consideration.[35] The self-declared realists in contemporary political theory do not offer any consolation. They barely touch on violence, and when they do, it is to address questions of legitimacy or to piously recall that all legal and political order ultimately rests on violence.[36] By contrast, Machiavelli observes that timeless and ostensibly universal theorizations of violence are ultimately vacuous. One of his principal criticisms of his contemporaries is that they systematically overestimated the historical solidity of their present, an assessment that seems as pertinent today as it was five hundred years ago. Times change, as Machiavelli frequently notes, and so must the assessment of political strategies. As a thinker deeply concerned with the unpredictable vagaries of political life, one of Machiavelli's main theses is that the analysis of political violence must be conjunctural – that formations of violence need to be evaluated with respect to "the quality of the times" [*la qualità de'tempi*], that is to say, in terms of the particular relations of forces

---

[33] Carr, *The Twenty Years' Crisis*, esp. 191–202.

[34] Morgenthau, *Politics among Nations*, 33.

[35] There are exceptions. For more historically attuned versions of IR realism, see the essays in Duncan Bell, ed. *Political Thought and International Relations: Variations on a Realist Theme* (Oxford: Oxford University Press, 2009).

[36] See for instance Walzer, "Political Action: The Problem of Dirty Hands," 163–64, 174; Williams, *In the Beginning Was the Deed*, 62–63; Geuss, *Philosophy and Real Politics*, 34–35. Bellamy adds more depth to the discussion, but his claim that the "prime Machiavellian lesson concerns the need to remove all political rivals and their armed supporters from the scene, often with the use of extreme force" flattens the political distinctions Machiavelli draws between popular and elite violence. Bellamy, "Dirty Hands and Clean Gloves," 425.

at work in a given historical moment (P 25; D 3.8).[37] And thus his realism is distinctly historicist.[38]

Radicalism. Along similar lines, Machiavelli does not share conventional realism's partiality to the status quo. As Antonio Gramsci points out, Machiavelli's realism is misconstrued as "superficial and mechanical" if one interprets him as defending the status quo instead of what might be or what ought to be.[39] True, Machiavelli famously accords priority to the "effectual truth" over the "imagination" (P 15). Yet *verità effettuale* is not synonymous with the present state of affairs. If it were, Gramsci writes, it would confine readers to their present and prevent them from seeing "beyond their own noses." A political actor of Machiavelli's ilk takes sides and seeks to "create new relations of force." Such an actor has no choice but to move beyond the status quo and deal in ideals and representations. According primacy to the effectual truth, then, is not to prioritize "is" over "ought" but to evaluate whether the ideals that animate a political project are abstract or concrete. Abstract ideals, fashioned by historically arbitrary wishful thinking, are a far cry from concrete ideals, informed by analyses of existing social forces. A political actor who promotes an abstract ideal is guilty of the cardinal Machiavellian sin: letting go "of what is done for what should be done" (P 15). By contrast, a political actor who defends a concrete ideal seeks to bring about a new equilibrium by strengthening socially operative forces considered progressive. Such an actor is grounded in what Gramsci, in a tweak to Machiavelli's terminology, calls the *"realtà effettuale"* but seeks

---

[37] Hence Althusser's claim that Machiavelli is the "first theorist" of the conjuncture. Louis Althusser, *Machiavelli and Us*, trans. Gregory Elliott (London: Verso, 1999), 16, 18. Although the concept can be traced back at least to Diderot (where "conjuncture" is defined as the temporal coincidence of various circumstances that reciprocally affect and modify one another) in the Marxist literature, "conjuncture" refers to the way that the political balance of forces at a given historical moment renders certain tactics effective and others futile. See Denis Diderot, *Encyclopédie, ou dictionnaire raisonné des sciences, des arts et des métiers* (1751–1772), s.v. "conjoncture". http://encyclopedie.uchicago.edu. Antonio Gramsci, *Selections from the Prison Notebooks*, trans. Quintin Hoare and Geoffrey Nowell Smith (New York: International Publishers, 1971), 177–78; Louis Althusser and Étienne Balibar, *Reading Capital*, trans. Ben Brewster (London: New Left Books, 1970), 311; Louis Althusser, *For Marx*, trans. Ben Brewster (London: Verso, 2005), 250.

[38] Behind the repeated references to *nostri tempi, quelli tempi, presenti tempi* is an analysis of political conditions that points to the various forces that shape a constellation. Jean-Claude Zancarini, "Une philologie politique. Les temps et les enjeux des mots (Florence, 1494–1530)," *Laboratoire italien. Politique et société* 7 (2007), 63.

[39] Antonio Gramsci, *Quaderni del carcere*, ed. Valentino Gerratana (Turin: Einaudi, 2007), 3:1577–78.

to overcome and transform that reality. The "ought" in this scenario is concrete; it is "the sole realistic and historicist interpretation of reality, the only history in action and philosophy in action, the only politics." Machiavelli was a radical realist, not in the sense that his books brought about a wholesale transformation of his immediate present – an abstract fantasy – but that they interpret that reality in terms of the possibilities of its transformation.

Unlike some strands of realism that have no patience for representational categories, Machiavelli's realism is not opposed to imagination. On the contrary: It presupposes a political actor's ability to represent and imagine a different reality but anchors this imagination in the concrete forces that define the present.[40] Such a realism differs from the "superficial and mechanical" kind in two respects: It acknowledges the role of the imagination in envisaging alternative political arrangements and it underscores the importance of interpretation, insisting that political reality does not manifest itself transparently but requires interpretation. Because such a realism does not presume that reality is an unmediated category, it implies that a grasp of political reality depends on a set of interpretive skills and a degree of political literacy. Hence Gramsci's conclusion that Machiavelli's work is an exercise in political pedagogy.

Populism. Conventionally, realism is understood as a pedagogy for statesmen, as offering an education for rulers, highlighting the importance of leadership. Machiavelli, by contrast, puts forward what Gramsci calls a "popular realism."[41] Popular realism purveys a pedagogy for the people. It differs from conventional realism by turning realism into an anti-elitist force. Power, Machiavelli insists, can be shared. Like many contemporary scholars, I regard him as much more invested in republican and democratic politics than the conventional realist perspective allows. At the heart of his political project is the idea of political freedom. Freedom is incompatible with the relations of domination ingrained in monarchic and oligarchic regimes. It requires, Machiavelli

---

[40] Viroli glosses such a view as a "realism with imagination" and Del Lucchese refers to Machiavelli's "radical realism." Maurizio Viroli, "Machiavelli's Realism," *Constellations* 14, no. 4 (2007), 466; Del Lucchese, *Conflict, Power, and Multitude in Machiavelli and Spinoza*, 15. See also Joseph Femia, "Gramsci, Machiavelli and International Relations," *The Political Quarterly* 76, no. 3 (2005).

[41] Gramsci, *Quaderni del carcere*, 3:1691.

suggests, political participation and shared rule.[42] Following a distinguished tradition of readers that includes Gentili, Spinoza, Harrington, Rousseau, and Gramsci, I read Machiavelli as a democratic theorist of popular freedom.[43] Without romanticizing the people, he observes that the ends of the many are more "decent" [*onesto*] than those of the few (P 9), which is why his abiding concern is the popular state and the social and historical conditions under which it can be established and reproduced.[44] Popular and democratic government is preferable to its alternatives on grounds of freedom and the common good [*il bene comune*] (D 2.2) – not because the people always make judicious policy

---

[42] Contra elitist interpretations that consider only the "few" to be competent political actors and contra neo-republican scholars who attribute to Machiavelli a thin conception of freedom as non-domination. For examples of elitist interpretations, see Sebastian de Grazia, *Machiavelli in Hell* (New York: Vintage, 1989), 180–83; Mansfield, *Machiavelli's Virtue*, 307; J. Patrick Coby, *Machiavelli's Romans: Liberty and Greatness in the Discourses on Livy* (Lanham, MD: Lexington Books, 1999), 254–56. According to Philip Pettit and Quentin Skinner, the commitment to non-domination that Machiavelli ascribes to the people is a desire for security (Pettit) and protection from interference (Skinner), not an eagerness to rule. From this perspective, self-government and political participation have at best instrumental rather than intrinsic value, insofar as a republican regime is better equipped than others to guarantee security and protection from interference. Philip Pettit, *Republicanism: A Theory of Freedom and Government* (Oxford: Oxford University Press, 1997), 28; Quentin Skinner, *Visions of Politics: Renaissance Virtues* (Cambridge: Cambridge University Press, 2002), 197. By contrast, Mark Jurdjevic compellingly argues that Machiavelli, especially in his late work, conceived of political action and participation as an end in itself. Mark Jurdjevic, *A Great & Wretched City: Promise and Failure in Machiavelli's Florentine Political Thought* (Cambridge, MA: Harvard University Press, 2014), 70–78.

[43] Alberico Gentili, *De legationibus libri tres*, trans. Gordon J. Laing (New York: Oxford University Press, 1924), III.9; Benedictus de Spinoza, *Political Treatise*, ed. Michael L. Morgan, trans. Samuel Shirley (Indianapolis: Hackett, 2002), 5.7; James Harrington, "A System of Politics," in *"The Commonwealth of Oceana" and "A System of Politics"* (Cambridge: Cambridge University Press, 1992), §21, 293; Jean-Jacques Rousseau, *The Social Contract, and Other Later Political Writings*, trans. Victor Gourevitch (Cambridge: Cambridge University Press, 1997), 3.6; Antonio Gramsci, *Quaderni del carcere*, 3:1690. See also McCormick, *Machiavellian Democracy*; Vatter, *Between Form and Event*; Miguel E. Vatter, *Machiavelli's The Prince: A Reader's Guide* (London: Bloomsbury, 2013); Del Lucchese, *Conflict, Power, and Multitude in Machiavelli and Spinoza*; Filippo Del Lucchese, "Machiavelli and Constituent Power: The Revolutionary Foundation of Modern Political Thought," *European Journal of Political Theory* (2014); Filippo Del Lucchese, *The Political Philosophy of Niccolò Machiavelli* (Edinburgh: Edinburgh University Press, 2015); Christopher J. Holman, *Machiavelli and the Politics of Democratic Innovation* (Toronto: University of Toronto Press, forthcoming).

[44] As Althusser notes, "the prince's practice is unintelligible if it is not appreciated that this state is a state rooted in the people, a popular state. The popular character of the state determines the prince's political practice." Althusser, *Machiavelli and Us*, 81.

or because the many are inherently incorruptible. And while Machiavelli does not advance a comprehensive vision of the good, by *bene comune* he means more than just preserving the state.[45]

This popular perspective has implications for interpreting political violence. Machiavelli's realism is popular, because he differentiates forms of violence both in terms of their objectives and in terms of their provenance. Violence in the service of shared power is not the same as violence in the service of usurpation. And violence from above cannot be equated to violence from below. Kicking down is not the same as punching up, and the strategies available to elites differ from those available to the plebs. Elites tend to have resources at their disposal that allow them to assemble significant military and political forces to pursue their objectives. By contrast, plebeians must rely on numbers and on targeting elite privileges and social standing.

For Machiavelli, the degree and incidence of violence varies, and the primary determinant of that variation is political and socioeconomic inequality. Violence is the product of political dynamics that are centrally connected to inequality and class conflict. The more unequal a state is, the more violence it will need in order to reproduce its social and political formation. Machiavelli offers three reasons for treating violence as a function of inequality. First, he associates violence not with a generic technology of government but with struggles over the basic structure of social and political orders. All social orders, he asserts, are composed of two antagonistic classes – the people and the *grandi* – each animated by distinct aspirations or humors [*umori*]: the people by a desire not to be oppressed, and the *grandi* by an appetite to command and dominate (P 9; see also D 1.5; FH 2.12). By *grandi* Machiavelli means not just the hereditary nobility but anyone who benefits from economic and political privilege, whether that privilege is based on birth, wealth, power, or prominence. Accordingly, Machiavelli calls the *grandi* by a variety of different names, sometimes labeling them *ottimati, nobili, signori, potenti, ricchi*, and *gentiluomini*.[46] While the conflict between these asymmetric dispositions can be directed into nonviolent outlets and does not always precipitate bloodshed, it forms the background structure for all incidences

---

[45] Christian Nadeau, "Machiavel: Domination et liberté politique," *Philosophiques* 30, no. 2 (2003), 324.

[46] This lexical range testifies less to the sundry sources of elite status than to their equivalence. Alfredo Bonadeo, "The Role of the 'Grandi' in the Political World of Machiavelli," *Studies in the Renaissance* 16(1969), 10–12.

of political violence. By emphasizing what Filippo Del Lucchese has called the "conflictual structure of reality," Machiavelli proposes a schema that makes political violence thinkable not simply as a last resort but also as a series of heterogeneous strategies of concrete struggles. [47]

The second reason why violence is a function of inequality has to do with Machiavelli's understanding of corruption. For Machiavelli, corruption is not the result of moral decline but of inequality, and to the extent that violence tracks political decay, it is a symptom of such inequality rather than of moral turpitude. Early fifteenth-century humanists such as Leonardo Bruni (1370–1444) and Poggio Bracciolini (1380–1459) had regarded private wealth as a means for civic virtue, but by the early sixteenth century, the Florentine intellectual circle in which Machiavelli was a prominent participant had developed a much more critical perspective on private fortunes.[48] Free cities, Machiavelli argues, need to keep the public rich and the individual citizens poor – an idea that would have been inconceivable to Bruni or Bracciolini.[49] Socioeconomic equality, Machiavelli contends, is a condition for a "political and uncorrupt way of life" (D 1.55). Inequality, by contrast, causes corruption and decay. It subverts public life, establishes unaccountable forms of social power, and introduces patron–client relationships that erode and ultimately ruin political freedom (D 1.7, 1.17, 3.22, 3.28).[50]

---

[47] Del Lucchese, *The Political Philosophy of Niccolò Machiavelli*, 41. See also Lefort, *Machiavelli in the Making*.

[48] See Felix Gilbert, "Bernardo Rucellai and the Orti Oricellari: A Study of the Origins of Modern Political Thought," *Journal of the Warburg and Courtauld Institutes* 12(1949).

[49] Machiavelli's assessment in *Discourses* 1.37 is foreshadowed by Guicciardini's *Discorso di Logrogno*. See Francesco Guicciardini, "How the Popular Government Should Be Reformed [Discorso Di Logrogno]," in *Cambridge Translations of Renaissance Philosophical Texts*, ed. Jill Kraye (Cambridge: Cambridge University Press, 1997), 230–32. Quentin Skinner remarked on the gulf separating the fifteenth- and sixteenth-century republicans on this point. See Skinner, *Foundations of Modern Political Thought*, 1:170.

[50] Contra Pocock, who advances the baffling claim that for Machiavelli, "inequality ... connotes neither inequality of wealth nor inequality of political authority – there is no reason to suppose that Machiavelli objected to either." Pocock, *The Machiavellian Moment*, 209. Gisela Bock follows Pocock in denying the relevance to Machiavelli of inequality of wealth but concedes his concern with inequality of status. Gisela Bock, "Civil Discord in Machiavelli's Istorie Fiorentine," in *Machiavelli and Republicanism*, ed. Gisela Bock, Quentin Skinner, and Maurizio Viroli (Cambridge: Cambridge University Press, 1990), 189. For critical perspectives, see Eric Nelson, *The Greek Tradition in Republican Thought* (Cambridge: Cambridge University Press, 2004), 77–85; Del Lucchese, *Conflict, Power, and Multitude in Machiavelli and Spinoza*, 70; Amanda Maher, "What Skinner Misses about Machiavelli's Freedom: Inequality, Corruption, and the Institutional Origins of Civic Virtue," *The Journal of Politics* 78, no. 4 (2016).

Third, because of their oligarchic ambitions, the most serious danger to freedom comes from the *grandi*.[51] Their intrinsic desire to dominate can never be entirely satisfied because domination, unlike freedom, has no obvious terminus and can always be further intensified. Thus, the ambitions of the great give rise to incessant intra-elite struggles as well as to relentless attempts to seize more power and wealth, usurp public offices, and procure clients. Elite ambitions fuel both oligarchic and anti-oligarchic violence. And while he deplores the former, Machiavelli often defends the latter as both appropriate and legitimate. It is impossible, Machiavelli writes, to "satisfy the great with decency and without injury to others" (P 9), which is why he categorically recommends that states be built on popular rather than elite support. The *grandi* have both the motivations and the resources to deploy violence for their political objectives. Unless their aspirations to oppress are curbed by the power of the people or by a popular prince, the predictable outcome is endemic violence. As an anti-oligarchic, even democratic, populist, Machiavelli expresses a strong preference for broad-based republican government. Yet his appraisal of the social and political power of elites leads him to argue that under conditions of severe inequality, a principality with a popular base is preferable – on grounds of freedom – to an aristocratic republic.

Hence violence, for Machiavelli, is not an abstract constitutive feature of politics or the state but has social and historical determinations. Set against the background of a social theory of conflict, he makes violence intelligible as elite and popular strategies. Rendering violence intelligible as event, mechanism, and strategy of a popular politics is one of Machiavelli's signal contributions to political theory. His commitment to popular freedom and anti-oligarchic politics is thus central to his account of violence.

THE STRUCTURE OF POLITICAL VIOLENCE

Machiavelli's distinctive approach to violence becomes clear if he is compared to the theorist who is often cited as his heir and who has

---

[51] Russell Price, "Ambizione in Machiavelli's Thought," *History of Political Thought* 3, no. 3 (1982), 401; McCormick, *Machiavellian Democracy*.

offered the most influential characterization of the modern state: Max Weber.[52] In his lecture "Politics as a Vocation," Weber famously argues that "the modern state can be defined sociologically only by the specific means that is peculiar to it: namely, physical violence."[53] For Weber, violence has three defining characteristics: It is (1) an instrument, (2) a product of nature, and (3) an inescapable feature of the political. These three features are encapsulated in the claim that violence is the "specific" and "decisive" means of politics.[54] Lest readers conclude that politics is entirely overshadowed by violence, Weber qualifies his point concerning the importance of violence with two provisos. First, violence is neither the only nor the typical instrument of government, and second, political associations are not the only ones that use violence as their means. Yet violence is peculiar and "indispensable" to the character of a political organization because it "is always the last resort when others have failed."[55] Thus for Weber – and many contemporary social and political theorists follow him on this point – violence is a potentially hazardous but ultimately trivial feature of politics. It is hazardous, because its injudicious exercise by irresponsible political actors can undermine the legitimacy on which its successful monopolization rests; yet it is trivial to the extent that it is never an end in itself, always subject to calculations of instrumental rationality, and invariably coercive in function.[56]

---

[52] Frazer and Hutchings offer an insightful analysis of the concept of violence as developed by Machiavelli, Clausewitz, and Weber. While I concur with the defense of the distinctively *political* character of violence in the work of these three authors, in my view the differences between the three are more salient than Frazer and Hutchings allow. Elizabeth Frazer and Kimberly Hutchings, "Virtuous Violence and the Politics of Statecraft in Machiavelli, Clausewitz and Weber," *Political Studies* 59, no. 1 (2011).

[53] Max Weber, *The Vocation Lectures*, ed. David Owen and Tracy B. Strong, trans. Rodney Livingstone (Indianapolis: Hackett, 2004), 33, trans. mod.

[54] Weber, *The Vocation Lectures*, 84, 89. In *Economy and Society*, Weber refers to violence furthermore as the "specific" and "indispensable" [*unentbehrlich*] means of a political organization. Max Weber, *Economy and Society*, ed. Guenther Roth and Claus Wittich (Berkeley: University of California Press, 1978), 54–55; Max Weber, *Wirtschaft und Gesellschaft* (Tübingen: Mohr Siebeck, 1980), 29–30, see also 514.

[55] Weber, *Economy and Society*, 54–55.

[56] Andreas Kalyvas is right that implicit in Weber's argument is a recognition that "the subterranean meanings lurking below the use of . . . violence" are essential to the state and to politics more broadly. Yet unlike Kalyvas, I think Weber stops short of theorizing these subterranean meanings. Andreas Kalyvas, *Democracy and the Politics of the Extraordinary: Max Weber, Carl Schmitt, and Hannah Arendt* (Cambridge: Cambridge University Press, 2008), 41.

Because of its focus on the instrumental and coercive aspects of political violence, I call Weber's position a "coercive instrumentalism." In contemporary social science, social and political theory, and political philosophy, coercive instrumentalism is the dominant position. Presupposed by both realist and liberal conceptions of violence, coercive instrumentalism treats violence as a species of coercion and regards it as the ultimate "last resort" means available to a political association.[57]

Weber neglects to specify why violent coercion is the ultimate instrument available to political associations, an omission that is revealing because it insinuates that the answer is self-evident. Yet Weber can only omit an explanation for why violent coercion serves as the elementary instrument of politics by tacitly assuming as uncontroversial a highly contestable premise: that violence is a residual instrument of nature and that the propensity to inflict injury or death is a fundamental element of the human condition.[58] This claim treats political violence as the effect of an essential anthropological propensity rather than the result of an immanent political dynamic. Implicit is a view of violence as radical negation, defined by the capacity to kill and destroy. What this perspective neglects (and Machiavelli, by contrast, highlights) is the historical diversity and productivity of forms of violence. By positioning violence as a product of nature, coercive instrumentalists avoid the question of how violence acquires social and political determinations.

What coercive instrumentalists fail to see is that coercion is not the universal paradigm of political violence but a very specific, modern, configuration. Coercion is distinguished by its dyadic structure: It involves an agent using threats to force another agent to do something against their will. It takes the figurative form of a duel, evoked by Weber's definition of power as the ability to exercise "one's will despite resistance."[59] Yet this figure of the duel, while evocative, obscures more

---

[57] In "Politics as a Vocation," Weber shifts seamlessly between the terms *Gewaltsamkeit, Gewalt,* and *Zwang,* betraying a schema of violence that is isomorphic with coercion. Weber, *The Vocation Lectures,* 33, 29.

[58] "Violent social action is obviously something absolutely primordial. Every group, from the household to the political party, has always resorted to physical violence when it had to protect the interests of its members and was capable of doing so." Weber, *Economy and Society,* 904.

[59] Weber, *Economy and Society,* 53, see also 926. In what is a remarkable parallel, Clausewitz describes war in analogous terms, as "an act of force to compel our enemy to do our will." Just as Weber conceives of political violence as essentially dyadic, pitting agents against one another in a contest of coercive capacities, so Clausewitz imagines war as "nothing but a duel on a larger scale." Carl von Clausewitz, *On War,* trans. Michael

than it clarifies. One of the lessons readers can learn from Machiavelli is that most forms of political violence, whether deployed by states or other actors, do not take the form of a contest of two wills. A Machiavellian understanding of violence challenges the dyadic picture of coercion in three important respects. First, violence, for Machiavelli, is not only an instrument but also an act of signification. Second, violence is not a sufficient means but one that is mediated by the passions.[60] And third, the model of political violence is not dyadic but triadic.

Most political violence is effective not because it physically compels another agent who is thus coerced; rather, it produces political effects by appealing to an audience. It is uncommon for political violence to function as a transitive instrument and to take a single direct object as its target. Most forms of political violence are designed to be seen or at least to leave behind visible traces, even when they take place in the secrecy of the torture chamber. Rarely is political violence aimed at a target's will; more typically, it is destined for the senses and the passions of an audience. In this sense, political violence is not coercive, because the body on which it is administered is not its ultimate target. As Machiavelli demonstrates time and again, political violence is a performance, elaborately staged, and designed to be perceived, experienced, remembered, and narrated.

The spectacular, sensory, graphic, dramatic, and iconic dimensions of violence are central to how it generates political effects. This renders violence both more powerful and more limited than the Weberian picture would suggest. It is more powerful because the passions function as multipliers, propagating violence's effects. It is more limited because it challenges the fantasy of mastery that is implicit in liberal and realist conceptions of violence. While the perception, experience, memory, and narration of violence can be choreographed, they can never be fully controlled, rendering the deployment of political violence much more volatile than standard accounts of coercive instrumentalism might suggest. This unpredictability is compounded by the multiple passions evoked by violence. Because Machiavelli does not see in death and in

Howard and Peter Paret (Princeton, NJ: Princeton University Press, 1984), 75. See Reinhard Bendix, *Max Weber: An Intellectual Portrait* (Garden City, NY: Doubleday, 1960), 290.

[60] I use the term "passions" rather than "affect," "feeling," or "emotion" because it evokes the trans-individual and social scene of political desire. See Robyn Marasco, *The Highway of Despair: Critical Theory after Hegel* (New York: Columbia University Press, 2015), 4–5.

bodily pain the ultimate negation and bareness of life, his account of the passions stimulated by violence is more capacious than the ordinary focus on fear. Unlike realists or liberals who connect violence primarily to fear, Machiavelli argues that violence also generates a variety of other politically relevant passionate responses, including desire, hatred, and solidarity. Hence the response to violence is much more difficult to script than one might otherwise assume.

Scholars have yet to reckon with the extent to which violence for Machiavelli is not a transparent and uniform strategy but part of a political pedagogy. Central to this pedagogy is the theatricality of violence – the ways in which violence is staged and represented. On this topic, rhetorical approaches to Machiavelli have made important contributions, yet one of the limitations is that the "rhetoric" that has been analyzed is almost exclusively Machiavelli's, that is to say the relation between the Machiavellian text and its readers.[61] In terms of his study of violence, it is worth looking at Machiavelli not just as a practitioner of rhetoric but also as an *analyst* of the rhetorical and performative dimensions of violence. To think of political violence in terms of performances is to highlight its theatrical and communicative aspects – the ways in which forms of political violence are interlaced with practices of representation. Machiavelli understood that the effectiveness of political violence can only be assessed by asking how violence is seen by a third party. The upshot of this insight is that any meaningful account of political violence has to look at violence not just from the perspective of its immediate target but also from the vantage point of a wider audience.

If political violence is a performance, then subjects who want to be agents must be able to interpret violence, and to do so requires a certain measure of literacy. On this topic, Machiavelli recounts the story of Piero Albizzi, a fourteenth-century Florentine nobleman, who was hosting a banquet when someone sent him a silver goblet filled with sweets and a hidden nail (FH 3.19). When the nail was discovered, the guests at the banquet came up with an elaborate explanation. Rather than probing the most obvious scenarios, that the nail found its way into the goblet by mistake or that it represents a threat against Piero, those present regarded it "as a reminder that he should drive a nail into the wheel [of fortune]; since fortune had led him to the top, if it were to continue in its circle it

---

[61] Victoria Kahn, "Virtù and the Example of Agathocles in Machiavelli's Prince," *Representations* 13(1986); Kahn, *Machiavellian Rhetoric*; Rebhorn, *Foxes and Lions*; Maurizio Viroli, *Machiavelli* (Oxford: Oxford University Press, 1998), 73–113

could only drag him down to the bottom" (FH 3.19). The nail, in short, allegorizes the need to act in sync with fortune, or as Machiavelli puts it elsewhere, in accordance with the quality of one's time. Machiavelli declines to further comment on this story, but from his description it is clear that the Florentine elites are sophisticated readers of allegories.

But what about the people? Can the common people match the refined exegetical skills of the *grandi*? Machiavelli has little confidence in people's natural capacities. Political virtues, he insists, are not natural – they are learnt and practiced. Freedom and political judgment necessitate training in the art of the state, which is also an art of interpretation. To respond politically to a situation requires, as Antonio Vázquez-Arroyo notes, "a degree of political literacy that is attained and cultivated by way of difficult encounters, experiences, and actions."[62] As I show, especially in Chapter 1, Machiavelli offers a political pedagogy, an education on how to read violence, so that the people may hone their interpretive aptitudes and rise to the challenge. The scenes of violence that puncture his work are part of this didactic project: They provide lessons in political literacy.[63] They offer a popular education in the interpretation of violence that is of use to the people in advancing a politics of freedom.

One of the curiosities of late Renaissance Florence is that symbols that were traditionally associated with popular freedom and republican government were systematically coopted by elites. Representing themselves as champions of freedom, wealthy families used these symbols to build large patronage networks. Patrons would assist their "friends" with debts, dowries, and commercial activities; they would use their influence to ease access to political office and help with litigation. Through such largesse, patrons secured the loyalty of non-elite clients and their families, building expansive networks of power and authority.[64] No family was more successful at assembling a broad faction than the Medici, who appropriated the symbols of Florentine republicanism to portray themselves as

---

[62] Antonio Y. Vázquez-Arroyo, *Political Responsibility* (New York: Columbia University Press, 2016), xvii, see also 215–16, 251–56.

[63] Recent scholarship has emphasized Machiavelli's role as a teacher of interpretation. See Nancy S. Struever, *Theory as Practice: Ethical Inquiry in the Renaissance* (Chicago: University of Chicago Press, 1992), 147–81; Kahn, *Machiavellian Rhetoric*, 18–43; Pedullà, *Machiavelli in tumulto*, 93. Dante Germino notes that Machiavelli's work spreads "political knowledge to elites and non-elites alike." Dante Germino, "Machiavelli's Thoughts on the Psyche and Society," in *The Political Calculus: Essays on Machiavelli's Philosophy*, ed. Anthony Parel (Toronto: University of Toronto Press, 1972), 76.

[64] Dale V. Kent, *The Rise of the Medici: Faction in Florence, 1426–1434* (Oxford: Oxford University Press, 1978).

champions of freedom.[65] This is the context for Machiavelli's political pedagogy. When the emblems and codes conventionally associated with popular freedom are appropriated by Florence's leading families, the capacity to accurately identify political symbols becomes a crucial political skill. Under these conditions, political literacy means being able to analyze and evaluate events, situations, and forces with respect to the kinds of political projects they advance.

THE ROMAN VOCABULARY OF VIOLENCE

A cursory look at Machiavelli's terminology makes clear that he does not have a concept that corresponds to what a twenty-first century English speaker might call "violence." From Roman political theory, Machiavelli inherits a pair of concepts – *vis* and *violentia* – which structure theoretical considerations of violence during the classical and medieval periods.[66] *Vis* means physical force and referred to both legal and illegal forms of violence.[67] *Violentia* [vehemence, impetuosity] and the associated verb *violare* [to outrage, dishonor] have a narrower semantic range, referring to destructive force and connoting a violation. Unlike *vis*, *violentia* always signifies a transgression, and in postclassical usage, *violentia* is nearly always identified with *iniura*, unlawfulness, and injustice.[68]

On the one hand, Roman law recognized certain forms of private and public force as legitimate.[69] On the other hand, especially in the late republic, Roman political theorists increasingly regarded the use of *vis publica* to be a great danger to Roman political life. Both Cicero

---

[65] Alison Brown, "De-Masking Renaissance Republicanism," in *Renaissance Civic Humanism*, ed. James Hankins (Cambridge: Cambridge University Press, 2000); Sarah Blake McHam, "Donatello's Bronze 'David' and 'Judith' as Metaphors of Medici Rule in Florence," *The Art Bulletin* 83, no. 1 (2001).

[66] I am grateful to Peter Stacey for his helpful comments on the relation between *vis* and *violentia*.

[67] Andrew Lintott, *Violence in Republican Rome* (Oxford: Oxford University Press, 1999), 22–23.

[68] Fritz Kern, *Gottesgnadentum und Widerstandsrecht im früheren Mittelalter: Zur Entwicklungsgeschichte der Monarchie* (Munster and Cologne: Böhlau, 1954), 143 n307.

[69] That force could legitimately be repulsed by force [*vim vi repellere licet*] was considered a precept of the *ius naturale*, and under Roman civil law, the use of violence to secure one's legal or natural rights was permissible. August Friedrich Pauly and Georg Wissowa, eds. *Real-Encyclopädie der classischen Altertumswissenschaft* (Stuttgart: Metzler, 1890–1980), s.v. "vis."

and Seneca – the principal philosophical authorities for the Florentine humanists – treat *vis* as corrosive of moral and political life.[70] As Cicero writes in *De legibus*, "There is nothing more destructive for states, nothing more contrary to right and law, nothing less civil and humane, than the use of violence [*agi per vim*] in public affairs in a duly constituted republic [*composita et constituta re publica*]."[71] But what counts as a "duly constituted republic?" Cicero was no pacifist, and as much as he abhorred violence in principle, he had little qualm about justifying its liberal use against political enemies. In Andrew Lintott's words, Cicero "exemplifies the incongruous attitude of most Romans to violence in politics … You may disregard the constitution and employ limited violence to resist violence on the ground that the law of the jungle now prevails, but you must not use too much violence as that will permanently destroy the state whose laws you are disregarding."[72]

Machiavelli's theory of violence constitutes a critical engagement with his Roman sources.[73] Like most Renaissance authors, Machiavelli maintained the conceptual distinction between *vis* and *violentia* inherited from Roman political theory. Akin to the Latin *vis*, Machiavelli's *forza* has no normative charge. It stands for forms of actions associated with arms; it is synonymous with "armed force" or simply "arms" and connotes a technical quality grounded in physical or military strength. Yet in contrast to the Roman Stoics, who were markedly ambivalent about *vis* – disavowing it in principle while defending it in practice – Machiavelli takes a much more pragmatic stance. Rejecting Cicero's moralistic (and hypocritical) disavowal of *vis*, Machiavelli emphasizes its constitutive nature. *Forza*, he argues, is a primary mechanism by which princes acquire and lose states or by which republics acquire and lose subject cities. More generally, *forza* is a euphemism for Machiavelli, one that refers to the deployment or threat of physical violence, to the infliction of injuries, and to executions. It describes, as I argue in Chapter 2, a generic, instrumental modality of

[70] Gilbert, *Machiavelli and Guicciardini: Politics and History*, 179; Skinner, *Foundations of Modern Political Thought*, 1:88–94; Pitkin, *Fortune Is a Woman*, 48.

[71] Marcus Tullius Cicero, *On the Commonwealth and on the Laws*, trans. James E. G. Zetzel (Cambridge: Cambridge University Press, 1999), 172, trans. mod.

[72] Lintott, *Violence in Republican Rome*, 62.

[73] On Cicero's influence on Machiavelli, see Marcia L. Colish, "Cicero's *De Officiis* and Machiavelli's *Prince*," *The Sixteenth Century Journal* (1978); J. J. Barlow, "The Fox and the Lion: Machiavelli's Reply to Cicero," *History of Political Thought* 20, no. 4 (1999). As Barlow rightly points out, Machiavelli inverts Cicero's conclusion nearly point for point.

political violence, where violence appears as a versatile and malleable technique to be deployed in different contexts for different ends.

Like the Latin *violentia*, Machiavelli and his contemporaries used *violenza* to refer to injustice.[74] *Violenza* is associated with criminal behavior, with a lack of legitimacy, and with unjust force used against free cities and institutions (FH 2.34). To hold a state with violence [*tenere con violenza*] is to hold it without the legitimacy of lineage, investiture, or popular support (FH 5.3).[75] When Machiavelli refers to a government as *insopportabile e violento* (FH 7.4), to an unjust war as *violento* (FH 5.8), or to a proposed coup d'état as *troppo violento* (FH 4.30), he indexes not the physical force and arms that were deployed but the lack of political legitimacy and the disregard for republican institutions and democratic practices. Because of this moral and legal baggage, *violenza* in fact plays a minor role in Machiavelli's political works and is eclipsed by other terms, notably *forza* and *crudeltà*.

Crudeltà is a more complex term in Machiavelli's lexicon. It characterizes actions that inflict gratuitous and shocking forms of injury. In contrast to force, cruelty is a decidedly non-euphemistic category. It refers to an essentially offensive, provocative, and often scandalous mode of violence. Unlike force, it has a more complicated instrumental valence. Cruelty involves a transgression that strategically elicits shock and awe. It often appears irrational and senseless, but this appearance is part of its modus operandi. In contrast to force, cruelty systematically violates the symbolic terms of the socio-political order. Unlike force, which is subject to a logic of efficiency, Machiavellian cruelty inflicts violence beyond what is objectively necessary. This surplus, however, is not redundant. It is class-specific, directed against the privileges and expectations of the *grandi*, and constitutes, as I argue in Chapter 3, a challenge to the terms of social hierarchy. This challenge makes cruelty a formidable political strategy and renders Machiavelli's theorization (and defense) of *crudeltà*

---

[74] Contra Frazer and Hutchings, who argue that Machiavelli uses *violenza* "when referring to personal and excessive acts of physical violence." Frazer and Hutchings, "Virtuous Violence," 70n3.

[75] We find the same usage, for example, in Coluccio Salutati's fourteenth-century treatise *On Tyranny*, where *violentus* is used as a synonym for *tyrannicus* or in Francesco Guicciardini's *Dialogue on the Government of Florence* (written in the 1520s), where *governo violento* is synonymous with *governo usurpato* to indicate an illegitimate regime. Coluccio Salutati, *Political Writings*, ed. Stefano U. Baldassarri, trans. Rolf Bagemihl (Cambridge, MA: Harvard University Press, 2014), 115; Francesco Guicciardini, *Dialogue on the Government of Florence*, trans. Alison Brown (Cambridge: Cambridge University Press, 1994), 158–59.

one of his most significant innovations in the discourse of political violence. In the history of Euro-Atlantic political theory and philosophy, cruelty has rarely been accorded serious consideration. By contrast, Machiavelli develops a theory of cruelty as a type of physical violence that traffics in appearances and that deploys these in a calculated manner.

Forza and *crudeltà* set up the scaffolding for my argument in the first part of the book, and I devote a chapter to each. While these terms are not always used consistently, they convey what I call two distinct *modes* of political violence. Imbued with their own mechanisms, protocols, and logics, each mode gives rise to distinct political effects. Cruelty and force are not new terms. As so often, Machiavelli doesn't invent these categories anew but instead appropriates existing ones, radically transforming their sense and meaning.[76] In contrast to *violenza, forza* and *crudeltà* are terms that qualify the materiality, appearance, and political effects of violence rather than its legal or moral grounds.

INTERPRETIVE CROSSROADS

This book offers an interpretation of Machiavelli's text that challenges both those who attribute to it a moderate republicanism and those who see in it the kernel of modern *raison d'état*. Yet my aim, in doing so, is not to substitute an ostensibly more authentic rendition of Machiavelli's political beliefs for the ones that currently circulate. My interest is in the lines of thought the text opens up and makes available. Texts in the history of political thought are shaped by the conditions of their production, by the languages, vocabularies, and historical archives available at the moment of their composition, and by the legacies and traditions through which they are read. Part of the reconstructive work of expounding Machiavelli's political theory of violence consists in identifying the legacies, problems, and rationales that inform the texts. By contextualizing the work in this way, lines of thought open up that may exceed the intentions of the author and that may not even have been fully discernible to him.[77]

I take as a starting point Machiavelli's vocabulary and historical context. Words matter and so do historical conditions of possibility.

---

[76] See Del Lucchese, *Conflict, Power, and Multitude in Machiavelli and Spinoza*, 67.

[77] Even Pocock recognizes that historical actors are never fully "in command of the 'meaning' of [their] own utterance." J. G. A. Pocock, *Political Thought and History: Essays on Theory and Method* (Cambridge: Cambridge University Press, 2009), 24.

Yet to begin with terminology is not to yield to the reduction of political theory to semantics.[78] By focusing on Machiavelli's vocabulary, I accept a couple of key contextualist claims: that the range of concepts and arguments available to an author are historically limited and that texts are concerned with problems specific to their time. Yet as much as I acknowledge a debt, it is also necessary to recognize the limitations of the contextualist paradigm. Machiavelli emphasizes the groundbreaking character of his own work, and even though he uses a conventional vocabulary, he frequently wrenches terms from their established meanings and imparts an original sense to them. Moreover, there are indications that he intended his work not for his contemporaries but for an audience of future readers.[79] Accordingly, to read his writings solely from the vantage point of his immediate addressees is to imprison them in an interpretive straightjacket.

The divergence between Machiavelli's lexicon and that of a twenty-first century reader tells contemporary readers nothing about whether they can learn anything from his texts for their own time. But it does allow readers to face up to a basic interpretive truth: The questions that readers bring to historical texts are not the author's but those of their own period. And this is as it should be. It is neither necessary nor desirable to dissolve past texts into their – linguistic, cultural, social, or political – contexts. To read Machiavelli's text in view of what it can teach twenty-first century readers about violence while conceding that this question may have been incomprehensible to the author is to acknowledge a historical difference but not an unbridgeable chasm.

Even though Machiavelli, in *The Prince* and the *Discourses*, articulates a set of political principles concerning the use of violence in politics, the explicit claims about how violence should be deployed are notoriously unclear. Moreover, they are often inconsistent with the scenes and episodes that function as their ostensible examples or that provide the

---

[78] The linguistic approaches to Machiavelli that became popular in the 1950s and 1960s have contributed much to our understanding, even though they have not provided the methodological panacea their pioneers had anticipated. See, for example, Fredi Chiapelli, *Studi sul linguaggio del Machiavelli* (Florence: Felice Le Monnier, 1952); J. H. Whitfield, "On Machiavelli's Use of Ordini," *Italian Studies* 10(1955); J. H. Hexter, "*Il principe* and *lo stato*," *Studies in the Renaissance* 4(1957); Giorgio Cadoni, "Libertà, repubblica e governo misto in Machiavelli," *Rivista internazionale di filosofia del diritto* series III, 39 (1962); Marcia L. Colish, "The Idea of Liberty in Machiavelli," *Journal of the History of Ideas* 32, no. 3 (1971).

[79] Catherine Zuckert, *Machiavelli's Politics* (Chicago: Chicago University Press, 2017), 6, 21.

dramatic structure for the historical narratives. To take a famous example, chapter 9 of *The Prince*, "Of the Civil Principality," sets out to describe a nonviolent mode of becoming prince. In Machiavelli's words, the civil prince comes to power using neither "crime nor other intolerable violence." Yet the chapter cites as the sole successful specimen of such a civil prince Nabis, who became ruler of Sparta by executing the last two claimants of the royal dynasty. Not only did Machiavelli's sources – Polybius and Livy – both consider Nabis a brutal despot, but so apparently did Machiavelli, at least in *Discourses* 3.6 where he refers to him as a tyrant.[80] Leaving aside the tension between *The Prince* and the *Discourses*, how does killing the pretenders to the Spartan throne qualify as a nonviolent mode of becoming prince? What makes it different from the acts of Agathocles, which Machiavelli in the previous chapters qualifies as criminal?

One could pile on the illustrations. Puzzles such as these require readers to look not only at what Machiavelli explicitly says about the role of violence in politics but also at the illustrations, figures, and narrative devices in his work. Philosophically inclined readers tend to privilege conceptual argument over narrative, the "general rule" over the particulars. By contrast, I pay special attention to the examples – the scenes and episodes that purportedly illustrate the conceptual claims. As it turns out, the examples often do not fit the theoretical arguments they are meant to epitomize, and the reader is left to adjudicate whether to follow the abstract claim or the illustration. My tendency is to go with the latter, in keeping with what I regard as Machiavelli's method. In his text, there are three kinds of examples: those that illustrate a claim and corroborate it, those that contradict and complicate a claim, and those that substitute for a claim, which the reader is expected to inductively derive.

OVERVIEW

The orders of Machiavellian violence encompass both a conceptual typology and analyses of specific formations of political violence. I treat the taxonomy of violent modes in Chapters 1–3 and the formations that exemplify these modes in Chapters 4–6. The first half of the book offers an analysis of spectacular violence (Chapter 1), of force (Chapter 2), and

---

[80] Livy, 34.27; Polybius, *Histories*, trans. William. R. Paton (Cambridge, MA: Harvard University Press, 1922–1927), 13.6–8.

of cruelty (Chapter 3). The second half of the book maps these modes onto the main formations of violence that Machiavelli analyzes: founding violence (Chapter 4), reproductive violence (Chapter 5), and plebeian violence (Chapter 6).

There is nothing quite like a memorable execution to disempower oligarchic elites and to simultaneously gratify the multitude. Accordingly, this book begins and ends with violence as spectacle. Chapter 1, "Spectacle," focuses on the famous scene in chapter 7 of *The Prince* that recounts the execution of Cesare Borgia's deputy, Remirro de Orco. Against the conventional Weberian readings of that scene, I interpret Machiavelli's Cesare as using violence to address the political passions and the imagination of his Romagnol subjects. In Machiavelli's narration, Cesare's assassination of Remirro becomes a detective story, a puzzle that the audience is invited to piece together.

Chapters 2 and 3 examine Machiavelli's terminology. Turning to his taxonomy of violence, they distinguish the two principal modes of political violence. Chapter 2, "Force," reconstructs Machiavelli's concept of force and contrasts it with contemporary models of coercion. I contend that force is an unstable and precarious mode of action that is stabilized when mediated through law and religion. Force is most effective when it operates not as an alternative to consent but when it directly manufactures such consent.

Chapter 3, "Cruelty," untangles Machiavelli's concept of cruelty. It puts forward an interpretation of cruelty as a quintessentially anti-oligarchic tactic. I regard Machiavellian cruelty as a type of physical violence that traffics in appearances: It refers to seemingly irrational violations of social status and dignity. Machiavelli inherits this notion of cruelty from the Romans, specifically from Seneca, but he transforms the Roman idea in crucial ways.

Chapter 4, "Beginnings," offers an analysis of cruelty as a transitional strategy. The chapter focuses on the violence of founding moments, especially on two central founding myths of Rome. Machiavelli turns the violent beginnings of Rome into a paradigm for founding and regenerating republics, which raises the question of what such "founding violence" means. Against empiricist and transcendental accounts of founding violence, I argue for a materialist interpretation that highlights the role of political memory.

Chapter 5, "Institutions," investigates forms of republican violence. Renaissance humanists traditionally regarded republics as peaceful alternatives to the repressive and conspiratorial violence that rattles principalities.

Machiavelli challenges this perspective by insisting that republics both partake in the political violence that defines the life of all states and unleash distinctive forms of violence of their own. This chapter looks at how violence is embedded in institutions and practices that assure the political reproduction of republican orders, in particular class conflict, punishment, and imperial warfare.

Chapter 6, "Tumults," turns from institutional and state-organized forms of violence to insurrectionary practices. Focusing on the notorious 1378 revolt by plebeian wool workers known as the Ciompi, the chapter examines how – in Machiavelli's rendition – the event's protagonists theorize insurrectionary violence. Unlike most of his predecessors or contemporaries, Machiavelli takes seriously the plebs as political actors along with legitimate interests, objectives, and strategies. In Machiavelli's telling, the Ciompi justify their rioting on resolutely partial and anti-universalist grounds, a point that interpreters frequently cite as evidence that Machiavelli regarded such violence as illegitimate. I disagree. Challenging current trends that rehabilitate plebeian politics insofar as they are harbingers of liberal democratic universalism, I argue that Machiavelli offers a compelling, unapologetically partisan, and antagonistic model of plebeian politics.

Spectacle

Such executions have in them something of the great and the generous.
— Niccolò Machiavelli, *Discourses on Livy*

It seems that Machiavelli's intentions, in writing *The Prince* were more complex and also 'more democratic' than the 'democratic' interpretation suggests.
— Antonio Gramsci, *Quaderni del carcere*

Acts of political violence are often designed to be witnessed. Executions, massacres, rapes, and lynchings are frequently performed in front of audiences or carried out in ways that leave traces for all to see. And even when such acts are ostensibly concealed, they are sometimes covered up so neglectfully that one is left to wonder whether the discovery isn't part of the perpetrators' strategy. Such formations of violence produce political effects in part through their theatricality. Staged violence elicits a range of affective responses from audiences, including fear, shock, and horror but also pleasure. As scholars in fields from gender studies to African American studies have shown, such practices of public violence also have more mediated political effects, for instance to enforce racial supremacy, the subjection of women, or the binary gender code.[1]

---

[1] See for instance Catharine A. MacKinnon, *Toward a Feminist Theory of the State* (Cambridge, MA: Harvard University Press, 1989), 172–83; Ta-Nehisi Coates, *Between the World and Me* (New York: Spiegel and Grau, 2015), 103–6.

Thus Frederick Douglass argues that the brutal public punishment of slaves was central not only to the making of an individual slave but also to the maintenance and reproduction of slavery as a system.[2] Moreover, as Saidiya Hartman has shown, spectacles of violence have an afterlife in discursive and visual form: Racial domination is reproduced not only by the violent acts themselves but also by the circulation of narratives and representations of such acts.[3] The dissemination of visual and narrative depictions of cruelty tends to reinscribe the subjection enacted in the original scenes.

By examining the function of theatrical violence in the reproduction of subjection, scholars like Hartman highlight the tendency of such violence to reproduce social and political orders and to maintain the status quo. But staged violence is neither intrinsically tyrannical nor does it necessarily prop up oppressive orders. Spectacular violence can also function as a mechanism of political change. In *The Prince*, Machiavelli puts forward such an account of spectacular violence by analyzing the strategy of Cesare Borgia in the Romagna.[4]

Cesare Borgia has long kindled controversy among Machiavelli's readers. On the one hand, Machiavelli depicts Cesare as a model for how to "found a state," and a role model for other princes (P 7, 8, 13). On the other hand, the brevity of Cesare's political life, his brutality, and the fleeting nature of his influence and power have led readers to question the sincerity of Machiavelli's praise. The secondary literature is divided over whether Machiavelli approved of Cesare's violence or whether he regarded him as a tyrant.[5] In the modern scholarship, three positions can be distinguished: There are those who, anxious to avoid tarnishing Machiavelli's credentials with the infamous murders and intrigues

---

[2] Frederick Douglass, *My Bondage and My Freedom* (New York: Penguin, 2003), 92–93, 192, 305.

[3] Saidiya V. Hartman, *Scenes of Subjection: Terror, Slavery, and Self-Making in Nineteenth-Century America* (New York: Oxford University Press, 1997), 17–23.

[4] I use the term "spectacle" as a synonym for theater and performance and as the English translation for Machiavelli's *spettaculo*. Contra the Situationist emphasis on the surface – on the image and its visibility – "spectacle" here is not a matter of sensible perception but of imagination.

[5] The topos of Cesare Borgia as glorious center of *The Prince* was first introduced by the Anti-Machiavellians, above all Bodin, who sought to discredit Machiavelli by associating him closely with Borgia. Bernard Guillemain, *Machiavel: L'anthropologie politique* (Geneva: Librairie Droz, 1977), 79.

associated with the Borgia name, deny the sincerity of Machiavelli's esteem for the condottiere.[6] On the other side are readers who emphasize the importance of state-formation for Machiavelli's thought and who argue that his esteem is based on Cesare's creation of a strong and unitary state.[7] And finally, there are readers who take the lesson of Cesare's violence to be that constitutional government relies on unconstitutional beginnings.[8]

In this chapter, I examine the mechanics of spectacular violence as deployed by Machiavelli's Borgia. Unlike the conventional interpretations, I read Cesare's violence in light of Machiavelli's counsel that a prince should ally himself with the people and build popular support. In chapter 9 of *The Prince*, Machiavelli puts forward a vision of the "civil principality" that contrasts with the kinds of states he discusses in earlier chapters of the book. What distinguishes the civil prince, Machiavelli writes, is that he becomes prince "with the aid of the people" and is sustained by popular rather than aristocratic support. What exactly constitutes a civil principality is a much-disputed issue, but as I argue in more detail in Chapter 3, the absence of violence is definitively not one of its characteristics. If, as Machiavelli suggests, popular support is what makes a civil prince, then Cesare Borgia can arguably be understood as a specimen of this rare breed of princes. To say that Cesare is a civil or popular prince does not imply that he is a paragon of democratic virtue but that his principal accomplishment consists in gaining the trust and

---

[6] Meinecke, Cassirer, and Baron regard Cesare as a tyrant. Friedrich Meinecke, *Die Idee der Staatsräson in der neueren Geschichte*, ed. Walther Hofer (Munich: Oldenbourg, 1957), 48; Cassirer, *The Myth of the State*, 145–46; Hans Baron, *In Search of Florentine Civic Humanism: Essays on the Transition from Medieval to Modern Thought* (Princeton, NJ: Princeton University Press, 1988), 114–15. Skinner and Najemy interpret Machiavelli's ultimate verdict on Borgia as negative. Quentin Skinner, *Machiavelli* (Oxford: Oxford University Press, 1981), 12; John M. Najemy, "Machiavelli and Cesare Borgia: A Reconsideration of Chapter 7 of the Prince," *The Review of Politics* 75, no. 4 (2013). Sullivan suggests that he is a cautionary tale for the Medici. Vickie B. Sullivan, *Machiavelli's Three Romes: Religion, Human Liberty and Politics Reformed* (De Kalb, IL: Northern Illinois University Press, 1996), 23–24. Mattingly and Benner view Machiavelli's praise of Borgia as satirical or ironic. Garrett Mattingly, "The Prince: Political Science or Political Satire?" *The American Scholar* 27(1958), 487–89; Erica Benner, *Machiavelli's Prince: A New Reading* (Oxford: Oxford University Press, 2013), 93–110.

[7] Roberto Ridolfi, *The Life of Niccolò Machiavelli*, trans. Cecil Grayson (London: Routledge & Kegan Paul, 1963), 57; Chabod, *Machiavelli and the Renaissance*, 69; Federico Chabod, *Scritti su Machiavelli* (Turin: Einaudi, 1964), 62n; Sasso, *Machiavelli e Cesare Borgia*, 207–8; Pocock, *The Machiavellian Moment*, 175; Negri, *Insurgencies*, 41–45.

[8] Mansfield, *Machiavelli's Virtue*, 187; Vatter, *Between Form and Event*, 119.

backing of the people.[9] And if spectacular violence plays an important role in generating this support, then Borgia's "rationally trained cruelty" is neither simply an illustrious example of how to use violence effectively nor motivated by narrow self-interest.[10]

BORGIA'S STATE-MAKING

The Prince relays multiple instances of spectacular violence – dazzling and memorable executions that are publicly staged and function as political turning points. But among the various master choreographers of such displays – Agathocles of Syracuse, Liverotto of Fermo, Nabis of Sparta, Hannibal, and Septimius Severus – Machiavelli showers none with more praise than Cesare. Here is how Machiavelli extols him:

> If I summed up all the actions of the duke, I would not know how to reproach him; on the contrary, it seems to me he should be put forward, as I have done, to be imitated ... So whoever judges it necessary in his new principality to secure himself against enemies, to gain friends to himself, to conquer either by force or fraud, to make himself loved and feared by the people, and followed and revered by the soldiers, to eliminate those who can or might offend you, to renew old orders through new modes, to be severe and pleasant, magnanimous and liberal, to eliminate an unfaithful military, to create a new one, to maintain friendships with kings and princes ... can find no fresher examples than the actions of that man.

(P 7)

A close observer of Cesare's career, Machiavelli was well acquainted with his actions as a result of two diplomatic missions that sent him to his court.[11] In *The Prince*, he retraces Cesare's rise and fall over the course of multiple chapters. First introduced in chapter 3 as "Valentino," the name

---

[9] My reading follows Sasso, who insists that chapter 7 of *The Prince* exhibits both Machiavelli's admiration for Cesare's actions, which he witnessed at Urbino and Imola, as well as his criticisms of the Duke's major political mistake: allowing Giuliano Della Rovere to be elected pope. I contest Inglese's view that the example of Cesare collapses political and military force. Sasso, *Machiavelli e Cesare Borgia*, 125–26; Giorgio Inglese, *Per Machiavelli* (Rome: Carocci, 2007), 65.

[10] The expression is Meinecke's. Meinecke, *Die Idee der Staatsräson*, 48. Contra Strauss who argues that princes' "selfish" concerns with their "own well-being, security, and glory" motivate the "immoral policies" advocated in *The Prince*. Strauss, *Thoughts on Machiavelli*, 80.

[11] The first, to Urbino, in June 1502, lasted only a few days; the second, to Imola and Cesena, had Machiavelli in Cesare's company for three months, from October 1502 to January 1503. During this period, Machiavelli wrote almost daily reports to the Florentine government, tracking Cesare's every move, describing his negotiations with the envoys of France, Venice, and Milan, and his skillful scheming with and against the

by which the people called him, Cesare is the main subject of chapter 7, where Machiavelli commends him for the good foundations he laid. He is mentioned again in chapter 8, as the topic of "grave discussions" and as having outwitted Liverotto. In chapter 11, he figures as the "instrument" of the distinctive political form that Machiavelli calls the "ecclesiastic principality" invented by Cesare's father, Pope Alexander VI. Cesare is further adduced in chapter 13 as the example of a prince who, after experimenting with troops borrowed from others, established his own forces. In chapter 17, he is cited as evidence that well-used cruelty is more merciful than badly used mercy; and in chapter 20 as proof for the uselessness of fortresses. In *The Prince*, there is no other figure, historical or mythical, that commands as much attention, occupies as much space, and draws so much of Machiavelli's admiration as Borgia.[12]

The illegitimate son of Alexander VI who becomes cardinal upon his father's election to the papacy but then turns in his ring and cassock for the sword, Cesare is somewhat of a conundrum. Like the dedicatee of *The Prince*, Lorenzo de'Medici, whose uncle Giovanni had become Pope Leo X in 1513, Cesare Borgia starts his political career indebted to the Vatican. With troops borrowed from the King of France and the Orsini family, he conquers the Romagna and transforms it into his *stato*. Yet in doing so, he is confronted with three challenges: an apprehensive population, an oppressive nobility intent on defending its plundering ways, and unreliable military allies. Through a series of tactically skillful and ruthless uses of violence, he overcomes each of these challenges and establishes himself – but only for a few brief years – as one of Italy's most feared warlords.[13]

Orsini and Vitelli condottieri. Even though Borgia sought a formal alliance with Florence or even a commission, Machiavelli was under strict orders to avoid any commitments and to learn as much as he could about Cesare's plans and intentions. At the time of the second mission, Borgia had conquered the cities of the Romagna as well as the duchy of Urbino. The Florentine *signoria* started to get nervous about the formidable warlord who now pushed toward Tuscany. Corrado Vivanti, *Niccolò Machiavelli: An Intellectual Biography*, trans. Simon MacMichael (Princeton, NJ: Princeton University Press, 2013), 24.

[12] Machiavelli continues to extol Borgia's virtues years after finishing work on *The Prince*. In a letter to Vettori from 1515, he mentions him and reiterates that he would "imitate" Valentino's deeds "on all occasions were I a new prince." Letter to Vettori, January 31, 1515, James B. Atkinson and David Sices, eds., *Machiavelli and His Friends: Their Personal Correspondence* (DeKalb: Northern Illinois University Press, 1996), 313.

[13] Contemporary sources attest to the *grande paura* inspired by Valentino. Sasso, *Machiavelli e Cesare Borgia*, 6; Francesco Guicciardini, *The History of Florence*, trans. Mario Dommandi (New York: Harper & Row, 1970), 194.

Machiavelli treats Borgia as an example of a prince who acquired his state through fortune but who "laid for himself great foundations" (P 7). Even though the condition for Cesare's initial military conquest was his fortune of being the pontiff's son, he successively expands his political autonomy. Having started the first military campaign with unreliable allies, Valentino "decided to depend no longer on the arms and fortune of others." His state-making involves two crucial moves: obtaining the loyalty of his troops and acquiring "the friendship of the Romagna." In order to secure his fickle troops, he first neutralizes the major clients of the Orsini by offering them patronage, allowances, and honors. He then tricks and kills the heads of the Orsini family, along with some of his allies who had turned against him. With the undivided loyalty of his army, he subsequently turns his attention to the Romagna and consolidates his state.

Cesare, whom the plebs [*il vulgo*] call "Duke Valentino," does everything "that should be done by a prudent and virtuous man to put his roots in the states that the arms and fortune of others had given him" (P 7). Like the plebs, Machiavelli calls Cesare "the Duke" and "Valentino," thereby reminding readers of the promise in *The Prince*'s dedication, that in discussing princes, Machiavelli will articulate the perspective of the people, for "to know well the nature of princes, one needs to be of the people" (P, DL).[14] This popular perspective is appropriate, not least because the Duke himself was particularly proud of how he "had gained all those people to himself" by improving their security and well-being. Since the approval by the Romagnol seemed especially important to him, it merits our attention to see how violence factors into building popular support.

The difficulty Cesare faced in the Romagna was not so much military as political. Over the course of the preceding years, he had overthrown the papal vicars in the Romagna, first accompanied by a French army and later by his own mercenary army, paid for by papal funds. One by one, the cities of Imola, Forlí, Pesaro, Rimini, and Faenza fell, as did Urbino, Camerino, Senigallia, Città di Castello, and Perugia. Yet even though he had asserted himself as the principal military power, political authority

---

[14] That Cesare is popularly called "Valentino" has been noted by McCormick, who sees it as a sign of popular allegiance, and by Benner, who interprets the sobriquet as dragging Cesare "down to the demotic level instead of elevating him above the people." John P. McCormick, "Prophetic Statebuilding: Machiavelli and the Passion of the Duke," *Representations* 115, no. 1 (2011), 2; Benner, *Machiavelli's Prince*, 96.

remained elusive. In Machiavelli's telling, Cesare faced a province "full of robberies, quarrels, and every other kind of insolence" (P 7). Replete with what Machiavelli in the *Discourses* calls "gentlemen" – those who live idly from the returns of their land and are "altogether hostile to every civilization" – the Romagna was the kind of place where "no republic or *vivere politico*" could ever have emerged (D 1.55).

Located between the Adriatic, the Apennines, and the Po river, the Romagna consists of a series of towns along the old Roman Via Emilia, which ran from Rimini on the Adriatic coast in a north-west direction toward Bologna. Prior to Cesare's conquest, the province had been divided into feudal lordships with each town ruled by a different family and riven by aristocratic rivalries.[15] Authority was parceled out and diffuse. Each of the towns was surrounded by a rural subject territory, or *contado*, stretching into the Apennine mountain range in the West and into the plains in the East.

Formally, the lordships of the Romagna were subjects of the pope. In the language of the fifteenth century, the lands of the Romagna were *terre mediate subiecte* as opposed to the lands that were immediately administered by the papal government [*terre immediate subiecte*].[16] The *signori* who ruled these *cittadine* were acting as apostolic vicars, an office introduced in the fourteenth century that required the princes to acknowledge papal supremacy and pay a yearly census. Many vicars failed to pay up and tacitly denied the supreme authority of the pontiff. As the papacy lacked the military resources to enforce its claims, the vicars progressively increased their political autonomy.[17]

Ever since featuring in Dante's *Divine Comedy* as a site of crime and lawlessness, the Romagna had been known in Italy as a province of tyrants "*mai senza guerra,*" never without war.[18] And even though the civil and political conditions had improved since its incorporation into the papal states in 1278, the Romagna remained a perilous region, "the

---

[15] See John Larner, *The Lords of Romagna* (London: Macmillan, 1965).

[16] Sandro Carocci, "The Papal State," in *The Italian Renaissance State*, ed. Andrea Gamberini and Isabella Lazzarini (Cambridge: Cambridge University Press, 2012), 72.

[17] Gustavo Sacerdote, *Cesare Borgia: La sua vita, la sua famiglia, i suoi tempi* (Milan: Rizzoli, 1950), 338.

[18] Dante Alighieri, *The Divine Comedy: Inferno, Vol. 1 Part 1*, trans. Charles S. Singleton (Princeton, NJ: Princeton University Press, 1990), 27.37; Larner, *The Lords of Romagna*, 50.

hotbed of every ferocious passion."[19] The smaller their fief, the historian Jacob Burckhardt observes, the more brutal, vicious, and disreputable the petty tyrants tended to be.[20] The Romagnol *signori* were unable or unwilling to control the mountainous area. In addition to boundary disputes and blood feuds, historians report regular incidences of cattle raiding, bride kidnapping, robbery, and assault, giving credence to Machiavelli's bleak description of the province.[21] By the 1480s, the volatile conditions in the Romagna had further been destabilized by the collapse of civil government in the main towns. In the cities of Cesena, Imola, and Forlì, the breakdown was a result of violent conflict between the *signori* and the local aristocracies. In Faenza, popular riots erupted following attempts to increase the price of grain.[22] It was in this context that Cesare dispossessed the local princelings of their fiefs.

Following his military conquest, Cesare cleaned house. His strategy was to delegate the violence to a deputy, Don Ramiro de Lorqua (known in Italy as Remirro de Orco), whom Machiavelli describes as "a cruel and ready man [*uomo crudele ed espedito*], and to whom Cesare gave the fullest powers [*plenissima potestà*]" (P 7). Remirro was one of the Spanish noblemen associated with the Borgia family.[23] Machiavelli says little about his tactics, but by calling him an *uomo crudele* with plenipotentiary powers, he suggests that the pacification was a brutal affair. Remirro quickly establishes order in the Romagna, introducing peace, obedience, and unity.

Machiavelli's defense of Cesare's violence hinges on his successful consolidation of peaceful order in the Romagna, turning it from a den of robbers, despotic aristocrats, and feudal tyrants into a province with "good government" characterized by "peace and unity" (P 7). In contrast to the *signori* who had failed to protect the people of the Romagna, Cesare seems to have been successful at establishing order. His edicts and proclamations show his concern for keeping his troops disciplined and protecting cities and towns from marauding soldiers,

---

[19] Jacob Burckhardt, *The Civilization of the Renaissance in Italy*, trans. S.G.C. Middlemore (London: Penguin, 1990), 53.

[20] Burckhardt, *The Civilization of the Renaissance in Italy*, 35.

[21] John Larner, "Order and Disorder in Romagna, 1450–1500," in *Violence and Civil Disorders in Italian Cities, 1200–1500*, ed. Lauro Martines (Berkeley: University of California Press, 1972), 40–41.

[22] Larner, "Order and Disorder in Romagna, 1450–1500," 50–58.

[23] Sacerdote, *Cesare Borgia*, 598.

while remaining approachable to his subjects in the Romagna and supporting local artisans.[24]

In one of his letters, written about a year after completing *The Prince*, Machiavelli emphasizes how Cesare produced *unity* in the Romagna by subjecting the entire province to the authority of a single governor. Unlike a state in which every city has its "own head," which is therefore always divided, the duke "made those peoples united, fearful of his authority, fond of his power, and trustful in it; and all the love they felt for him, which was great, considering his newness, resulted from this decision."[25] Cesare's unification of the Romagna betokens an even grander military and political aspiration on behalf of the Borgias: a territorial strategy to unify central Italy or even Italy in its entirety.[26] For Machiavelli, this ambition was particularly interesting. An ardent advocate of Italian unity, Machiavelli was captivated by the prospect of fusing temporal and religious authority. Moreover, he regarded such a project as a departure from the Church's historical role in preventing political unity in Italy. In his view, the Church had retarded political unity because it was too timid to unify Italy but strong enough to prevent any other power from doing so (D 1.12).[27] Cesare represents the possibility of a new role for the Church, allowing it to mobilize its considerable spiritual and ideological resources alongside a military strategy in pursuit of Italian unity.

Did Cesare introduce good government to the Romagna? Machiavelli certainly thought so, pointing to the "civil court" that Valentino set up in the province, "with a most excellent president, where each city had its advocate" (P 7). Machiavelli also mentions the loyalty that the Romagnol subjects had toward Cesare, even after Alexander's death. So did Guicciardini, who notes that Cesare was greatly admired by his subjects because of the justice and integrity with which he ruled the Romagna.[28] Historians tend to agree, citing Cesare's *buon governo*, while Roberto Ridolfi, Machiavelli's finest biographer, reports that when Valentino

[24] Michael Mallet, *The Borgias: The Rise and Fall of a Renaissance Dynasty* (London: Bodley Head, 1969), 203; Sacerdote, *Cesare Borgia*, 442–43.
[25] Letter to Vettori, January 31, 1515. Atkinson and Sices, *Machiavelli and His Friends*, 313.
[26] Sacerdote, *Cesare Borgia*, 338. See also Mallet, *The Borgias*, 201–12.
[27] A judgment that is shared by modern historians such as Burckhardt, *The Civilization of the Renaissance in Italy*, 20.
[28] Guicciardini, *The History of Florence*, 194.

moved his troops through Umbria, the people in nearby cities rose with cries of "*duca, duca.*"[29] To be sure, the bar was low, given the failure of the vicars to maintain peace and order. Nonetheless, the historical records – edicts, proclamations, and testimony – tend to support Machiavelli's view that the Romagna was well governed and that Cesare's regime was both just and popular.[30]

The primary casualties of Cesare's state-making were families belonging to the local and regional nobilities.[31] By unseating these oppressive elites from their positions, Cesare redeemed the Romagnol population from abusive regimes of domination. It is this engagement, on behalf of the people (rather than his having built a unitary state or having established a judicial institution) that distinguishes him in Machiavelli's view. It is no wonder, then, that the people or "il vulgo" honored Cesare by calling him "Duke."

CENTRALIZING THE MEANS OF VIOLENCE

Conventional interpretations of Borgia's state-making focus on the productivity of fear, the consolidation of territory, and the violent establishment of law and order.[32] From the vantage point of a theory of state-formation, Borgia's conquest of the Romagna can be analyzed as the centralization of the means of violence in what Weber would call a

---

[29] Edoardo Alvisi, *Cesare Borgia: Duca di Romagna* (Imola: Ignazio Galeati, 1878), 391; William Harrison Woodward, *Cesare Borgia* (London: Chapman and Hall, 1913), 313–18; Ridolfi, *The Life of Niccolò Machiavelli*, 63.

[30] Clemente Fusero, *Cesare Borgia* (Milan: Dall'Oglio, 1963); Sacerdote, *Cesare Borgia*, 443–44, 600; Ignazio dell'Oro, *Il segreto dei Borgia* (Milan: Ceschina, 1938), 48. Najemy dissents and regards the "friendship of the Romagna" as more of an aspiration than an accomplishment. Najemy, "Machiavelli and Cesare Borgia," 544.

[31] The aristocracy that had previously governed the province and now lost their positions – families such as the Malatesti, Montefeltro, Varano, Manfredi, and Alidosi – had obtained their positions through usurpation. In the mid-fourteenth century, Pope Benedict XII legalized and granted post-facto legitimacy to the various "tyrants" who had usurped cities formally subject to the Empire. In response, Emperor Louis IV officially granted all "tyrants in the towns of the Church" their municipalities (FH 1.30; 1.39).

[32] Chabod, *Scritti su Machiavelli*, 62; Viroli, *Machiavelli*, 55–56; Mansfield, *Machiavelli's Virtue*, 186–87; Giovanni Giorgini, "The Place of the Tyrant in Machiavelli's Political Thought and the Literary Genre of the Prince," *History of Political Thought* 29, no. 2 (2008), 243; Alissa M. Ardito, *Machiavelli and the Modern State: The Prince, the Discourses on Livy, and the Extended Territorial Republic* (Cambridge: Cambridge University Press, 2015), 52–53.

process of "political expropriation."[33] Historically minded scholars may frown on the anachronism of invoking a twentieth-century author to explain a sixteenth-century text, yet readings of *The Prince*'s seventh chapter routinely draw on Weber's model even if they do not name it.[34] This is especially true for interpreters who view Machiavelli as a theorist of the state and who explain Machiavelli's esteem for the Duke by virtue of the strong state the latter had created in the Romagna.[35]

A Weberian reconstruction of Cesare's Romagnol state-making might look like this: In the first step, Borgia uses his delegate to remove competing centers of power; in a second step, he eliminates this deputy who has risen to be a potential rival and a political liability; and in the third step, he creates a court, thus institutionalizing power not as prerogative but in juridically codified terms. In the secondary literature, Cesare's court has become something of a fetish, providing interpreters who would rather not get their hands dirty with Cesare's violence a way to discuss the episode in the Romagna.[36] Such readings draw on a well-established mytho-political schema where cycles of private violence are overcome through the establishment of the state. The classic paradigm of this sequence in Euro-Atlantic political theory is found in Greek tragedy, especially in the *Oresteia*, where the creation of Athena's court seemingly resolves the titanic battle between old and new gods, replacing unmediated violence and revenge by language, logos, and discourse. Both in Athens and in the Romagna, a new social order is established through the court, replacing uncontrolled feuds with rationalized public violence.[37]

---

[33] Weber, *The Vocation Lectures*, 38. See for instance Peter Breiner, "Machiavelli's 'New Prince' and the Primordial Moment of Acquisition," *Political Theory* 36, no. 1 (2008); Bellamy, "Dirty Hands and Clean Gloves."

[34] For explicit acknowledgments of a Weberian lens, see, for example, Vatter, *Between Form and Event*, 117; McCormick, "Prophetic Statebuilding," 3, 9.

[35] Ridolfi, *The Life of Niccolò Machiavelli*, 57; Chabod, *Machiavelli and the Renaissance*, 69; Chabod, *Scritti su Machiavelli*, 62n; Sasso, *Machiavelli e Cesare Borgia*, 207–08; Pocock, *The Machiavellian Moment*, 175.

[36] See for instance Elena Fasano Guarini, "Machiavelli and the Crisis of the Italian Republics," in *Machiavelli and Republicanism*, ed. Gisela Bock, Quentin Skinner, and Maurizio Viroli (Cambridge: Cambridge University Press, 1990), 32.

[37] Here, I can do justice neither to the complexities of violence and founding in the *Oresteia* nor to tragedy as a genre. In fact, as Peter Euben contends, Greek tragedy can itself be understood as a political pedagogy. See Peter J. Euben, "Justice and the Oresteia," *The American Political Science Review* 76, no. 1 (1982); Peter J. Euben, *The Tragedy of Political Theory* (Princeton, NJ: Princeton University Press, 1990). On the Oresteia, see also Simon Goldhill, *Aeschylus, the Oresteia* (Cambridge: Cambridge University Press, 1992). On the curse as a figure for how violence is inherited across

Machiavelli no doubt opens the door to such a reading, yet the story remains woefully incomplete. For one, it fails to attend to the popular character of Cesare's state. By removing the *signori* and executing Remirro, Cesare exercises power for the benefit of the people. As Sasso has observed, if the "civility" of the civil prince consists in the use of power for the sake of the people, then there is no question that Cesare Borgia must be considered a civil prince.[38] Cesare becomes a civil prince by building a state designed to contest the dominance of the feudal nobility and by converting himself into a champion of the people. The court he establishes in the Romagna is, as Vatter emphasizes, not an impartial and disinterested institution that dispenses formal legal opinions. Rather, it marks an alliance between the prince and the people, and it materializes, in institutional form, Cesare's promise to defend the people against the nobility.[39]

Relatedly, the Weberian story leaves out the meticulously staged and choreographed nature of Remirro's execution. Here is how Machiavelli describes the scene:

Then, the duke judged that such excessive authority was not necessary, for he feared it might become hateful; and he established a civil court in the middle of the province, with a most excellent president, where each city had its advocate. And since he knew that the harshness of the past had generated some hatred, to purge the spirits of the people and to gain them entirely to himself, he wished to show that if any cruelty had been committed, it had not come from him but from the harsh nature of his minister. And having seized this occasion, he had him placed one morning in the piazza at Cesena in two pieces, with a piece of wood and a bloody knife beside him. The ferocity of the spectacle left the people at once satisfied and stupefied.

(P 7, trans. mod.)

On Machiavelli's interpretation, the principal aim of Remirro's execution was to dissociate Cesare from his agent's cruelty. Rather than using discursive means – a proclamation or a public indictment – Valentino disavows Remirro's cruelty through a performance of public violence. By emphasizing the *spettaculo* that the Duke created for the people of

generations, see Yves Winter, "Violence and Visibility," *New Political Science* 34, no. 2 (2012).

[38] Gennaro Sasso, *Machiavelli e gli antichi e altri saggi*, 2:361. See also Del Lucchese, *The Political Philosophy of Niccolò Machiavelli*, 78; McCormick, "Machiavelli's Inglorious Tyrants."

[39] Vatter, *Between Form and Event*, 118–19. See also Vatter, *Machiavelli's* The Prince, 65–66.

Cesena, Machiavelli makes clear that state-making is both witnessed and staged and that the theatricality of such acts is crucial to their political function. Throughout his work, Machiavelli attributes great importance to theatricality and stagecraft. To act politically is to be on stage, to be an actor, to play a role, to manipulate an audience, and to engage in the "engineering of imagination."[40] Political actors stage spectacles: from the carnivals and public performances favored by the Medici, the street processions of thousands of children orchestrated by Savonarola, to the public games and jousts organized by Cesare.

Political violence is no exception. The terrifying scene in the piazza of Cesena manifests an intense and austere visual choreography. For someone who was an eyewitness to this *spettaculo*, Machiavelli's illustration of the scene is remarkably sparse. Remirro "in two pieces, with a piece of wood and a bloody knife beside him." The ostentatious visual nature of this exhibition is emphasized by the omission, in Machiavelli's narrative, of the killing itself. The text moves seamlessly from the speculation about the duke's motives to the horrific scene in the piazza, as if Machiavelli's Borgia were intent on concealing the act of the execution.

In a letter written the day of the gruesome discovery, December 26, 1502, Machiavelli was not so confident about the prince's motives. There he observes that "[n]obody feels sure of the cause of [his] death, except that so it has pleased the prince."[41] On that ominous day, when the inhabitants of Cesena awoke to find the sundered body of Remirro in the piazza, they were faced with a puzzle that called for interpretation. Based on Machiavelli's rendition, there was no question as to who was responsible for the deed; yet the people could not immediately ascertain the reasoning behind it and the implications that followed. Instead, they (along with Machiavelli's readers) were left with the traces of a crime scene, forced to piece together the rationale behind Remirro's execution. In leaving behind the clues without further explanation, Machiavelli compels his readers to come up with their own interpretations.

---

[40] Kenneth Robert Minogue, "Theatricality and Politics: Machiavelli's Concept of Fantasia," in *The Morality of Politics*, ed. Bikhu Parekh and Robert Nandor Berki (London: Allen & Unwin, 1972), 155. On the importance of theater for Machiavelli's politics, see Maurice Merleau-Ponty, "Note sur Machiavel," in *Signes* (Paris: Gallimard, 1960); Norman Jacobson, *Pride & Solace: The Functions and Limits of Political Theory* (New York: Methuen, 1986), 21–50; Kahn, "Virtù and the Example of Agathocles in Machiavelli's Prince"; Brown, *Manhood and Politics*, 102–04; Rebhorn, *Foxes and Lions*, 86–134, esp. 110.

[41] Legations, December 26, 1502 (CW 142, EN 5.2, 520).

This injunction to interpret is a key feature of Machiavelli's account of Remirro's assassination, and its distinctiveness becomes clearer if it is compared to another contemporary rendition of the killing.[42] In contrast to Machiavelli, Agostino Nifo's 1521 *De regnandi peritia* (a replica – probably plagiarized – of *The Prince* in Latin) has Cesare executing Remirro in broad daylight.[43] Nifo's account includes the presence in Cesena of all the "advocati" who had been injured by Remirro and who were invited to witness the execution. For Nifo, the spectator's gaze on the actual punishment plays a major part in the psycho-political effect Remirro's execution has on the Romagnol. Whether Nifo's more detailed account has a historical source or is simply a creative elaboration of Machiavelli's narrative is unknown, but the scene Nifo paints offers a useful contrast that allows us to think through Machiavelli's depiction.

Practices of punishment were highly didactic occasions to affirm not only legal codes but also social norms and moral truths. This pedagogical nature of punishment is emphasized by chroniclers whose narratives frequently stylize punishments, weaving cautionary anecdotes into the descriptions.[44] From the public exposure to various forms of torture and the way the corpse was disposed, the body of the condemned was subject to an elaborate visual spectacle. As Foucault notes in his discussion of the famous opening scene of *Discipline and Punish*, early modern judicial executions were theatricalized scenes, organized according to detailed choreographies and scripted in such a way that participants perform designated roles in front of spectators.[45] In her study of early modern theatrical performances of beheadings, the cultural theorist Margaret Owens argues that there was a convergence of expectations that audiences brought to the scene. Informed by the conventions of theater,

---

[42] Apparently, Machiavelli was not the first to dramatize Borgia's conquest; a comedy from Urbino did likewise but is unfortunately lost. Ronald L. Martinez, "Machiavelli and Traditions of Renaissance Theater," in *The Cambridge Companion to Machiavelli*, ed. John M. Najemy (Cambridge: Cambridge University Press, 2010), 208.

[43] *The Prince* was not published until 1531, ten years after Nifo's *De regnandi peritia*. Yet Machiavelli's work circulated widely in manuscript form, especially in Florence and Rome. On the status of Nifo's text (and whether or not it is plagiarized), see Anglo, *Machiavelli – the First Century*, 59–60; Gabriele Pedullà, "Disputare con il *Principe*," in *Atlante della letteratura italiana*, ed. Gabriele Pedullà and Sergio Luzzatto (Turin: Einaudi, 2010).

[44] Trevor Dean, *Crime and Justice in Late Medieval Italy* (Cambridge: Cambridge University Press, 2007), 60–62.

[45] Michel Foucault, *Discipline and Punish: The Birth of the Prison*, trans. Alan Sheridan (London: Penguin, 1991), 34.

viewers of public executions increasingly demanded the dramatic protocols of capital punishment to mirror that of the stage and vice versa.[46]
Nifo's version of Remirro's execution appeals to the conventions of such
a visual spectacle, in which the audience plays an active participatory role.

On Nifo's account, the execution resembles a public trial, in which the
meaning of the scaffold is communicated both verbally and symbolically.
By contrast, in Machiavelli's rendition, the people are stupefied, at least in
part, because the meaning of Remirro's death and dismemberment is
ambiguous. This ambiguity is important, because it compels the people
to try to make sense of the scene rather than fall back on existing cultural
patterns of public executions.[47] Had Remirro been publicly charged with
a crime and had the execution taken place in broad daylight, there would
be no need for interpretation. Had the execution taken place publicly,
Cesare would also have run the risk that Remirro might blame him
directly for the violence and repression used in the pacification of the
Romagna.[48] Yet in contrast to Nifo's, Machiavelli's Borgia is involved in
a project of civic pedagogy, in which the people – along with the readers –
are confronted with the clues of a crime scene that they are left to
reconstruct. The category of the scene organizes the traces of the event
spatially. Facing the traces of cruelty, the people are forced to piece
together the act, identify the agent, and attribute a motive. There is no
question that Machiavelli thought his contemporaries able to rise to the
occasion. After all, he describes the people of Florence as "subtle interpreters of all things [*sottile interprete di tutte le cose*]," and there is no
reason to expect any less of the Romagnol or of his readers (FH 8.19).

Starting with the arrangement of Remirro's corpse, an interpretation
can take recourse to the symbolic language of dismembered bodies.
Machiavelli's depiction of the mortal remains "in two pieces, with a piece
of wood and a bloody knife beside him [*in dua pezzi ... con uno pezzo di
legne e uno coltello sanguinoso accanto*]" provides important cues but
also leaves out key information. Remirro was bisected but what were the

---

[46] Margaret E. Owens, *Stages of Dismemberment: The Fragmented Body in Late Medieval
and Early Modern Drama* (Newark: University of Delaware Press, 2005), 115–43.

[47] McCanles notes that the display of Remirro's corpse was a signal to the Romagnol that
the spectacle was an act of communication with a content that required decoding.
Michael McCanles, "Machiavelli's 'Principe' and the Textualization of History," *MLN*
97, no. 1 (1982), 7. For insightful attempts at such decodings, see Rebhorn, *Foxes and
Lions*, 116–34; McCormick, "Prophetic Statebuilding."

[48] Rebhorn, *Foxes and Lions*, 120.

"two pieces"? Was he decapitated? If so, the protocol associated with the execution would point to the register of political crimes.

In the changing landscape of how political crimes are punished and how dead bodies are invested with meaning, a decapitated body might suggest that Remirro was guilty of treason. Along these lines, the knife and the piece of wood could stand for the ax and the block of wood that were employed in Florence for decapitation until about 1470, when a contraption similar to the guillotine started to be used.[49] As decapitation was traditionally reserved for those guilty of homicide or of crimes against the state, the visual language Machiavelli ascribes to Cesare may well be an attempt to emphasize Remirro's criminality. The implication of this particular choreography is that the killing is not a settlement of scores but an execution. As such, it is a penal and judicial act, even if it is one of summary justice.

Yet Machiavelli's text leaves open whether the two pieces of Remirro's body are head and trunk or whether Remirro was quartered.[50] As for the piece of wood, it might represent the executioner's block. But in the visual register of executions, it could also evoke the stake that executioners were sometimes ordered to drive through a corpse as if to simulate live burial.[51] Alternatively, the block of wood might be an allusion to the cross and the severed body of Remirro a belated Christmas (or rather Saint Stephen's Day) gift for the people of Cesena.[52] Finally, it could also point to a butcher's implements, the wood representing a butcher's wedge used to break up carcasses.[53] If so, perhaps Remirro was not decapitated but split

[49] Andrea Zorzi, "Le esecuzioni delle condanne a morte a Firenze nel tardo medievo tra repressione penale e ceremoniale pubblico," in *Simbolo e realtà della vita urbana nel tardo medioevo*, ed. Massimo Miglio and Giuseppe Lombardi (Rome: Vecchiarelli, 1993), 188; de Grazia, *Machiavelli in Hell*, 327.

[50] De Grazia writes that "in two pieces" implies that Remirro was quartered and the presence of the knife intimates that it was done by a butcher. Similarly, Sacerdote suggests that Remirro's body was quartered "and his head planted on a spear." De Grazia, *Machiavelli in Hell*, 327–28; Sacerdote, *Cesare Borgia*, 600. In the Italian context of the time, punishments involving the display of dismembered body parts were exceedingly rare, and in early modern Florence, the four modes of executions that are found in historical sources are hanging, decapitation, burning at the stake, and live burial. See Zorzi, "Le esecuzioni delle condanne a morte," 184; Andrea Zorzi, "Rituali e ceremoniali penali nelle città italiane (secc xiii–xvi)," in *Riti e rituali nelle società medievali*, ed. Jacques Chiffoleau, Lauro Martines, and Agostino Paravicini Bagliani (Spoleto: Centro italiano di studi sull'alto medioevo, 1994).

[51] Richard Evans, *Rituals of Retribution: Capital Punishment in Germany 1600–1987* (Oxford: Oxford University Press, 1996), 86.

[52] Ridolfi, *The Life of Niccolò Machiavelli*, 62; McCormick, "Prophetic Statebuilding," 7.

[53] Martinez, "Machiavelli and Traditions of Renaissance Theater," 209.

like a hog and carved like a piece of meat. Such a bisection might point to
the bestial nature of Remirro's acts in the Romagna or to the visceral and
quasi-cannibalistic pleasure of revenge. Cesare's message to the people
might be something like "look, this is how I will butcher your enemies."
And the bloody knife? It could be Remirro's, if the intended meaning
of the execution is to dissociate Valentino's rule from Remirro's cruelty.
It could also be Cesare's, in which case it might indicate an unconcealed
but indeterminate threat against his representatives and subjects alike. Or,
by leaving his knife behind, he might be signaling a promise – that now
that the Romagna is pacified, the knife is no longer needed and no more
violence will be visited upon the province.[54]

The abundance of possible interpretations invites readers of *The Prince*
to become participants in the inquiry.[55] By turning Remirro's execution
into a pedagogical moment, Machiavelli draws on the traditional didactic
elements of public executions. In Florence, executions tended to be highly
formalized and ritualistic affairs. They were increasingly taking place
inside rather than outside city walls to maximize their visibility, and
as the frequency of executions declined, the staging became more
elaborate.[56] There was a trend to emphasize the ceremonial and symbolic
dimensions of punishment and inscribe it in a political semantic of signs,
symbols, gestures, and images.[57]

Those punished for the most serious political crimes such as treason
were often subjected to further vilification following their execution or
banishment. The city of Florence traditionally painted dishonorable
portraits [*pitture infamanti*] of its public enemies on its walls or public
buildings. Following the expulsion of the despised despot Walter of
Brienne (Duke of Athens), his picture was painted as an effigy of shame
on the wall of the Palazzo del Podestà. In the 1440s, the painter Andrea
dal Castagno portrayed the enemies of Cosimo de'Medici on the facade
of the Palazzo del Podestà. After the Pazzi conspiracy of 1478, Sandro
Boticelli received a commission to paint the murderers of Giuliano de'Medici on the wall above the Dogana. When, during the 1529 siege of
Florence, mercenary captains escaped from the city along with some

---

[54] McCormick, "Prophetic Statebuilding," 8.

[55] Struever argues that Machiavelli's text forces the reader "addressed as noninquirer, into
the role of inquiry." Struever, *Theory as Practice*, 175.

[56] In 1504, the Florentine pillory, known as the *gogna* was moved to a prominent location
in the Mercato Vecchio. Robert Davidsohn, *Geschichte von Florenz: Vierter Band. Die
Frühzeit der Florentiner Kultur* (Berlin: E.S. Mittler & Sohn, 1922), 326, 330, 333.

[57] Dean, *Crime and Justice in Late Medieval Italy*, 63.

citizens, Andrea del Sarto was hired to portray them as traitors on the walls of the Mercanzia and the Palazzo del Podestà.[58] The image on the cover of this book is one of del Sarto's sketches for these defaming portraits. It depicts a man hanged by his foot, and it is one of seven surviving studies in red and black chalk prepared for these frescoes.[59] These iconic representations were part of a civic pedagogy, teaching Florentines how to read and interpret public practices of violence. The *pitture infamanti* were designed to develop a political literacy and to enable Florentines to become better readers of the political world. And just as Castagno and del Sarto painted disparaging portraits of the city's enemies on the Palazzo del Podestà, so Machiavelli defames Remirro by immortalizing the exposure of his sundered body in *The Prince*.

CATHARTIC VIOLENCE

Machiavelli figures the execution as cathartic and remedial. Cesare's objective in executing Remirro is to cleanse and "purge" [*purgare*] the infuriated spirits (P 7). His cruelty "restores" [*raccioncia*] the Romagna. In fact, Cesare's violence is depicted in exactly the same terminology as Romulus's fratricide, which as I show in Chapter 3, Machiavelli also justifies as an act of restoring or mending.[60] In both the case of Romulus and of Cesare, the verb *racconciare* – to restore, reorder, or repair – portrays violence as an act of reconciliation. The reader, it seems, is called upon to invoke the same principle that "he who is violent to spoil, not he who is violent to mend, should be reproved" (D 1.9).

By executing Remirro for the benefit of the public, Cesare enacts a maxim Machiavelli spells out in the *Florentine Histories*: "he who does not hope for good does not fear evil" (FH 2.14). The public *spettaculo* of violence leaves the people of the Romagna "satisfied and stupefied" [*satisfatti e stupidi*] and provides them with the hope for good Machiavelli

---

[58] Giorgio Vasari, *The Lives of the Artists*, trans. Julia Conaway Bondanella and Peter E. Bondanella (Oxford: Oxford University Press, 1998); Davidsohn, *Geschichte von Florenz, Bd. IV*, 327–30; Samuel Y. Edgerton, Jr., *Pictures and Punishment: Art and Criminal Prosecution During the Florentine Renaissance* (Ithaca, NY: Cornell University Press, 1985), 59–125; Wendy J. Wegener, "'That the Practice of Arms Is Most Excellent Declare the Statues of Valiant Men': The Luccan War and Florentine Political Ideology in Paintings by Uccello and Castagno," *Renaissance Studies* 7, no. 2 (1993).

[59] Edgerton, *Pictures and Punishment*, 114–22.

[60] Ezio Raimondi, "The Politician and the Centaur," in *Machiavelli and the Discourse of Literature*, ed. Albert Russell Ascoli and Victoria Kahn (Ithaca, NY: Cornell University Press, 1993), 157.

considers necessary. Note that it is the "ferocity" that fulfils this political role. Remirro's "harshness" generates a socialized affective response – hatred – which in turn is converted into a political resource by another transgression: the gruesome display of the violated violator. The public staging of dismemberment produces pleasure and satisfaction for its audience, leaving the Romagnol *satisfatti e stupidi* and with purged spirits. This excess turns spectacular violence into a remedial force with therapeutic effects: "strong medicine," as Machiavelli calls it elsewhere. It restores, repairs, and reorders, a point Machiavelli signals through the repeated use of the verb *racconciare*.

As I will argue in more detail in Chapter 6, various episodes in the *Discourses* and the *Florentine Histories* recount similar but not exactly equivalent moments of cruelty-induced purges. Take for instance the popular upheaval that brought down Walter of Brienne, discussed in book 2 of the *Florentine Histories*. There, the people are described as tearing apart the bodies of the duke's supporters "with their hands and their teeth" as well as engaging in a "rabid fury" of ritual cannibalism. This cruelty, Machiavelli observes, "purged" the multitude and made them able to conclude an accord (FH 2.37). The expiatory dimension of awe (exercised by the people in the case of Duke Walter or exercised on their behalf by Duke Valentino) bespeaks the political demand for catharsis.[61] But who exactly, among the Romagnol, is galvanized by hatred and what are the mechanisms that produce the cathartic release?

On Nifo's rendition, the presence of the *advocati* at Remirro's execution suggests that the killing is a public act of reconciliation with the elites that were harmed by the governor. Read through Nifo's lens, the "hatred" was the nobles', on account of the loss of power, privilege, and honor they suffered at Remirro's hands. Nifo's depiction thus suggests that Cesare sacrifices Remirro to mollify the *signori*. By contrast, on Machiavelli's account, the beneficiaries of Remirro's execution are not the nobles but the people. Whereas Nifo's Borgia reinstalls the old order by appeasing the *signori*, Machiavelli's Borgia attends to the people. Recall that Machiavelli introduces the episode to demonstrate Cesare's skill in building popular support. The spirits Machiavelli's Cesare must purge are not the elite's but the people's [*li animi di quelli populi*]. But this gives rise to a puzzle: If the targets of Remirro's cruelty are the *signori* who are reviled by the people, why would Remirro's attack on

---

[61] This is why, contra Zuckert, awe is not "akin to fear." Zuckert, *Machiavelli's Politics*, 210.

these elites trigger the people's hatred? And why would the people be "satisfied" by the execution of the official who has liberated them from bitter domination?

The interpretive framework of popular realism is helpful in answering these questions. Rather than treating the popular hatred against Remirro as an effect of elite manipulation, it suggests that the Romagnol had good reason to loathe Cesare's representative. There is no doubt that Romagnol elites would have sought to exploit local loyalties and to represent the assault against their privileges as illegitimate. If such efforts had been successful, then the people's hatred for Remirro could have been interpreted as an effect of popular confusion. On this reading, Remirro would be an innocent victim who is sacrificed to the unjust hatred of his beneficiaries.

Yet this is decidedly not the interpretation Machiavelli seeks to elicit. Rather than representing the people as naïve victims of elite manipulation with no capacity for political judgment, he depicts their hatred as a sound response to injustice. Implicit in Machiavelli's account is that Remirro used his *plenissima potestà* not only against the *signori* but also against the people. Such an interpretation is supported by records that accuse Remirro of corruption, extortion, and profiteering; it seems that he reaped advantage from grain shortages by illicit trafficking in wheat.[62] An aristocrat ruling with an iron fist, Remirro releases the people from the domination by the *signori* but substitutes his own authoritarian and brutal ways. Remirro's crime, then, is his inability or unwillingness to contain his brutality and target the elites. It is this leakage of cruelty that, in Machiavelli's rendition, ultimately costs him his life and his honor.

Having established the subjects affected by the hatred against Remirro, it now remains for us to examine the mechanisms that generate the cathartic release. Remirro's execution functions to dramatically expunge popular hatred. Such purges, Machiavelli suggests, happen in the course of gratifying the people's passions. The expiatory language of purging and mending indicates that the execution is intended to evoke intense affective responses that produce political bonds. Such affective responses and cathartic release were a staple of early modern executions; yet the cloaked nature of Remirro's assassination requires some additional interpretive work.

---

[62] Sacerdote, *Cesare Borgia*, 599.

In a judicial execution, the cultural grammar for catharsis was conventionally drawn from the religious register, especially from Christian hagiographic and martyrological traditions. Like Christian saints and martyrs, the condemned were expected to suffer physical pain.[63] In exchange for the agony, a wrong or crime is purged. Thus, the martyrological motif invests the execution with a transactional protocol: expiation at the price of suffering. And just as the suffering bodies of Christian saints had salvific powers, so the physical pain of the condemned was understood in a redemptive register. Consequently, the tortured and executed body testified not only to the power of the state but also to the redemptive capacity of visceral pain.

In view of this expiatory schema, it is all the more puzzling that Remirro's pain is not on display for either the people of Cesena or for Machiavelli's readers. In contrast to the tortured bodies of Christian saints, which were imbued with salvific power owing to the physical pain they suffered, the cathartic force of Remirro's execution does not emanate from his agony. Not only did he not die for an ideal or a righteous cause, but the expiatory logic of his execution does not conform to the martyrological motif. In fact, Remirro is more like a scapegoat. He is killed by Cesare as a substitute, though he is not a scapegoat in the technical sense that this term has in the Torah or in the sense that Girard's theory of sacrificial violence ascribes to it.[64] A scapegoat is typically chosen by lot and is publicly sacrificed not because of individual guilt but as atonement for a collectivity's wrongdoings. If, along the lines of the reading I rejected earlier, the people's hatred was a product of elite manipulation, then Remirro's death could indeed be interpreted as a kind of expiation of popular guilt. On this account, the catharsis produced by the ferocious spectacle does not primarily relieve hatred but redeems the people's guilt for their complicity in the unmerited killing. For Machiavelli, however,

---

[63] Saints, writes Margaret Owens, were represented as beheaded, "flayed alive, roasted on grills, tortured with hot pincers, disemboweled, thrown into lions' dens, and subjected to an assortment of amputations and mutilations. Eyes are poked out, tongues are torn out, breasts severed, and hands lopped off." Owens, *Stages of Dismemberment*, 28. See also Mitchell B. Merback, *The Thief, the Cross and the Wheel: Pain and the Spectacle of Punishment in Medieval and Renaissance Europe* (London: Reaktion, 1999).

[64] In Leviticus (16:5–28), the goat that is released into the wilderness bears all the community's sins and transgressions; the goat thus substitutes for the community. Similarly, for Girard, scapegoating is a mechanism whereby the death of one individual atones for the sins and transgressions of a collectivity. René Girard, *Violence and the Sacred*, trans. Patrick Gregory (London: Continuum, 2005), 41.

Remirro is not innocent, the killing is not unmerited, and the purge that is effected by his death expiates not the Romagnols' sins but Cesare's.

Yet even though Remirro is neither a conventional martyr nor a scapegoat in the technical sense, the scene of his execution remains shot through with Christian motifs. These motifs – the ominous date of the execution just after Christmas and visual cues, including the piece of wood, have led McCormick to interpret Remirro's execution as a Passion play, with Remirro's sundered body playing the role of a belated Christmas gift for the people of the Romagna. This clever allegorical reading raises important questions for understanding Machiavellian violence: If founding moments need religious consecration, are spectacular executions elements of a political theology? Put differently, does Machiavelli advance a political theology of violence?

The idea that political events follow a theological script is familiar in political theory. The premise for such views is that Christianity suffused European society with theological themes such that secularization is but a continuation of theology in disguise.[65] Recent work in this vein suggests not only that political and philosophical modernity is saturated by religious ideas and imagery but that it is entirely parasitic on theological categories.[66] Scholars who attribute a political theology to Machiavelli argue that his prince is a redeemer, that spectacular executions sacralize founding moments, or that symbolizations of power cannot but invoke theological motifs.[67] From this perspective, Remirro's execution is modeled on (or at the very least haunted by) Catholic paradigms and rituals.

[65] Warrants for this view come for instance from Carl Schmitt's famous line in *Political Theology* that "all significant concepts of the modern theory of the state are secularized theological concepts" or from Karl Löwith's thesis of the structural analogy between philosophies of history and theologies of salvation. Carl Schmitt, *Political Theology: Four Chapters on the Concept of Sovereignty*, trans. George Schwab (Chicago: University of Chicago Press, 2005), 36; Karl Löwith, *Meaning in History* (Chicago: University of Chicago Press, 1949). See also Claude Lefort, "The Permanence of the Theologico-Political?" in *Democracy and Political Theory* (Cambridge: Polity, 1988).

[66] Michael Allen Gillespie, *The Theological Origins of Modernity* (Chicago: University of Chicago Press, 2008); Giorgio Agamben, *The Kingdom and the Glory: For a Theological Genealogy of Economy and Government*, trans. Lorenzo Chiesa and Matteo Mandarini (Stanford, CA: Stanford University Press, 2011).

[67] For the prince as redeemer, see Rebhorn, *Foxes and Lions*, 132. For the sacralization of founding moments, see Jesse Goldhammer, *The Headless Republic: Sacrificial Violence in Modern French Thought* (Ithaca, NY: Cornell University Press, 2005), 6. For theology as language of power, see Graham L. Hammill, *The Mosaic Constitution: Political Theology and Imagination from Machiavelli to Milton* (Chicago: University of Chicago Press, 2012), 5; Graham Hammill and Julia Reinhard Lupton, eds. *Political Theology and Early Modernity* (Chicago: University of Chicago Press, 2012).

The trouble with these versions of political theology is that they get Machiavelli's conception of religion wrong and pay no heed to the political logic of violence. A politically literate response to violent spectacles involves interpreting them to ascertain their logics. These logics are, however, mystified when spectacles of violence are construed as divine acts, inscribed in schemas of punishment and redemption. This is not to say that religion plays no role. That Machiavelli considers religion central to political life is undeniable. His treatment of Roman religion and of the "armed prophets" suggests nothing less (P 6; D 1.11–15). Having experienced the power of prophecy in the person of the Dominican friar Girolamo Savonarola, whose apocalyptic sermons had gripped and convulsed Florence in the early 1490s, Machiavelli was well aware of the sway religion can have. Savonarola inspired a movement of spiritual, social, and political reform that attracted a large number of followers. Although the friar was burnt at the stake in 1498, his disciples continued to influence Florentine politics for decades thereafter.[68] Yet, what Machiavelli admires about Roman religion (in contrast to Savonarolan millenarianism) was that it directly strengthened civic life rather than weakening it. He praises ancient rituals and devotional practices because they are resolutely immanent. Rather than advancing a political theology that mystifies political events by figuring them in theological terms, Machiavelli defends a civil religion that is politically enabling.[69] A civil religion harnesses religious metaphors and images in order to create convenient narratives for political life, but it does not bear the scraps of theology as a kind of early modern hangover.

Earlier I noted the prominent motif, in traditional European mytho-political founding narratives, of the conversion of violence into law

---

[68] See Alison Brown, *Medicean and Savonarolan Florence: The Interplay of Politics, Humanism, and Religion* (Turnhout: Brepols, 2011); Felix Gilbert, "Florentine Political Assumptions in the Period of Savonarola and Soderini," *Journal of the Warburg and Courtauld Institutes* 20, no. 3/4 (1957); Jurdjevic, *A Great & Wretched City*, 16–52. Alison McQueen, "Politics in Apocalyptic Times: Machiavelli's Savonarolan Moment," *The Journal of Politics* 78, no. 3 (2016); Lorenzo Polizotto, *The Elect Nation: The Savonarolan Movement in Florence, 1494–1545* (Oxford: Clarendon Press, 1994); Donald Weinstein, "Savonarola, Florence, and the Millenarian Tradition," *Church History* 27, no. 4 (1958).

[69] John M. Najemy, "Papirius and the Chickens, or Machiavelli on the Necessity of Interpreting Religion," *Journal of the History of Ideas* 60, no. 4 (1999); Ronald Beiner, *Civil Religion: A Dialogue in the History of Political Philosophy* (Cambridge: Cambridge University Press, 2011), 17–45; Victoria Kahn, *The Future of Illusion: Political Theology and Early Modern Texts* (Chicago: University of Chicago Press, 2014), 83–113.

through mechanisms of expiation. Machiavelli's grisly scene in Cesena serves as a counterexample to these schemas of political and juridical founding moments. Unlike the heroes of Greek tragedy, whose violence brings guilt and persecution upon them, which they can only escape through acts of expiation, if at all, Cesare evades guilt through a multiplication of violence. In tragedy, the conversion of violence into legal authority typically occurs – for instance in Aeschylus's *Oresteia* – through the establishment of legal or quasi-legal public institutions that guarantee the peace. While Machiavelli retains the juridical motif (Cesare establishes a "civil court in the middle of the province"), it is not the court that purges the hatred but the public display of Remirro's severed body.

This claim is distinct from the social anthropology of sacrifice, a leading strand of which has long understood the sacrificial ritual as a mechanism whereby a social group releases tension. The anthropologist Victor Turner has argued that social arrangements such as hierarchies, laws, roles, and authority invariably generate conflict. According to Turner, sacrifice is the ritualistic matrix or "quintessential process" whereby societies rid themselves of such "negative sentiments" and generate unity.[70] While Machiavelli shares the view that political violence can generate unity, unlike Turner, he does not understand that unity as being generated by group boundaries. Whereas Turner follows Durkheim in conceptualizing violence as a mechanism of producing such boundaries, Machiavelli remains focused on the question of how violence transforms the exercise and representation of power in a given constellation. If Remirro's execution is sacrificial, it is not because of a universal social need to discharge negative emotions but because of the specific political context of corruption and elite domination.

The irony of Remirro's execution is that it allows Cesare to disavow political violence by exercising it. Cesare appears as a savior who rescues the people from the cruelty of his deputy. The spectacular display of the traces of cruelty has the paradoxical effect of making the previous violence invisible. In the process, the main witness of Remirro's brutality – the people – become an accomplice in violence's abnegation. Had Remirro been put on the scaffold in front of an audience, Cesare's implication in his ruthless brutality would have been revealed. By assassinating his governor in secret and then displaying the remains in the piazza, Cesare publicly repudiates his responsibility

[70] Victor Turner, "Sacrifice as Quintessential Process Prophylaxis or Abandonment," *History of Religions* 16, no. 3 (1977), 197.

for Remirro's incontinent use of violence. The execution thus stands for the symbolic threshold at which the state publicly acknowledges past abuses, punishes the perpetrator, and emphatically promises reform. This dual function of violence is one of the reasons why this story is of such interest to Machiavelli. Cesare manages to turn violence from a liability into an asset, using violence's spectacular traces to renounce violence. The popular hatred aroused by Remirro's cruelty is what allows Cesare to deploy violence in order to displace it. He cleans his hands of one type of violence not by making peace or declaring an amnesty but through a second act of violence. This suggests that the way to disavow violence is by deploying it, and the best route to turn hatred into legitimacy is through an execution.

THREE POLITICAL PASSIONS

The conventional modern story about how violence produces political effects is one about fear. It is generally traced back to Hobbes and treats fear, specifically the fear of death, as the central emotion of modern politics, the mediating factor between the individual and the collectivity.[71] Hobbes is credited not with the idea that fear serves as the transmission mechanism for violence but that it is the bedrock of social and political life, that the right kind of fear is both rational and virtuous, and that it must be assiduously cultivated. While Hobbes offers a far more elaborate defense of a pedagogy of fear, the idea goes back to Machiavelli. Fear, Machiavelli argues, forges the most reliable political bonds because "men love at their own convenience but fear at the convenience of the prince" (P 17). But fear creates not merely obedient subjects. More than just terror, fear is a force of unity; it unifies a people under the law. And lest the passage from *The Prince* be interpreted as a blanket vindication of cruelty, Machiavelli insists that fear is induced not only by violence but also by religion (D 1.11–15). The former engenders fear of the state; the latter fear of the gods. Fear of the gods disciplines people, makes them obey the law, and enables them to act as a collective subject. As I will argue in more detail in the next chapter, one of Machiavelli's insights into

---

[71] For the preference for Hobbes over Machiavelli on fear, see for instance Corey Robin, *Fear: The History of a Political Idea* (Oxford: Oxford University Press, 2004), 39.

how fear works politically is that fear of the law is insufficient to bind people together. Laws must be supplemented by violence or religion.[72]

Cesare's *spettaculo* in the square of Cesena is one of the forms such a supplementation can take. Yet on Machiavelli's narrative, Remirro's killing is only peripherally concerned with fear; the primary passions that govern the episode are love and hatred. In order to make sense of these affective responses to Remirro's actions and eventual demise, we need a brief detour through Machiavelli's political psychology, his theory of the three political passions: love, fear, and hatred.[73] Machiavelli conceives of the passions as feelings that humans experience involuntarily and for which they can therefore be neither praised nor blamed. Because emotions are fundamental drivers of human actions, understanding these passions and learning how to manage and exploit them is key for political success, whether one is founding a new state, addressing a republic, conspiring against a tyrant, or revolting against an elite.

From the Roman Stoics, Machiavelli inherits both the triad of political passions – love, fear, and hatred – and the focus on how the passions affect the ruled. This focus on the ruled is distinct, for instance, from Aristotle, for whom the primary political problem posed by the passions is how to prevent them from perverting the minds of rulers.[74] Yet whereas both Cicero and Seneca preached the primacy of love and the ineffectiveness of fear, Machiavelli famously inverts their teachings. For Machiavelli, love and fear are both regime-preserving whereas hatred is regime-endangering. Hence princes and republics must know how to evoke both fear and love and how to minimize the effects of hatred.

Love is the least prominent, yet it plays a central role as a generator of political unity. By love, Machiavelli means not a romantic sentiment but loyalty and fidelity.[75] This political concept of love resembles

---

[72] As D 1.15 demonstrates, religion is an important supplement but no substitute for violence.

[73] In the *Discourses* and the *Florentine Histories*, Machiavelli expands his political psychology by also discussing hope. Unlike fear, love, and hatred, which are central to governance, hope is more relevant to foreign policy, in particular to decisions about war. Hence Machiavelli argues in the *Florentine Histories* that "men are moved so much more by the hope of acquiring than by the fear of losing, for loss is not believed in unless it is close, while acquisition, even though distant, is hoped for" (FH 4.19).

[74] Aristotle, *The Politics and the Constitution of Athens*, trans. Steven Everson (Cambridge: Cambridge University Press, 1996), 1286a19, 1287a30.

[75] Romantic love or eros is decidedly not a political passion for Machiavelli. See for instance FH 5.21, where a Florentine envoy addresses the Venetian Signoria and refers to the "love" of the Florentines for Venice and its government. See also Catherine Zuckert,

Cicero's, for whom popular love [*amor multitudinis*] consists of goodwill [*benivolentia*]. Such goodwill creates strong political bonds. Thus, Cicero remarks in *De officiis*, "there is nothing at all more suited to protecting and retaining influence than to be loved."[76] Yet whereas Cicero thought that goodwill is elicited through "kind services" and through the reputation of moral virtue, above all justice, liberality, and faithfulness, Machiavelli offers a very different account.[77] Machiavelli's concept of love is at work, for example, in the "friendship" that he says Cesare acquired in the Romagna. Cesare's objective of executing Remirro, Machiavelli writes, was to "gain" the people "entirely to himself." That connection is based on esteem and gratitude. The Romagnol, he says, are "fond" [*affezionati*] of Cesare's power – hence he speaks of the people's "love" for Borgia [*tutto lo amore gli portavono*].

Despite the vital role of love in the formation of political unity, Machiavelli considers fear a more potent force. Fear is stronger than love, because "men love at their convenience and fear at the convenience of the prince" (P 17, see also D 3.21). Fear is the effect of an imagined future harm or pain. It is not only safer than love but also stronger than other passions, for in a contest between the passions, it is the one that tends to prevail (FH 5.13). Aristotle notes that the powerful are feared, especially when they are seen as unjust or angry, or when they themselves are afraid, have been wronged, or have wronged others.[78] People fear the powerful because of the latter's capacity to cause harm. What Machiavelli adds is that power is a necessary but insufficient condition to inspire fear. For the powerful to be feared they must also use their power and publicly demonstrate some amount of violence on a regular basis. Princes can induce both love and fear, and just as the promotion of love requires liberality, that of fear demands violence.

Fear's privileged status in Machiavelli's pantheon of the passions is explained by its mechanism. Politically, the power of fear lies in its capacity to isolate individuals. We hate collectively, but we fear individually. This is especially true for the fear of punishment. As Machiavelli

"Fortune Is a Woman – but so Is Prudence," in *Feminist Interpretations of Niccolò Machiavelli*, ed. Maria J. Falco (University Park: Pennsylvania State University Press, 2004), 202.

[76] Marcus Tullius Cicero, *On Duties*, trans. M. T. Griffin and E. M. Atkins (Cambridge: Cambridge University Press, 1991), 2.23.

[77] Cicero, *On Duties*, 2.32.

[78] Aristotle, *Rhetoric*, trans. W. Rhys. Roberts (Princeton, NJ: Princeton University Press, 1984), 1382a27–b27.

notes in *Discourses* 1.57, such fear is a distinctively particularizing passion; it functions by isolating people and by breaking up the unity of a multitude. When they are united, multitudes are strong; yet when everyone is isolated, multitudes lose all their political force. This makes fear a potent political mechanism.

Among the political passions, fear is peculiar in that it is built around uncertainty. Unlike other political emotions, what is specific about fear is that the threat of loss, whether to a person, possession, or a state of affairs, is uncertain. As Rebecca Kingston writes, "[d]espair, horror, and terror acknowledge the inevitability and indeed the experience of great loss, while fear only portends it."[79] The threat heralded by fear may be real and valid or not, but what distinguishes fear from anxiety, Kingston notes, is that there is a conception of threat, even if the extent of fear may not be proportional to the degree and type of loss imagined. This suggests that to be useful for a political actor, fear must be of a certain kind: It must be directed and channeled toward certain objects rather than diffuse and unspecific. That is, it must remain fear rather than become general anxiety. The unpredictability and doubt that attends the threat of loss also implies that as part of fear there is a hope that the menace not be realized. As a political passion, fear feeds off this hope, and it is what distinguishes the operation of fear, for instance, from that of terror, where hope is absent.

Despite its efficaciousness, fear has an important Achilles heel. Machiavelli notes that it has a tendency to turn into hatred (D 2.P). Fear is generated by violence and religion, but whereas excessive religious fear generates passivity, excess violence makes a prince "most hateful to all the world," something a prudent prince should avoid at all cost because it will lead to conspiracies and revolts against his rule (P 17, 19). Hatred is a kind of vengefulness, a desire to retaliate. Following Roman convention, Machiavelli understands hatred as an expression of general hostility, especially political hostility.[80] Indeed, for the Romans, the principal meaning of *odium* was "aversion."[81] One might expect Machiavelli to distinguish between hatred and anger, but the two concepts are largely isomorphic. When hatred affects a multitude, Machiavelli sometimes

---

[79] Rebecca Kingston, *Public Passion: Rethinking the Grounds for Political Justice* (Montreal: McGill-Queen's University Press, 2011), 165.

[80] Joseph Hellegouarc'h, *Le vocabulaire latin des relations et des partis politiques sous la république* (Paris: Les belles lettres, 1972), 192.

[81] G. Mahlow, "Lateinisches 'odi'," *Zeitschrift für vergleichende Sprachforschung auf dem Gebiete der indogermanischen Sprachen* 56, no. 1/2 (1929).

speaks of anger or rage [*rabbia*], but hatred is the preferred term (D 1.16–17, 3.12; FH 3.5, 3.24). It designates the one political passion that can generate popular rebellions and ultimately lead to a prince's downfall.

The tendency of fear to turn into hatred is evident in the story about Remirro, whose cruelty, Machiavelli says "had generated some hatred." Civil religion offers one solution to this dilemma, because it can elicit fears that trump hatred. Discussing the power of Roman rituals, Machiavelli reports the story of the tribune Marcus Pomponius, whose fear of breaking an oath was so strong that he could "put aside" his hatred (D 1.11). If Roman religion could engender the kind of fear that eclipses hatred, then it functioned as an effective supplement to violence.

If violence is unavoidable, Machiavelli opines, it is best deployed with a view to minimizing hatred. Here Machiavelli contests the conventional maxim attributed to tyrants: *oderint dum metuant* – may they hate me as long as they fear me.[82] In contrast to this classical formula, credited to Caligula, Machiavelli argues that princes cannot so easily dispense with the problem of hatred. Hatred is not just an interpersonal emotion, arising out of disappointed love and frustration, but a complicated political passion. Unlike fear, which tends to individualize, hatred produces the possibility of unifying a multitude. Hence Machiavelli's warning that collectivities become weak through fear and strong through hatred.[83] From the point of view of the prince, this yields the problem of how to deploy violence without generating hatred. (From the point of view of a rebellion, it yields the opposite problem: how to nurture collective hatred and avoid fear, especially in the face of repression.) Machiavelli's response to this problem is, paradoxically, that the theatrics of cruelty properly disposed can make violence not only palatable but productive. As the Remirro story makes clear, a good choreography of violence allows the prince to disavow violence and deny both authorship and responsibility.

The danger that popular fear flips to popular hatred regulates the deployment of violence by the state, yet, as is evident from Valentino's pursuit, popular hatred can be converted into gratification or pleasure.

---

[82] Cicero, *On Duties*, 1.97; Marcus Tullius Cicero, *Philippics*, trans. D. R. Shackleton Bailey, John T. Ramsey, and Gesine Manuwald (Cambridge, MA: Harvard University Press, 2010), 1.34. The line is originally from Accius' *Atreus*.

[83] For the corrosive role of fear on multitudes, see D 1.57. I discuss the role of hatred in unifying multitudes in more detail in Chapter 6.

Vengeance, Machiavelli writes, has the appearance of bringing "advantage and pleasure" [*utile e piacere*] (FH 4.10). The line is Tacitus's, and Machiavelli quotes it in full in *Discourses* 1.29.[84] The upshot of the Tacitean point is that there is an asymmetry between obtaining a benefit and suffering an injury. People are more likely to take revenge for an injury than to be grateful for a benefit. That is so because gratitude seems burdensome, while revenge creates the appearance of gain. Revenge, the gratification of hatred, is, in short, a powerful pursuit. And when hatred is converted – either back into fear or into pleasure – it is transformed from a liability into a political resource.

The psychological premise presupposed by this logic of the political passions is that people take pleasure in their enemies' misfortune, something Machiavelli takes for granted. Oppression causes hatred and resentment, and the more oppressed people are, the more likely they are to rejoice in the public display of revenge. Because the people are "many times, deceived by a false image of good" (D 1.53), the object of hatred is frequently displaced, leading to public violence that targets the perpetrators of oppression but not their beneficiaries.[85] What makes spectacular violence effective, then, is that it turns third parties from witnesses into spectators. Summoned to become part of the theatrics of cruelty, the audience is invited to enjoy the spectacle and revel in the common gratification of seeing their enemies punished.

If violence is politically functional to the extent that it addresses the passions, then a number of consequences follow. In order to inspire fear, violence must satisfy certain conditions. For one, it must not give rise to further violence and revenge. Second, violence must be understood semiotically, that is to say as the meaning generated through the production and circulation of signs. Political violence must have an audience; there has to be an addressee in place. Moreover, such violence is subject to formal constraints: It is embedded in signs and symbols. For acts of violence to signify, they are subject to the formal rules by which signs operate. Or, in a more Machiavellian language, violence must "appear" in a certain way and take a particular "form" or "nature" to become "effectual." This form is not arbitrary. It derives from the communicative process, from the practices and circumstances of reception, and the broader social and historical relations that shape

---

[84] Tacitus, *Histories*, 4.3.
[85] This, incidentally, is the meaning of Machiavelli's seemingly anti-popular claim in the *Florentine Histories* that it is the "nature" of the plebs to "rejoice in evil" (FH 2.34).

the conditions of intelligibility. Strategies of violence, in short, must take the form of an address, the symbolic terms of which are intelligible to an audience.

For a spectacle of violence to reach the passions, it would first travel through the filter of the imagination. Mediated by the imagination, the perception of violence could then trigger the passions Machiavelli ascribes to it. Machiavelli did not formulate an explicit account of how this works, yet in a famous letter known as the *Ghiribizzi*, he insists on the importance of the imagination for explaining human action. There, he writes that humans act according to their natural talent [*ingegno*] and imagination [*fantasia*].[86] Individuals and collectivities have different imaginations that mediate between sensation and understanding and explain variations in perception and action.

If spectacular violence is a procedure that generates political effects by way of the passions, then the individual and collective imagination act as conveyor points between sensory experiences and political affects. Understood this way, the imagination is not opposed to the *verità effettuale* but its mechanism. By effectual truth, Machiavelli means that human action or *virtù* must create sensory effects in the world that address the imagination. In Harvey Mansfield's words, "The effectual truth of governing requires that a prince get an effect by creating an effect; in the two meanings of effect, it is not only efficient but showy."[87] The adjective *effettuale* refers both to a truth that produces certain effects in the world, and to a truth that is efficacious in its operations.[88]

CONCLUSION

Cesare's state-making in the Romagna is poorly understood by conventional Weberian accounts of European state-formation that focus on the centralization of the means of violence. Drawing on Althusser's dictum that the "popular character of the state determines the prince's political practice," I have proposed an interpretation of Machiavelli's Cesare as a teacher of political literacy. The scene, orchestrated by Valentino, with

---

[86] Letter to Giovan Battista Soderini, September 13–21, 1506. Atkinson and Sices, *Machiavelli and His Friends*, 134–36. For interpretations, see Gennaro Sasso, "Qualche osservazione sui *Ghiribizzi al Soderino*," *Machiavelli e gli antichi e altri saggi*, vol. 2.

[87] Mansfield, *Machiavelli's Virtue*, 30.

[88] As Del Lucchese notes, the adjective *effettuale* is a neologism, coined by Machiavelli, and references the fact [*factum*], the effect [*effectus*], and the verb to do [*facere*]. Del Lucchese, *The Political Philosophy of Niccolò Machiavelli*, 26.

the material evidence of scandal, violence, and cruelty, elicits an effort at reading. Remirro's remains in the piazza call for interpretation: They invite readers to reconstruct the act, identify the agent, and impute a motive for the assassination and dismemberment. The staged scene invokes theatrical protocols and appeals to cultural codes that make violence intelligible. By aiming to induce awe and address its spectatorship on the affective level, such violence relies centrally on an aesthetic dramaturgy. The bewildering scene demands of readers that they pause and evaluate, and step out into the piazza to look at the corpse so as to interpret the logic of violence.

Political catharsis, Machiavelli suggests, is not produced by reconciliation but by the double-pronged strategy of disempowering beneficiaries of injustice (the papal vicars, noble families, and warlords that formerly ruled the province) and producing a memorable execution that gratifies the hatred and vengefulness of the people. Presupposed by such a schema of cathartic violence is a political psychology of the passions that I have sought to reconstruct. By tapping the political passions through the filter of the imagination, the scene produces a catharsis that is not exactly that of a martyr or a scapegoat (although allusions to both schemas are present) but a political mechanism of disavowal.

2

Force

You must know that there are two kinds of combat: one with laws, the other with force. The first is proper to man, the second to beasts; but because the first is often not enough, one must have recourse to the second.

– Niccolò Machiavelli, *The Prince*

A prudent man used to say that to hold a state with violence, there must be proportion between the one who forces and the one who is forced. And whenever such proportion is in place, one can trust that the violence will endure; but when the one who is forced is stronger than the one using violence, one can expect it to cease any day.

– Niccolò Machiavelli, *Discourses on Livy*

In a short speech composed in 1503, while he was serving as secretary to the Florentine republic, Machiavelli writes: "without force, cities do not maintain themselves but come to their end."[1] The recourse to force imposes itself, Machiavelli says, because states must consider as enemies all those who have the capacity to conquer it. The speech was probably written for Piero Soderini, who presided over the Florentine republic from 1502 to 1512 and faced a challenging political constellation. Externally, renewed French interventions in Italy and Cesare Borgia's conquests to the east portended insecurity. Even though the French were traditional

---

[1] "Parole da dirle sopra la provisione del danaio, facto un poco di proemio et di scusa," OP 1:13; CW 3:1439–1443. See Maurizio Viroli, *Machiavelli's God* (Princeton, NJ: Princeton University Press, 2010), 118–19.

allies, Louis XII had made his aversion to the republican regime very clear, demonstrating that he would rather deal with the Medici than with the official representatives of the Florentine republic. Domestically, the *ottimati* were discontent about Soderini's anti-oligarchic policies and his refusal to do away with the popular institutions that deprived them of their traditional influence. Enmity – both domestic and foreign – had become a permanent and structural feature of Florentine politics.

Under these conditions, force, which for Machiavelli is synonymous with "armed force" or simply "arms," denotes an instrumental quality of violence grounded in military strength. Force involves offending and injuring others, and Machiavelli conveys this instrumental aspect of force through a constellation of contiguous terms, such as *ingiuria*, *offesa*, and the cognate verb *offendere*. More often than not such offenses are lethal and involve killing [*ammazzare*] or eliminating [*spegnere*] enemies by war or assassination. *Spegnere* – to eliminate – is a prominent term in Machiavelli's idiom.[2] It connotes extinguishing the light or flame of life. Along with another metaphor *ferro*, "iron" (or "steel" as it is often translated), the language of extinguishing vividly expresses the instrumental dimensions of violence.[3]

Both princes and republics, Machiavelli contends, must "measure" their forces, an expression that suggests that forces are quantifiable and commensurate (D 2.10, 2.23). *Forza* is a central Machiavellian concept because it encapsulates a mode of violence that is embodied and material yet also fungible and politically underdetermined. Due to its polysemy, *forza* is also one of the most slippery terms in Machiavelli's vocabulary. It not only designates the use of arms but also serves as a generic term for natural or supernatural powers. Force takes us both to the heart of Machiavelli's political theory and to his natural philosophy, his view that human and natural bodies, causes, and powers are continuous rather than radically distinct.

---

[2] Chiapelli, *Studi sul linguaggio del Machiavelli*, 57–59. As Stacey notes, the figure of extinguishing the light of life is a reversal of one of Seneca's favorite metaphors, namely the role of light and illumination that surrounds a virtuous monarch. Peter Stacey, *Roman Monarchy and the Renaissance Prince* (Cambridge: Cambridge University Press, 2007), 277–78.

[3] *Ferro* is a euphemism for arms and armed force (FH 2.15), hence Scipio is described as forcing the fearful Romans to swear an oath to defend the republic "with naked steel in hand" [*col ferro ignudo in mano*] (D 1.11) and Machiavelli refers to "so many princes killed with steel" [*morti col ferro*] (D 1.10).

This chapter pursues two objectives. First, by situating Machiavelli's discussion of force in the context of early sixteenth-century Florentine political debates, I show that his conception of force is not merely technical but tied to a popular and anti-oligarchic politics. Second, I reconstruct Machiavelli's concept of force and contrast it with contemporary models of coercion. In doing so, I show that for Machiavelli, force is unstable and in need of supplements such as law, religion, and ideology. Far from glorifying force or envisaging it as a universal panacea in politics, Machiavelli demonstrates that force cannot successfully operate without legal, religious, or ideological supports.

THE MEDICI RESTORATION AND THE DISCOURSE OF FORCE

The oligarchic coup against the Florentine republic that occasioned the return of the Medici in 1512 elicited a burgeoning debate about enmity and the role of force in domestic politics. In contrast to the earlier humanist credo that sees in unity and concord the foundations of communal citizenship, Florentine authors of the early sixteenth century engaged in a theoretical reflection about conflict, war, and struggle. This difference is evident if one compares the works of Machiavelli or Guicciardini to that of the fifteenth-century humanist Leon Battista Alberti, who a few decades prior briefly treats enmity in his book *Della famiglia*. Alberti insists that enmity, conflict, hatred, and vengeance are to be avoided at all cost. Enmity, he writes, is "hardened, deep hatred," which derives from envy and ambition.[4] "Those who love me wish me well, grieve at my misfortunes, and are happy to strive for my welfare. My enemies wish me ill, rejoice at my every affliction, and take pleasure in hindering my acquisition of honest profits and praise."[5] By associating it with character flaws, Alberti offers a moralistic, individualized, and depoliticized account of enmity. The emotions aligned with enmity, especially hatred and anger, are treated as unworthy of virtuous men and as signs of incontinence and immaturity.

When enmity emerged as a major topic of interest in early sixteenth-century Florentine political discourse, it was disconnected from the concern with moral vices such as envy and hatred. Instead, the political controversy about force became a contest between the two principal

---

[4] Leon Battista Alberti, *The Albertis of Florence: Leon Battista Alberti's Della Famiglia* (Lewisburg, PA: Bucknell University Press, 1971), 308.
[5] Alberti, *Della Famiglia*, 309.

factions among the Florentine elite: the Mediceans and anti-Mediceans. Friends and allies of the Medici advocated the use of force to preempt another popular regime while their foes defended the conventional association of force with tyranny. Machiavelli intervenes in this debate by introducing a popular and anti-elitist perspective.

In the period following 1512, when the Medici family restored its power in Florence, recourse to force became a topic of debate in the various political and constitutional proposals that circulated. Historically, Florentine policy, both foreign and domestic, had been based on the belief that for a territorially small and militarily weak state like Florence, reason and wit [*ragione* and *ingegno*] were more effective political strategies than *forza*.[6] It was hence incumbent on political leaders to do the utmost to avoid and defer situations in which *forza* was decisive, using a tactic of delay and stalling that Florentines referred to as *temporeggiare* – to temporize.[7] Alberti, for instance, while acknowledging that "they say that force can only be met with force," insists on the primacy of vigilance and precaution, and emphasizes that if force must be used, it should be done honorably, in a just and open manner rather than by trickery.[8] The historian Felix Gilbert reports that in the late fifteenth century, there was "an almost religious conviction in this Florentine belief in the triumph of reason." Hence in 1496, as the city came under pressure by other Italian powers because of its alliance with France, and the Florentines had to choose whether to respond "by force or with ingenuity," the widespread assumption was that ingenuity was by far the better option.[9]

Yet, the political upheavals between 1494 and 1512, which ultimately led to the overthrow of the republic and to the return of the Medici, converted many Florentine elites to the idea that force, rather than wit or ingenuity, is the determinant factor in politics.[10] As Gilbert and other historians of the period have noted, during these turbulent years the political discourse in Florence changed markedly.[11] A new vocabulary emerged to describe the divisions of the body politic with terms

---

[6] Gilbert, "Florentine Political Assumptions," 201.
[7] On the strategy of temporization, see Hörnqvist, *Machiavelli and Empire*, 98–102.
[8] Alberti, *Della Famiglia*, 314.
[9] Gilbert, "Florentine Political Assumptions," 201.
[10] Gilbert, *Machiavelli and Guicciardini: Politics and History*, 129.
[11] Hörnqvist, *Machiavelli and Empire*, 281; Jean-Louis Fournel, "La connaissance de l'ennemi comme forme nécessaire de la politique dans la Florence des guerres d'Italie," in *L'Italie menacée: Figures de l'ennemi*, ed. Laura Fournier-Finocchiaro (Paris: L'Harmattan, 2004), 33.

such as *divisione, discordie, tumulti, odio, fazioni, inimicizia*, and, of course, *forza*. Both in domestic and foreign policy, previous inhibitions about naming the forms of dominion, empire, struggles, and forms of violence receded. Whereas previously, *forza* had been regarded as a blunt and inadequate political means, over these years a new paradigm had materialized, according to which politics was ruled by force.

The acquiescence to the role of *forza* was not, however, a conversion of dreamy idealists to the hard truths of political reality. As much as students of political theory might wish that the new paradigm of force emerged as a category through which astute observers made sense of the political earthquakes of the time, in fact, the new vocabulary of politics was part of a highly partisan struggle among the Florentine aristocracy. The struggle concerned the nature of Medici rule, the form that this rule should take, and the manner by which Florence's leading family should consolidate its political power.[12]

The Florentine nobility, and especially its leading families, had for the most part been opposed to the democratic republic that lasted from 1494 to 1512 and was headed by Piero Soderini. They overwhelmingly supported the Medici restoration. Yet while most *ottimati* shared an opposition to the inclusive and participatory institutions of the democratic republic, such as the Great Council [Consiglio Grande] established in 1494, there were significant disagreements about the form the renewed Medici rule should take.[13] Prior to 1494, Florence had been governed by the *ottimati* in a regime that was nominally republican but substantially oligarchic. The officials who served in the Signoria and the various councils that made up the Florentine government were selected by means of sortition [*tratta*], from the bags in which the names of all qualified candidates had been placed. Rather than interfering with the sortition itself, the powerful families, above all the Medici, exercised their influence by manipulating the names in the bags using various constitutional and

---

[12] Pocock, *The Machiavellian Moment*, 114–55; Rudolf von Albertini, *Das florentinische Staatsbewußtsein im Übergang von der Republik zum Prinzipat* (Bern: Francke Verlag, 1955), 197; John M. Najemy, *A History of Florence, 1200–1575* (Malden, MA: Blackwell, 2006), 422–26.

[13] Founded in 1494, the Great Council was the cornerstone of the popular regime established by the followers of Girolamo Savonarola, the Dominican friar who dominated Florentine politics between the overthrow of the Medici in 1494 and his execution four years later. Composed of some 3,000 members, it was a symbol of democratic popular government despised by many among Florence's elites. Nicolai Rubinstein, "Politics and Constitution in Florence at the End of the Fifteenth Century," in *Italian Renaissance Studies*, ed. Ernest F. Jacob (London: Faber & Faber, 1960), 156–61.

extra-constitutional mechanisms.[14] In the period since 1382, following the turbulent years of the Ciompi revolt, the Florentine aristocracy had perfected a form of narrow, elite-based republican government, known as a *governo stretto*, staffed by the *amici*, an inner circle of powerful families with the Medici at the helm.

During the first five decades of their rule, the Medici maintained the republican façade by preserving the traditional communal institutions, such as the Signoria, the Consiglio del Popolo, and the Consiglio del Comune.[15] In a triangular conflict between the *popolo*, the *ottimati*, and the Mediceans, Cosimo de'Medici resisted attempts to overthrow the republican institutions and positioned himself as a defender of the republic.[16] The Medici family protected its rule by manipulating the electoral system, ensuring that only allies would be elected to governing bodies, and by maintaining an expansive network of patronage. Having incorporated the bulk of the Florentine aristocracy into the regime, Cosimo and Lorenzo de'Medici managed to consolidate their family's power without ruffling traditional constitutional feathers.

Subsequent to the popular republican interlude of 1494 to 1512, many *ottimati* pleaded for a return to the pre-1494 regime: a narrow *governo stretto* dominated by the wealthy and powerful families, yet a regime that remains formally republican. Guicciardini, for instance, a defender of the traditional aristocracy but also an advocate of liberty, argued that the Medici should pursue a policy of moderation, both in dealing with their opponents and with the aristocracy as a whole.[17] Yet the nobility was split. Against traditionalists such as Guicciardini, a group of younger *ottimati* contended that the Medici should use force against their enemies. It was precisely the formal republicanism of the pre-1494 regime, they argued, that had allowed figures like Savonarola and Soderini to subvert the nobility and create a popular state.

These young "prophets of force" – the expression is Gilbert's – called for a transition to a Medici principate.[18] Their rationale was that the

---

[14] The best account of the Florentine political institutions in the fifteenth century remains Nicolai Rubinstein, *The Government of Florence under the Medici (1434–1494)* (Oxford: Clarendon, 1966).

[15] Albertini, *Das florentinische Staatsbewußtsein*, 15.

[16] See FH 7.3. Najemy, *A History of Florence*, 301.

[17] Pocock, *The Machiavellian Moment*, 143–48; Peter E. Bondanella, *Francesco Guicciardini* (Boston, MA: Twayne, 1976), 47.

[18] Gilbert, *Machiavelli and Guicciardini: Politics and History*, 129. Najemy calls them the "radical ottimati." Najemy, *A History of Florence*, 422.

political turmoil of the previous two decades was proof that *forza* was the key factor in politics, both domestic and foreign. A principate, they believed, was better able to deploy an authoritarian politics of force than an aristocratic republic. In a letter to Cardinal Giovanni de'Medici – the later Pope Leo X – Paolo Vettori announces that in contrast to their illustrious ancestors, who were able to "hold the state using industry rather than force" the post-Restoration Medici need to deploy "force rather than industry."[19] Pointing to the lack of political stability, to their numerous enemies, to the people's continued attachment to Soderini's republic, and to the unreliability of the *grandi*, Vettori contends that Florence can no longer be governed by the methods used by their predecessors.[20] He recommends sidelining the existing republican institutions, establishing a small council of close advisers, and, crucially, taking recourse to *forza*.

Vettori and others regarded a strong principate as the only way to prevent a possible recurrence of a popular government, which is why they advocated dissolving republican institutions. In 1516, Lodovico Alamanni, a pro-Medici politician, penned a *Discorso* to Lorenzo in which he discusses, as a conceivable course of action, killing all citizens that oppose the Medici. Alamanni ultimately rejects such callous use of force as nonviable and disgraceful. A statesman like Lorenzo, he exclaims, would disapprove of the bloody ways of "the godless Agathocles" and "the wicked Liverotto of Fermo."[21] Yet the fact that a recourse to political assassination could even be publicly contemplated and that it took the form of the very same examples to which Machiavelli appeals in chapter 8 of *The Prince* demonstrates that a discursive shift had taken place. Alamanni's proposal is extreme, but even Guicciardini, who rejected the project of a Medici principate, argued that states could not exist without recourse to force. Hence, his advice to the Medici to use a blend of "love and force." For Guicciardini, states must rely on force to induce men to pursue their natural inclination to be good. Men, he

[19] "Ricordi di Paolo Vettori al Cardinale de'Medici sopra le cose di Firenze," in Albertini, *Das florentinische Staatsbewußtsein*, 345.
[20] Albertini, *Das florentinische Staatsbewußtsein*, 33.
[21] "Discorso di Lodovico Alamanni sopra il fermare lo stato di Firenze nella devozione de'Medici," in Albertini, *Das florentinische Staatsbewußtsein*, 367. See also Gilbert, *Machiavelli and Guicciardini: Politics and History*, 137–38.

argued, need the help of a coercive institution to prevent passions and temptations from diverting them from the proper path.[22]

Previously, Renaissance authors would have regarded such uses of force (and especially political assassinations) as unacceptable and tyrannical. During the political crisis in 1458, a citizen proudly cited Sallust to argue that it was not by force of arms that a republic becomes great but, as Rome did, "by industry at home and just rule abroad."[23] *Tyranny* was the concept inherited from antiquity to describe the usurpation of power, its seizure, and its use in illegitimate and arbitrary ways.[24] Originally a Greek term used to describe usurpation, tyranny subsequently came to stand for a particular *quality* of rule. Hence Rousseau will later distinguish between the "vulgar sense" of tyranny, namely government "with violence and without regard for justice" and the "precise sense" in which "the Greeks understood the word," namely usurped government "without having any right to it."[25] As so often, Rousseau overstates his case. The "vulgar sense" was in fact already part of Aristotle's definition of tyranny.[26] Yet the distinction between the two ways of thinking about tyranny is nonetheless useful.

Linking the two prevailing understandings of tyranny, the fourteenth-century thinkers Bartolus de Saxoferrato and Coluccio Salutati distinguished between the *tyrannus ex defectu tituli*, a ruler who attained the throne illegitimately, and the *tyrannus ex parte exercitii*, a ruler who governs unjustly albeit with legal title.[27] Underlying both conceptions of tyranny is the idea that a king's legitimacy is undermined by evil and injustice. The unjust king forfeits his right to rule, irrespective of

---

[22] Guicciardini, *Dialogue on the Government of Florence*, 75; Bondanella, *Francesco Guicciardini*, 51–52.

[23] Donato Cocchi, July 2, 1458, quoting *Bellum Catilinae* 52.19–21, cited in Alison Brown, "The Language of Empire," in *Florentine Tuscany: Structures and Practices of Power*, ed. William J. Connell and Andrea Zorzi (Cambridge: Cambridge University Press, 2000), 39.

[24] Strauss likes to emphasize that Machiavelli, in *The Prince* (but not in the *Discourses*) deliberately undermines the distinction between the king and the tyrant, but that's not my point here. See, for example, Leo Strauss, *On Tyranny* (London: Glencoe, 1963), 22–23.

[25] Rousseau, *Social Contract*, 3.10.

[26] For Aristotle, tyranny is the "arbitrary power of an individual which is responsible to no one, and governs … with a view to its own advantage; not to that of its subjects, and therefore against their will." Aristotle, *Politics*, 1295a19.

[27] Francesco Ercole, "Introduzione," in Coluccio Salutati, *Il trattato 'De tyranno' e lettere scelte* (Bologna: Nicola Zanichelli, 1942), xxxvii. See also Ronald G. Witt, "The *De Tyranno* and Coluccio Salutati's View of Politics and Roman History," in *Italian Humanism and Medieval Rhetoric* (Aldershot: Ashgate, 2001).

whether the unjust action was committed in the acquisition or execution of power. Having broken the inseparable bond between the terms *rex* and *rectus*, the unjust king loses his title before god; he becomes a usurper, "tyrannus."[28]

This natural law conception of tyranny shaped anti-Medicean politics in fifteenth- and sixteenth-century Florence. Renaissance Italians understood usurpation as an illegitimate albeit well-established way of attaining political power. From the della Scala in Verona through the Malatesta of Rimini, to the Visconti of Milan and the dozens of petty tyrants in the Romagna, Umbria, and Marche, many Italian cities were ruled by usurpers, condottieri, or their heirs. Nonetheless, the discourse of tyranny (and, by extension, the vindication of tyrannicide) remained a fixture of republican ideology.[29] Thus, when Piero de'Medici was expelled from Florence in 1494, the newly established Great Council resoundingly proclaimed the advent of freedom and the demise of tyranny.[30] Savonarola in his *Treatise on the Government of Florence* insists that even though the Medici had not technically usurped power but instead governed by retaining the formal structures of the Florentine republic, they nonetheless qualify as tyrants because they governed for their own benefit rather than for the common good.[31] Savonarola makes the link between tyranny and force very explicit: "Tyrant is the name for a man of evil life, the worst among all those people who want to rule above all others through force [*per forza*]."[32] Painting a picture of a ruthless and homicidal ruler, Savonarola sees tyranny as the epitome of violence. A tyrant cannot but rely on force because his entire government is founded on vice and sin and because force is the only mechanism that can maintain a regime based on

---

[28] Kern, *Gottesgnadentum und Widerstandsrecht*, 187.

[29] J. K. Hyde, "Contemporary Views on Faction and Civil Strife in Thirteenth- and Fourteenth-Century Italy," in *Violence and Civil Disorders in Italian Cities, 1200–1500*, ed. Lauro Martines. (Berkeley: University of California Press, 1972).

[30] Nicolai Rubinstein, "Florentine Constitutionalism and Medici Ascendancy in the Fifteenth Century," in *Florentine Studies*, ed. Nicolai Rubinstein (London: Faber and Faber, 1968), 462.

[31] Girolamo Savonarola, "Treatise on the Rule and Government of the City of Florence," in *Selected Writings of Girolamo Savonarola: Religion and Politics, 1490–1498*, ed. Anne Borelli and Maria C. Pastore Passaro (New Haven, CT: Yale University Press, 2006), 179, 183. See Pocock, *The Machiavellian Moment*, 105–13; Giovanni Silvano, "Florentine Republicanism in the Early Sixteenth Century," in *Machiavelli and Republicanism*, ed. Gisela Bock, Quentin Skinner, and Maurizio Viroli (Cambridge: Cambridge University Press, 1990), 46–49; Weinstein, "Savonarola, Florence, and the Millenarian Tradition"; Brown, *Medicean and Savonarolan Florence*.

[32] Savonarola, "Treatise on the Rule and Government of the City of Florence," 187.

avarice, hatred, and fraud. Because tyranny depends on *forza delle arme* and because "such force cannot be resisted with reason" Savonarola concedes that "we cannot give any instructions concerning this."[33]

By disassociating the instrument of force from the discourse of tyranny, the young oligarchs whom Gilbert calls prophets of force signal a shift in the political concerns of the Florentine elites. Whereas older generations of *ottimati* were anxious about a concentration of power in a single person or family and viewed such developments as preludes to tyranny, authors such as Vettori and Alamanni were more concerned about the potential threat to their privileges and prerogatives arising from another popular democratic regime. They did not, in other words, contest the conventional link between force and despotic government but were, in marked contrast to their elders, willing to bargain with despotism.

FORCE AND THE DEMOCRATIC REPUBLIC

Unlike Savonarola who claimed to have no *instruzione* to give concerning *forza*, Machiavelli was more than ready to do so. Yet unlike the young prophets of force whose concern was to leverage force against the people in the defense of aristocratic privilege, Machiavelli dismisses the use of force against the people as ineffective. "I say that for the prince or the republic that fears his or its subjects and their rebellion, such fear must first arise from the hatred one's subjects have for one, the hatred from one's bad behavior, and the bad behavior either from believing one can hold them by force or from the lack of prudence of whomever governs them" (D 2.24). For Machiavelli, the belief that the people can be subdued by force is hubristic; the effective and decent way of holding a state is to rely on the people's "benevolence" and support. Machiavelli was interested in force not as an instrument to subjugate the people but as a mechanism for defending a democratic regime.[34] Responding to the failure of both Savonarola and Soderini to maintain the popular governments they headed, Machiavelli's intervention in the

---

[33] Savonarola, "Treatise on the Rule and Government of the City of Florence," 197.

[34] Contra the revisionist tendency to depict Machiavelli as a mere "bureaucrat" under Soderini (Bausi) and deny his commitment to the cause of Soderini's republic (Black), I follow the conventional interpretation by Ridolfi and others, according to which Machiavelli was a champion of the popular republic. Ridolfi, *The Life of Niccolò Machiavelli*, 15–132; Francesco Bausi, *Machiavelli* (Rome: Salerno, 2005), 72; Robert Black, *Machiavelli* (London: Routledge, 2013), 40.

early sixteenth-century discourse of force consists in an attempt to account for the role of force in a *governo largo*.

Machiavelli's critique of Savonarola focuses on the friar's inability to wield force when elites turned against him. In a well-known passage in chapter 6 of *The Prince*, Machiavelli opposes the "most excellent princes" Moses, Cyrus, Romulus, and Theseus to the "unarmed" Savonarola, who ended up burning on the stake. What distinguishes the most excellent princes, Machiavelli writes, is their capacity "to use force" [*possono forzare*]. They are "armed prophets" and rely for their persuasive power not exclusively on prayer and preaching, as did Savonarola, but on the ability to make people "believe by force" [*fare loro credere per forza*]. In the *Discourses*, Machiavelli further contrasts the failures of Savonarola and Soderini to construct a stable popular regime with the successful founding of such a polity by Moses. In contrast to Savonarola and Soderini who were unable (Savonarola) or unwilling (Soderini) to use force against conspiratorial patricians, Moses successfully confronted his opponents, killing "infinite men" in the process (D 3.30).[35]

In that same chapter of the *Discourses*, Machiavelli saves his harshest criticism for Soderini. Opposed, as a matter of principle, to the use of force against domestic political adversaries, Soderini trusted that envy would eventually be cured by time and largesse (D 3.30). By criticizing Soderini for his refusal to use force against his oligarchic rivals, Machiavelli makes clear that the choice of political means is not simply a matter of personal moral deliberation but of political responsibility. Soderini's reluctance to "strike his opponents vigorously and to beat down his adversaries" cost him and Florence dearly. As a result, "he lost not only his fatherland but his state and his reputation" (D 3.3). Soderini's humanist pieties led to the overthrow of the most democratic government the city had enjoyed in over a century and ultimately to the consolidation of the Medici principate over the course of the following decades. As Wolin puts

---

[35] Machiavelli's likely reference is Exodus 32, when Moses, following the episode of the Golden Calf, orders a massacre in which three thousand Israelites are murdered. As Jurdjevic notes, the most probable source for Machiavelli's Moses are Savonarola's sermons on Exodus from March 2 and 3, 1498. Jurdjevic, *A Great & Wretched City*, 41. On Machiavelli's Moses, see John H. Geerken, "Machiavelli's Moses and Renaissance Politics," *Journal of the History of Ideas*, 60 no. 4 (1999); Hammill, *The Mosaic Constitution*; Warren Montag, "'Uno mero esecutore': Moses, *fortuna*, and occasione in *The Prince*," in *The Radical Machiavelli: Politics, Philosophy, and Language*, ed. Filippo Del Lucchese, Fabio Frosini, and Vittorio Morfino (Leiden: Brill, 2015); Najemy, "Papirius and the Chickens."

it: "Here was a gentle, well-intentioned man forced by the imperatives of politics to choose between the objective necessity of destroying his enemies or of observing legal niceties which would allow his enemies to destroy him. Being a good man, he chose the latter, thereby inflicting grave harm on his country and himself."[36] By elevating the amicable and peaceful resolution of conflicts into a moral principle, Soderini failed to discharge his political responsibility toward the city. The blame Machiavelli attributes to Soderini is all the more serious because, unlike Savonarola who lacked the resources to deploy force, Soderini had the capacity but decided, on the grounds of his convictions, to forgo violence.

Soderini's weak point was that he was ultimately a moralist. That is, he believed that decisions about political means, including force, require an appeal to moral principles. By elevating moral considerations over the unscripted contingency of politics, Soderini implicitly positions the wellsprings of moral precepts (religion, tradition, or moral philosophy) as authoritative and ostensibly apolitical sources for settling political questions. Entailed in such a view is that politics consists in applying principles and values specified elsewhere; that political actors must seek the ethical ground for politics outside political life itself, a framework that Machiavelli categorically rejects.[37]

Machiavelli's account of force is a response to Savonarola and Soderini on the one hand and to the prophets of force on the other. Like Vettori, Alamanni, and others, Machiavelli dismisses the traditional link between tyranny and force. Yet unlike the young patricians, Machiavelli's aim is not to legitimize a Medici principate but to theorize the conditions, forms, and limits of political violence for a popular regime. Whereas the prophets of force simply invert the traditional proscription of *forza* in order to secure an oligarchic regime against the people, Machiavelli's political and theoretical projects are different.

Politically, Machiavelli is aligned with the people rather than the nobility, and he argues for recourse to *forza* on behalf of the people.[38] His critiques of Savonarola and Soderini for their respective failures to deploy force show this very well: In both cases, Machiavelli criticizes

---

[36] Wolin, *Politics and Vision*, 186.

[37] For a compelling critique of such a view, see Vázquez-Arroyo, *Political Responsibility*, 25–62.

[38] Contra Martelli, who has argued that Machiavelli became a Medici partisan in 1512, once the Medici were the only political force that could confront the traditional *ottimati* faction. Mario Martelli, "Introduzione," in Niccolò Machiavelli, *Il principe.* (Rome: Salerno, 2006).

leaders of popular regimes for neglecting the conditions that might allow such regimes to prosper. Machiavelli's advice to the Medici is in tune with these positions. In a letter penned in late 1512, he advises the Medici not to trust the *ottimati*, who are wont to pursue their own interests, and instead to ally themselves with the people against the nobility.[39] The real enemies of the Medici state, he contends, are not the democratic populists around Soderini but the aristocratic opposition. Oligarchs like the previously cited Paolo Vettori are always pleased to vilify the former *gonfaloniere* but are unreliable political allies.[40]

Theoretically, Machiavelli articulates *forza* in relation to political responsibility, law, and speech. Unlike the *ottimati*, who – without argument – presume it to be a universally effective, pliable, and transposable political instrument, Machiavelli examines the conditions, limits, and modalities of force. It is to these conceptual aspects of force that we will now turn. As I will show, Machiavelli rejects a common and rarely interrogated cliché about political violence, namely that it is an obviously effective "last resort." Machiavelli's discussion of *forza* calls into question this self-evidence, highlights the instability of force, and prompts a differentiation between force and coercion.

POLITICAL AND NATURAL FORCES

The idiom of force ties Machiavelli's political theory of state and legal violence to an ontology and natural philosophy. In *Discourses* 3.22, Machiavelli gestures to such an ontology by postulating that there must be "proportion between the one who is forcing [*da chi sforzava*] and that which is forced [*a quel che era sforzato*]," suggesting that the idiom of force provides a medium for comparing and evaluating such instrumental potentials.[41] As is suggested by the language of "proportion," force designates not just military measures but serves as a generic term for

---

[39] "Ai Palleschi" in OP 1:87–89.

[40] Marchand notes the "violent language" Machiavelli uses to describe the aristocracy. Jean-Jacques Marchand, *Niccolò Machiavelli. I primi scritti politici (1499–1512): Nascita di un pensiero e di uno stile* (Padua: Antenore, 1975), 308.

[41] This is the dimension of force that Wolin has captured so well with the felicitous expression of an "economy of violence." Such an economy, Wolin proposes, would be a "science of the controlled application of force" with the aim to maintain the distinction "between political creativity and destruction." The appropriate measure of force will vary, depending on the specific social and historical conditions. Wolin, *Politics and Vision*, 198.

natural or supernatural powers. Hence Machiavelli describes a great storm in 1456 as "driven by superior forces, natural or supernatural" (FH 6.34). Force, as used in this passage, is the impetus behind the storm, that which propels it.

This expansive sense of force is also evident in Machiavelli's use of the verb *forzare*. Especially in its passive mode, *forzare* expresses necessity, a lack of options and available alternatives. To be forced is to be exposed to constraints that restrict one's available courses of action, a condition that Machiavelli frequently labels *necessità*.[42] *Necessità* is Machiavelli's metaphor for natural forces that are too strong for humans to overcome. It is a category of Machiavelli's naturalism, designating the limits of human *arte* and *industria*. According to Friedrich Meinecke, *necessità* stands for an overarching causality that governs and coerces human and nonhuman natural life.[43] As such, it manifests both the power that forces the prince to act "against faith, against charity, against humanity, against religion" (P 18), as well as that which compels men to be good (P 23). Necessity, in other words, describes both the elementary condition of political action and the matrix of a latent deployment of force.

A key passage in the *Discourses* supports this interpretation of *forza*. Writing about the Roman institution of the dictatorship, Machiavelli contests the view that the dictatorship had undermined Rome's freedom. It was not "the name nor the rank of dictator" that corrupted Rome but rather the "forces" that extended the dictatorial authority beyond its constitutional term of six months (i.e. Sulla and Caesar). For "it is forces that easily acquire names, not names forces" [*sono le forze che facilmente si acquistano i nomi, non i nomi le forze*] (D 1.34). Here force is not a means of violence but a generic metaphor for a cause that sets something in motion, a social or natural power.

The adage that forces easily acquire names and that names do not beget forces implies a materialist social ontology, in which the building blocks of social reality are not names but moving forces. Understood this way, *forze* are the invisible relations that are responsible for the motion of

---

[42] As various scholars have noted, the language of coercion and necessity (in expressions, such as *debbe*, *è necessario*, *fu forzato* and *bisogna*) is all over Machiavelli's texts, pointing to the importance of a generic logic of constraint in the architecture of the work. Giorgio Barberi-Squarotti, *La forma tragica del 'Principe' e altri saggi sul Machiavelli* (Florence: Leo S. Olschki, 1966), 139; Guillemain, *Machiavel: L'anthropologie politique*, 246; Herfried Münkler, *Machiavelli: Die Begründung des politischen Denkens der Neuzeit aus der Krise der Republik Florenz* (Frankfurt a.M.: Fischer, 2004), 246–56.

[43] Meinecke, *Die Idee der Staatsräson*, 46.

objects in the world. Force, in short, is motile force. In contrast to forms of violence that aim at possessing, using, expending, or exploiting the body, force is not interested in what a body can do. Its focus, instead, is on the body as a transferable and transposable object, something that can and must be relocated, transported to another place, or removed entirely.[44]

As a principle of movement, the Machiavellian conception of force is tied to a natural philosophy and, more specifically, to a theory of motion that Machiavelli inherits from Aristotelian physics. According to a basic principle of Aristotelian dynamics, an object's motion is proportional to the force that is applied to it.[45] Hence motion presupposes force, or as the fourteenth century philosopher Jean Buridan, who revised Aristotle's theory of motion, would have said "impetus."[46] That *impeto* and *impetuouso* are important terms for Machiavelli is not the only evidence for the influence that Buridan's theory of impetus and Aristotelian natural philosophy had on Machiavelli's conception of force. For Machiavelli, *forza* is the general medium of social and political relations that are structured by power. A political situation – the *qualità de'tempi* – is thus best understood as a force field. Political actors find themselves in networks of forces that determine their position and condition their courses of action. In this expansive sense, *forza* establishes a common denominator for comparing and assessing relations of power and capacity in the political world.

Framed this way, the concept of force functions as a heuristic for diagnosing the constellations of power at a given historical moment. In order to adequately deploy force, political actors must know how to evaluate forces; prior to acting "they should first measure and weigh their forces" (D 3.2). Forces, Machiavelli implies, have both measures and weights and the two are not identical. Actors must be able to read force fields and catalogue the heterogeneous modes of power and capability. Force, in this sense, is more than merely a synonym for violent action: It is

---

[44] Reemtsma calls this "locating violence" [*lozierende Gewalt*]. Jan Philipp Reemtsma, *Vertrauen und Gewalt: Versuch über eine besondere Konstellation der Moderne* (Hamburg: Hamburger Edition, 2008), 106.

[45] Aristotle, *Physics*, 256a1–3, 266b28–267a10.

[46] Whereas Aristotle held that a force must be exercised continually on an object, Buridan's theory of impetus held that an object may continue to move, if an impetus is implanted in it. Jack Zupko, "John Buridan," *The Stanford Encyclopedia of Philosophy* (Spring 2014 Edition), Edward N. Zalta (ed.) http://plato.stanford.edu/archives/spr2014/entries/buridan/.

a principle of intelligibility for the historico-political field.[47] By calling force a principle of intelligibility, I mean that it functions as a general schema that allows political situations to be plotted in terms of competing actors, capacities, and opportunities.

FORCE, LAW, AND COERCION

According to the nineteenth-century legal theorist John Austin, law has the structure of a command. What distinguishes a command from other expressions of desire is that the party issuing it has both the power and intention to "inflict an evil or pain in case the desire be disregarded."[48] Thus, for Austin, the sanction provoked by noncompliance is constitutive of the very idea of law, a definition that Machiavelli would have fully endorsed. In chapter 12 of *The Prince*, Machiavelli declares that states are founded on "good laws and good arms" but that "there cannot be good laws where there are not good arms." Laws, in short, must be backed up by armed force. Paralleling Austin, the twentieth-century legal theorist Hans Kelsen characterized law as a "coercive order." Its decisive criterion, Kelsen adds, "is the element of force – that means that the act prescribed by the order ... ought to be executed even against the will of the individual and, if he resists, by physical force."[49] Like Machiavelli, Austin and Kelsen consider enforcement to be central to the law and an important source of the duty to obey.

Machiavelli would add that a prerequisite for enforcing obedience is that "whoever forces be more powerful than whoever is forced" [*che sia più potente chi sforza che chi è sforzato*] (D 1.40). This seemingly pedestrian thought – that the agent who relies on force must be stronger than the one who is being forced – expresses the *instrumental* dimension of force. Force, here, stands for the medium of coercion, deterrence, or retribution. It is the capacity, when deployed to a degree that cannot be withstood by the target, of destroying or injuring that target. Force compels a target, under threat of destruction or injury, to perform or desist from performing certain acts.

---

[47] Achille Norsa, *Il principio della forza nel pensiero politico di Niccolò Machiavelli* (Milan: Ulrico Hoepli, 1936).

[48] John Austin, *The Province of Jurisprudence Determined*, ed. Wilfrid E. Rumble (Cambridge: Cambridge University Press, 2007), 21.

[49] Hans Kelsen, *The Pure Theory of Law*, trans. Max Knight (Berkeley: University of California Press, 1967), 34.

It is here that a couple of important differences between modern legal theory and Machiavelli's conceptions of force emerge. Whereas for Austin and Kelsen the state operates primarily by means of legal force, Machiavelli regards law and force as distinct and complementary. Hence, in his famous allegory of the centaur in chapter 18 of *The Prince*, Machiavelli distinguishes law and force as two opposed strategies:

> Thus, you must know that there are two kinds of combat: one with laws, the other with force [*l'uno con le leggi; l'altro con la forza*]. The first is proper to man, the second to beasts; but because the first is often not enough, one must have recourse to the second. Therefore it is necessary for a prince to know well how to use the beast and the man. This role was taught covertly to princes by ancient writers, who wrote that Achilles, and many other ancient princes, were given to Chiron the centaur to be raised, so that he would look after them with his discipline. To have as teacher a half-beast, half-man means nothing other than that a prince needs to know how to use both natures; and the one without the other is not lasting.
>
> (P 18)

In contrast to Kelsen's and Austin's models, which align force with law and conceive of force (or sanction) as law's instrument, Machiavelli introduces force as an antonym to law. In doing so, Machiavelli constructs an expansive concept of political force that includes not just physical violence but any type of extralegal deception and compulsion.[50]

The relation between force and law is further complicated by the fact that Machiavellian *forza* (like the Roman *vis*) sometimes operates within and sometimes outside the legal framework. Sometimes Machiavelli conveys the distinction between legal and extralegal force as that between "ordinary" and "extraordinary" modes, though, as I contend in Chapter 5, that typology is not stable. In the discussion of the centaur, Machiavelli insinuates that force is not on its own a *substitute* for consent. The meaning of the allegory, he explains, is that princes need to be adept at using *both* the human and the beastly nature, in other words both law and force, because "the one without the other is not lasting." In my discussion of the passions in Chapter 1, I argued that violence and religion are supplements to the law, because they foster the fear that the law requires yet is unable to generate on its own. Machiavelli's interpretation of the centaur implies that force and law supplement each other in another way, because neither is stable without the other. Law requires force to reproduce itself, just as force needs law to endure.

---

[50] Timothy J. Lukes, "Lionizing Machiavelli," *American Political Science Review* 95, no. 3 (2001), 564.

That law without force is unstable makes intuitive sense. It highlights the dependency of any legal framework on force.[51] Law relies on force most obviously as a means of enforcement but also as a rationale for its existence and as a means for founding a legal order. Well-ordered laws, Machiavelli insists in the *Discourses*, are insufficient unless propelled "by one individual who with an extreme force [*con una estrema forza*] ensures their observance" (D 1.17). It is force, in other words, that makes law binding.

Yet the reverse is also true. Not only does law rely on force but force also relies on law. On its own, force is fugitive, based solely on the strength of its wielder. Because force is only effective in a contest with other forces for as long as it is the greater force, it is subject to quick depletion. To maintain relations that are purely based on force is burdensome and costly, as they require the persistent expenditure of force. Unaccompanied by legal or ideological support, force has no claim to authority beyond the law of the stronger. While Machiavelli does not spell out in what way force is unstable, he later implies that it is the overt and blunt quality of force that limits its political usefulness. For force to be durable, it must be able to function in an intermittent and suspended mode. Suspended force relies on threats, on credible promises that non-compliance will be sanctioned, but also on legitimacy, in other words, on ideology. By ideology, I mean the discourses and practices that legitimate state force in the name of security, law, and freedom.[52] For force to last, it must function in the service of some other principle. To the extent that such a principle provides the normative justification for force, one might say that it operates in a law-like way, that force makes a claim to a law that is not the law of force.

Similar reflections have motivated contemporary legal philosophers to turn away from Austin's and Kelsen's coercive accounts of law. In what became one of the most important contributions to twentieth century jurisprudence, H. L. A. Hart contends that only a narrow subset of legal

---

[51] The complex relation between law and force is indicated, for instance, by the proliferation of categories of force in the legal lexicon. Thus, Burrill's *Law Dictionary* distinguishes between eighteen different types of force: vis ablativa, vis armata, vis clandestina, vis compulsiva, vis divina, vis expulsiva, vis exturbativa, vis fluminis, vis impressa, vis inermis, vis injuriosa, vis inquietativa, vis laica, vis licita, vis major, vis perturbativa, vis proxima, and vis simplex. Alexander M. Burrill, *A Law Dictionary and Glossary: Containing Full Definitions of the Principal Terms of the Common and Civil Law* (New York: Baker, Voorhis & Co., 1867), s.v. "vis".

[52] Vatter, *Machiavelli's The Prince*, 66–67.

situations take the form of a command. The command structure does not and cannot describe the standard operating procedure of the law, because no society could muster the forces necessary to secure every individual's compliance. While modern law requires a credible threat to dissuade people from noncompliance, for its day-to-day operation, law relies on a "general belief" in the consequences of disobedience and on widespread "general obedience," neither of which can plausibly be explained by the idea of coercive orders.[53] Machiavelli would agree. In the *Discourses*, he speaks of the "proportion" that is necessary for force to be effective. In *The Prince*, he suggests force is most effective when it does not *appear* as force, that is to say when it is mediated. Force is mediated through law and religion, through the state's legal and ideological apparatuses.

Yet whereas Hart seeks to detach law's authority from the state's coercive capacities, Machiavelli insists that law is a medium for force, an intermediary element that articulates force and bestows a measure of legitimacy on it. That law draws on other sources – notably ideology and religion – for its stability and authority does not change its coercive structure. The passage from *The Prince* cited earlier, where Machiavelli distinguishes between the armed and unarmed prophets, underscores the way in which force is interwoven in religion and ideology. Being an armed prophet means that "things must be ordered in such a mode that when [the people] no longer believe, one can make them believe by force" [*si possa fare loro credere per forza*] (P 6). Moses, Cyrus, Theseus, and Romulus were able to "make their peoples observe their constitutions" because they were armed, that is to say, willing to kill their rivals, whereas Savonarola is the example of a prince who was "ruined" as soon as cracks in public opinion started to appear.

The idea that force can coerce people into belief seems rather fanciful, which is why most readers do not interpret the passage literally.[54] Standard readings construe the armed prophets' force as eliciting obedience rather than belief. Conversely, I think a literal interpretation is both plausible and instructive. To "make them believe by force" intimates that force exercises power not only over bodies but also over the mind. More precisely, it suggests – contra Hart – that belief and ideas are susceptible

---

[53] H. L. A. Hart, *The Concept of Law* (Oxford: Oxford University Press, 1994), 21–24.

[54] See for instance Pocock, *The Machiavellian Moment*, 171; Viroli, *Machiavelli*, 110; Zuckert, *Machiavelli's Politics*, 58n35. Benner deems it "clearly paradoxical, if not absurdly unrealistic." Benner, *Machiavelli's Prince*, 81.

to change through the experience of force. The implication is that Machiavellian force is not a substitute for consent. Rather, it has a doxopoietic capacity; it participates in generating the belief in and habit of obedience. That Machiavelli calls Moses, Cyrus, Theseus, and Romulus armed *prophets* suggests that the nature of the beliefs that are at stake fall under the category of religion. The armed prophet's task is not just to enforce compliance among the disillusioned but to use force in such a way as to rekindle their faith. This may seem like a trivial point, but it isn't. For Machiavelli, force has the capacity to shape belief in what Victoria Kahn calls the "useful fiction" formulated by the prophet.[55] Religion functions as useful fiction, because it kindles beliefs and practices that can sustain citizenship, political autonomy, and popular politics (they can also be used more nefariously, to undermine the people's agency and capacities). When mediated by the right kind of civic religion, force can strengthen political bonds and civic virtue rather than act as their surrogate. Put differently, for Machiavelli, the role of the state is not complementary to the church. The state is a kind of church, operating ideologically and fostering consent by drawing on religion.

Machiavelli does not specify the precise mechanism whereby force can create or modify belief. The case of Moses is instructive: It is not the conspirators who challenge his authority by demanding an idol – the Golden Calf – whose minds are being changed. They do not survive their encounter with Mosaic force, for they are included among the "infinite number of men" Moses kills at Sinai. Rather, the use of force against the antagonists of a popular regime elicits a response from onlookers. The armed prophet uses the force of arms effectively when force impresses itself upon those who see it, when the images trigger and sustain political passions via the medium of the imagination. It is the encounter and apprehension of force by an audience that makes people "believe by force," thus rendering force politically stable. This is why ideology (or religion), force, and law, are inseparable. When force functions in the doxopoietic mode, when it compels some to believe, then agent A is forcing B in order to get C to believe. The implication of attributing to political force a doxopoietic power is that force and consent are not substitutes but that force can in fact fabricate consent (albeit not among

[55] Kahn, *The Future of Illusion*, 94–105.

its immediate targets).[56] Armed prophets produce consent not only through their doctrinal activities but also through the exercise of force.

By appealing to force as a supplement to speech, as that which can make people believe if they fail to do so on their own accord, Machiavelli alludes to a well-rehearsed topos in ancient and medieval debates about rhetoric. One of the traditional points of debate concerning persuasion has always been its coercive potential. An abiding concern of ancient critics of rhetoric was that oratory deploys a kind of seduction that enchants language and makes words irresistible, blurring the distinction between force and consent.[57] Yet whereas the anxiety about rhetoric has traditionally been about the danger of utterances slipping out of the constative and into the performative mode, Machiavelli emphasizes the flip side. Instead of the apprehensiveness about how to do things with words, *The Prince* highlights the possibility that words can be done with things. The implication is that language is not categorically distinct from but on a continuum with force. In politics (as well as in war), there is a continuity of words and swords.

The distinction between the human and beastly modes of combat is thus ultimately less important than their interdependence. This is not to say that Machiavelli reduces all politics to force. In fact, both the centaur allegory and the passage on armed prophets constitute evidence against the view that Machiavelli regards force as a sufficient condition or instrument for government. The figure of the centaur suggests that force is unstable without law and that law serves as a crucial mode of mediation for force. In the case of the armed prophets, it is persuasion and belief that mediate force. These passages thus sketch a theory of the state, where the state is understood as a complex of political practices that mutually articulate force and consent. Machiavelli's insight is that the moments of force and consent are not two separate and complementary mechanisms of government but that each relies on the other and cannot operate without it.

The remark about those who rely solely on the lion suggests that the centaur allegory is intended to dispel the idea that military coercion is a

---

[56] Elsewhere, Machiavelli also writes of the *grandi* making the people consent [*acconsentire*] "by force and with arms" [*per forza e con le armi*], suggesting that "consent" for him is not the opposite of force (FH 7.3).

[57] The locus classicus for this problem is Gorgias's *Encomium of Helen*, where Gorgias ascribes to persuasion "the form of necessity" even if it "does not have the same power." Gorgias, "Encomium of Helen," in *The Older Sophists*, ed. Rosamond Kent Sprague (Indianapolis: Hackett, 2001), 12.

sufficient mechanism for political control. Unlike the prophets of force – the political lions who regard force as a generic, polyvalent, and sufficient response to political uncertainty – Machiavelli highlights the importance of mediating force through ideology. What the prophets of force fail to see is that force describes a continuum of practices and that force works best when blended with deception.

Force, for Machiavelli, ultimately designates an unstable mode of violence. On the one hand, it stands for an instrumental, more or less measurable, fungible, and transitive mode of violence that is in principle substitutable. These aspects make the concept of force susceptible to an analysis that emphasizes the continuity (but not identity) of Machiavelli's political and military reflections. On the other hand, force is insufficient as a political instrument: It needs supplements such as religion and law to be effective. Force operates at its best when there is a continuity between words and swords, when physical violence blends into deception and hence does not appear as such.

CONCLUSION

By advising the Medici to use force in order to strengthen their hold on Florentine government and prevent the *popolo* from recapturing the state, the young prophets of force modify the conventional view that associates force with tyrannical government. Yet the effort to remove force's stigma and redeem it for the dominant political family preserves the association between force and a monarchic or despotic form of rule. In contrast to the oligarchic Mediceans' reclaiming of force, the principal aim of Machiavelli's discussion is to demonstrate why the leaders of popular and democratic regimes cannot renounce force without ruining the prospects of democratic government. A popular regime cannot abjure force, because it must confront the oligarchic elites that will inevitably conspire to overthrow it.

Besides the opposing political allegiances that differentiate his discussion from the dominant discourse of force in early sixteenth-century Florence, Machiavelli's theorization of force is also distinguished by an assiduous treatment of force as political mechanism. *Forza*, as I have argued, stands for the political use of arms. It is frequently metaphorized in military terms and refers to the deployment or threat of physical violence, to the infliction of injuries, and to executions. While physical violence does not exhaust the concept of force, it has a privileged status in politics, because it is the mode in which force, especially when exercised by states, often manifests itself.

By analyzing force at the level of its logic and mechanism, Machiavelli emphasizes the immanent and anti-metaphysical dimensions of political violence. Because force is subject to an economy of expenditure – its reservoirs are quickly consumed and depleted when in use – it is a constitutively unstable and precarious mode of action that is greatly stabilized when mediated through law and religion. Force works best, Machiavelli suggests, in what I have called a doxopoietic mode, when it operates not as an alternative to public opinion but directly manufactures consent, as modeled by the armed prophets and *più eccellenti* princes: Moses, Cyrus, Romulus, and Theseus.

The language of *forza* takes Machiavelli beyond the military and political spheres and into a more expansive conception of natural and supernatural powers. *Forza*, I have argued, designates not only political uses of violence but also the principle of motion that animates any moving object. As such, force is part of a natural philosophy beholden to a Renaissance gloss on Aristotelian physics. This naturalistic sense of force is important, because it allows force to morph into a principle of intelligibility that shapes Machiavelli's method of analyzing political situations. Machiavelli's discourse of force vacillates between these two senses of force – physical violence on the one hand, principle of intelligibility on the other. This vacillation suggests that one of the distinguishing features of the forms of power that structure political constellations is their capacity to marshal or metamorphose into violence.

3

Cruelty

The essential task of Marxism is to find a violence which recedes with the approach of man's future.

    – Maurice Merleau-Ponty, *Humanism and Terror*

One generation prior to Machiavelli, the Neoplatonist philosopher and founder of the Florentine Academy Marsilio Ficino (1433–1499) described cruelty as inhumanity. Echoing the common Renaissance opposition between humanism and cruelty, Ficino saw cruelty as a lack of *humanitas*. "Why," Ficino asks in one of his letters, "are boys crueler [*crudeliores*] than old men? Insane men crueler than intelligent men? Dull men crueler than the ingenious?" His answer is that they are "less men than the others."[1] Cruel men are incomplete men. Their deficiency in *humanitas* – the virtue of loving other human beings as one's fellows – expresses itself in their penchant for cruelty. In contrast to Ficino and the Florentine Platonists who see cruelty as inhuman, Machiavelli treats cruelty as a distinctively human trait. In doing so, he follows Aquinas, who identified cruelty as a *human* evil and juxtaposed it to savagery [*saevitia*] and brutality [*feritas*], which are evils because humans *fail* to be human.[2]

---

[1] Paul Oskar Kristeller, "The Philosophy of Man in the Italian Renaissance," *Italica* 24, no. 2 (1947), 104.

[2] The distinction between *crudelitas* and *saevitia* is already suggested, albeit imprecisely, by Seneca. Book 2 of *De clementia* differentiates them, while book 1 collapses the two. See Lucius Annaeus Seneca, "On Mercy," in *Moral and Political Essays* (Cambridge: Cambridge University Press, 1995), 1.5, 2.4.2. For Aquinas, savagery and brutality have no

By conceptualizing cruelty as distinctively human, Machiavelli challenges the facile dismissal of cruelty as inhuman and evil. Instead, he demands that his readers entertain the thought that cruelty may be a politically necessary and even salutary tactic. Such a vindication of cruelty is jarring for twenty-first century readers nourished on the liberal doctrine that regards cruelty as just about the worst thing humans can do.[3] Characteristic of modern liberal conceptions of cruelty is that they tend to identify it as quintessentially an offense of the strong against the weak. Torture and the gulag are the modern paradigms of cruelty, imagined as the exposure of naked and vulnerable individuals to the formidable and total power of the state. Judith Shklar, whose theorization of cruelty I take to represent this tendency, defines cruelty as the "willful inflicting of physical pain on a weaker being in order to cause anguish and fear."[4] Cruelty, in this account, is a gratuitous and perverse mode of violence, typically linked to absolute power and – in its modern form – to totalitarianism.

Machiavelli offers a (frequently misunderstood) defense of cruelty that contrasts with the liberal repudiation point by point. In this chapter, I reconstruct Machiavelli's concept of cruelty, distinguish it from his account of force, and elaborate its theoretical novelty. Unlike force, which, as seen in Chapter 2, is fungible, measurable, and deploys substitutable implements, Machiavellian cruelty has a different structure. Cruelty refers to a modality of lethal violence characterized by the public display of ferocity. When Machiavelli speaks about cruelty, he means primarily public executions, in particular, executions that are bloody or that feature – like Remirro's – ways of marking and stigmatizing the body of the condemned. Like force, cruelty targets the body, but unlike force, cruelty seeks to undo the body's integrity. It is a kind of excess violence beyond death. As such, cruelty – unlike force – is more difficult to dose.

---

moral dimension; they are committed for purely instrumental purposes. By contrast, what distinguishes cruelty is that it "exceeds in the mode of punishing: wherefore cruelty differs from savagery or brutality, as human wickedness differs from bestiality." Thomas Aquinas, *The Summa Theologica*, trans. Fathers of the English Dominican Province (London: Burns Oates and Washbourne, 1920), II, 159. Aquinas's considerations are in turn cited by Antoninus of Florence (1389–1459), the Dominican friar and archbishop of Florence and one of the Renaissance's outstanding scholastic theologians, whose *Summa Theologica* may have been familiar to Machiavelli. St. Antoninus Florentinus, *Summa Theologica in Quattuor Partes Distributa* (Verona: Ex Typographia Seminarii, Apud Augustinum Carattonium, 1740), 2.8.5.

[3] See, for instance, Rorty, *Contingency, Irony, and Solidarity*, xv.

[4] Judith N. Shklar, *Ordinary Vices* (Cambridge, MA: Harvard University Press, 1984), 8.

Machiavelli derives this excessive and transgressive dimension from Roman political discourse – especially from Seneca – but as I will show, he modifies Seneca's notion of cruelty in important respects. Whereas Seneca understood cruelty as a character vice, Machiavelli offers instead a *political* conception of cruelty.[5]

THE MEDICI REVENGE

On an April Sunday in 1478, a group of assassins attacked the two leading members of the Medici family, Lorenzo and Giuliano, during high Mass in the Florentine cathedral of Santa Maria del Fiore. The event became known as the Pazzi conspiracy.[6] Among the plotters were the archbishop of Pisa, a cardinal, and members of the Pazzi and Salviati families, banking dynasties that competed with the Medici for business and political influence.[7] One of the conspirators stabbed Giuliano in the chest with a dagger, and an accomplice struck him repeatedly with a sword until he was killed. The two priests tasked with assassinating Lorenzo were less successful. Lorenzo was wounded in the neck but managed to flee to the sacristy and escape. His survival saved the Medici regime and sealed the Pazzi's defeat. In spite of a desperate last-minute attempt to rally the people, the conspirators were crushed.

The Medici retaliation was swift and bloody. The diarist Luca Landucci reports that a number of conspirators and their associates were killed in the town squares, among them a priest who was quartered and whose severed head "was stuck on the top of a lance, and carried about Florence the whole day [while] one quarter of his body was carried on a spit all through the city."[8] That same day, pro-Medici crowds killed

---

[5] There are exceptions, where Machiavelli uses cruelty to refer to the desire to inflict pain (FH 5.11) or as a synonym for brutality (D 2.8; 3.32). But in general (and contra Strauss who conflates the two), Machiavelli tends to distinguish cruelty from harshness or severity. As I discuss in more detail in Chapters 4 and 5, Brutus is described as severe (D 1.17; 3.2; 3.3) and Manlius Capitolinus as harsh [*aspro*] (D 3.22) but neither is qualified as cruel. Mirroring Livy (22.60, 3–4), who refers to Manlius's *severitas*, Machiavelli distinguishes severity from cruelty. Elsewhere, Machiavelli uses the adverbs *acremente* (D 1.8) or *agramente* (D 2.24) as qualifiers to describe harsh punishment. The famous discussion of Tacitus is framed in terms of severity [*severità* and *durezza*] of punishment versus authority (D 3.19). See Strauss, *Thoughts on Machiavelli*, 187.

[6] For one of the best historical treatments, see Lauro Martines, *April Blood: Florence and the Plot against the Medici* (Oxford: Oxford University Press, 2003).

[7] Najemy, *A History of Florence*, 352–53.

[8] Luca Landucci, *A Florentine Diary From 1450 to 1516*, ed. Iodoco Del Badia, trans. Alice de Rosen Jervis (New York: E.P. Dutton, 1927), 16. See also Angelo Poliziano, "The Pazzi

dozens of men, many of whom were seen dangling from the windows of the palace of the Signoria. Others were dragged through the city, defenestrated alive, or hanged from the windows of the Palazzo del Podestà and the Casa del Capitano.[9] In the following days, dozens more suffered similar fates. Machiavelli writes that "everyone pursued the Pazzi with words full of anger and deeds full of cruelty" (FH 8.9). Jacopo Pazzi was exhumed twice. First, his corpse was removed from the family tomb and buried near the city walls. The next day, he was again exhumed, his naked body dragged through the city by the noose on which he had been hanged, and ultimately thrown into the Arno river.[10] All told, historians estimate that in the days following the attack more than eighty men were killed, with hangings from palace windows a favorite motif.[11]

Machiavelli remarked on the irony that a conspiracy which nearly cost Lorenzo his life left him stronger than ever before. His enemies were eliminated; he no longer had to share power or consult with his brother; and any lingering resentment harbored by rivals and suspicions held by popular republicans had dissipated (FH 8.9–10).[12] The event allowed Lorenzo to consolidate power and to present his family as selfless, civic-minded servants of the republic who had become innocent victims of jealousy, perfidy, and evil.

In Machiavelli's rendition, public performance of cruelty played a crucial part in solidifying the position of the Medici family at the helm of the Florentine state in the conspiracy's aftermath. The brutal choreography of hanged and decapitated bodies dangling from balconies and thrown out of windows left an enduring impression on the citizenry. Both the scale and genre of the bloody revenge were unprecedented. Before the mid-fifteenth century, political crimes were traditionally punished by exile, fines, bans on public office, or disenfranchisement.[13] Florence's political class, like that of other Italian city-states, frowned upon the

---

Conspiracy," in *Humanism and Liberty: Writings on Freedom from Fifteenth-Century Florence*, ed. Renée Neu Watkins (Columbia, SC: University of South Carolina Press, 1978), 178.

[9] According to Guicciardini, Florence had never experienced "a day of such travail." Guicciardini, *The History of Florence*, 35.

[10] Machiavelli's description of the desecration of Jacopo Pazzi's corpse is corroborated by Poliziano, "The Pazzi Conspiracy," 182.

[11] Najemy, *A History of Florence*, 357.

[12] See also Guicciardini, *The History of Florence*, 36.

[13] See Alison Brown, "Lorenzo de' Medici's New Men and their Mores: The Changing Lifestyle of Quattrocento Florence," *Renaissance Studies* 16, no. 2 (2002); Fabrizio Ricciardelli, *The Politics of Exclusion in Early Renaissance Florence* (Turnhout: Brepols,

death penalty and regarded it as divisive. Until very recently, executions were used to punish grave criminal matters but only rarely to subdue political opponents.[14] Under the Medici, this aversion to the death penalty had gradually changed.[15] Political dissent was increasingly criminalized and the death penalty was used more frequently. Executions, especially by hanging and decapitation, became associated with political crimes such as treason and conspiracy.

It was not only the scale of punishment that was unparalleled. The particular modes of killing and maiming were symbolically significant. By mutilating and defenestrating the conspirators, the Medici and their allies inscribed and marked these bodies. The bodies that dangled from windows and palaces and were paraded through town served as testament to the Medici's power. Contemporary reports suggest that these hangings and defenestrations were carefully scripted. Palace windows and balconies, increasingly important in Renaissance architecture, functioned as politically saturated stages of power – both princely and republican.[16] By turning them into loci of violence, the Medici signaled the dawn of a new era, one in which the public performance of cruelty became a technology to garner popular support. The revenge orchestrated by the Medici and their allies was destined to be seen, remembered, and narrated.

Born in 1469, Machiavelli was but nine years old and busy studying his Latin authors when the Pazzi conspiracy occurred.[17] Yet the events of 1478 form the background of his reflections on cruelty. What makes the public display of dismembered bodies an effective political tactic? What is the political function – in a republic or a principality – of the

---

2007); Marvin E. Wolfgang, "Political Crimes and Punishments in Renaissance Florence," *The Journal of Criminal Law, Criminology, and Police Science* 44, no. 5 (1954).

[14] Umberto Dorini, *Il diritto penale e la delinquenza in Firenze nel sec. XIV* (Lucca: Domenico Corsi, 1916); Davidsohn, *Geschichte von Florenz, Bd. IV*, 319–20.

[15] Following Cosimo's return from exile in 1434, his enemies were, in Machiavelli's words, "basely put to death" (FH 5.4). The centralization of authority that took place under Cosimo's successors, especially under Lorenzo the Magnificent, led to increased political repression. See Rubinstein, *The Government of Florence under the Medici (1434–1494)*, 195–206; Melissa Meriam Bullard, "Adumbrations of Power and the Politics of Appearances in Medicean Florence," *Renaissance Studies* 12, no. 3 (1998).

[16] As the historian Daniel Jütte has shown, defenestration was a comparatively rare form of punishment that was used most prominently in Renaissance Florence and was seen as having a characteristically political valence. Daniel Jütte, "Defenestration as Ritual Punishment: Windows, Power, and Political Culture in Early Modern Europe," *The Journal of Modern History* 89, no. 1 (2017), 21.

[17] Ridolfi, *The Life of Niccolò Machiavelli*, 6.

sorts of desecrations that the Medici encouraged? To address these questions, Machiavelli turned to Seneca.

A NEO-ROMAN CONCEPTION OF CRUELTY

The sixteenth century saw a surge of interest in questions of cruelty, in Renaissance philosophy, Elizabethan drama, travel writing, and literature.[18] That preoccupation with cruelty was fueled in part by a renewed circulation of Seneca's writings.[19] Seneca's treatise on mercy, *De clementia*, was the principal source for most discussions of cruelty, including Machiavelli's.[20] Starting in the 1470s, numerous new editions of and commentaries on Seneca's works were published; Erasmus issued an edition of *De clementia* in 1529, followed by a commentary on the same text by Calvin in 1532.

Seneca's *De clementia* is not just a treatise on mercy. It is the only surviving systematic theorization of Roman monarchy and the earliest remaining specimen of the Latin mirror-of-princes genre – the advice books that specify the virtues that make a good ruler.[21] Composed at the beginning of Nero's reign, it warns the young emperor against the vice of cruelty. Seneca defines cruelty as "grimness of mind in exacting punishment" [*atrocitas animi in exigendi poenis*], thus situating it in a specific penal context.[22] Cruelty denotes a lack of moderation in punishment and

---

[18] Daniel Baraz, *Medieval Cruelty: Changing Perceptions, Late Antiquity to the Early Modern Period* (Ithaca, NY: Cornell University Press, 2003); Jody Enders, *The Medieval Theater of Cruelty: Rhetoric, Memory, Violence* (Ithaca, NY: Cornell University Press, 1999); Pieter Spierenburg, "The Body and the State: Early Modern Europe," in *The Oxford History of the Prison*, ed. Norval Morris and David J. Rothman (Oxford: Oxford University Press, 1995).

[19] Baraz, *Medieval Cruelty*, 26.

[20] Quentin Skinner, "Introduction," in *The Prince* (Cambridge: Cambridge University Press, 1988), xvii; Stacey, *Roman Monarchy and the Renaissance Prince*.

[21] *De clementia* had a profound influence on the mirror-of-princes genre that developed from the thirteenth to the fifteenth century on the Italian peninsula. On the debt that this literary trend, which includes Machiavelli's *The Prince*, has to Seneca, see Stacey, *Roman Monarchy and the Renaissance Prince*, 4–5. See also Neal Wood, "Some Common Aspects of the Thought of Seneca and Machiavelli," *Renaissance Quarterly* 21, no. 1 (1968); Richard Tuck, *Philosophy and Government, 1572–1651* (Cambridge: Cambridge University Press, 1993), 20.

[22] Seneca, "On Mercy," 2.4. Seneca's terminology is inconsistent; for the purposes of this discussion, I rely on the more conceptually precise discussion in book 2 of *De clementia*. See Daniel Baraz, "Seneca, Ethics, and the Body: The Treatment of Cruelty in Medieval Thought," *Journal of the History of Ideas* 59, no. 2 (1998), 198.

betrays a sadistic desire to inflict suffering unworthy of the human soul.[23] Thus cruelty refers to an individual's moral disposition; it marks a character trait attributed to wicked emperors.

For Seneca, cruelty is primarily a character vice rather than a political crime or violation of the law. By defining cruelty – as well as its opposite: mercy – as ethical qualities, Seneca makes an important intervention in the political theory of monarchy. Such moral integrity acquires manifest importance in imperial (as opposed to republican) political life, when political virtue was no longer embedded in institutions but in the moral psychology of rulers. For the first time in Latin political thought, virtuous kingship is not tied to the lawful exercise of power but to the character and moral disposition of the office holder.[24] In the process, *clementia* becomes, as Stacey notes, the "quintessential virtue of absolutism."[25] Conversely, cruelty becomes absolutism's exemplary vice.

Mercy represents a core masculine virtue in the Roman moral imagination, and it is of special importance for the Stoics.[26] The Stoics regarded mercy as the ultimate political virtue because humans are fallible. In the face of another's moral failings, the preeminently human thing to do is to show leniency and restraint. Cruelty, by contrast, describes a "lack of self-control" in dealing with others' moral shortcomings.[27] This lack of moderation leads Seneca to define cruelty as a kind of excess, an irrational and unwarranted surplus of violence. The precise nature, form, or purpose of that surplus is of no relevance. What is important is that such excess lacks rational ground. Comparing cruelty to "bestial madness," Seneca insists on the irrationality of taking delight in killing and of inflicting unwarranted punishments.

Seneca's notion of cruelty shaped the way a number of his Roman contemporaries and near-contemporaries used the term. In the works of Valerius Maximus, Tacitus, and Suetonius, cruelty describes a modality

---

[23] Seneca, "On Mercy," 2.4.3.
[24] For Cicero, for instance, the idea of virtuous kingship is a contradiction in terms, for he associates kingship with slavery and makes no distinction between *rex* and *tyrannus*. *On Duties*, 2.7.23. Seneca's view is not without precedent in Greek political thought. Both Isocrates and Xenophon elaborated theories of virtuous monarchy. See Isocrates, "Nicocles," and "To Nicocles," in *Isocrates I* (Austin: University of Texas Press, 2000); Xenophon, *The Education of Cyrus*, trans. Wayne Ambler (Ithaca, NY: Cornell University Press, 2001).
[25] Stacey, *Roman Monarchy and the Renaissance Prince*, 33.
[26] Melissa Barden Dowling, *Clemency and Cruelty in the Roman World* (Ann Arbor: University of Michigan Press, 2006), 2, 19, 27.
[27] Seneca, "On Mercy," 1.3.2, 2.4.1–2.4.2.

of violence that satisfies one of the following two conditions: either it has no rational purpose or it fundamentally defies the status of the person who is targeted.[28] At the dawn of the Empire, cruelty was thus understood to be a noninstrumental modality of violence characterized by irrationality and degradation. According to the historian Andrew Lintott, cruelty "was performed not in the pursuit of an identifiable interest" but for emotional satisfaction. Moreover, "the cruelty of an act was determined not so much by the act itself but by the character and merit of the sufferer: hence it was thought to lie more in the destruction of *dignitas* through humiliation than in the infliction of physical harm."[29] Thus, political and military leaders were not habitually condemned for violent acts per se but for ones directed against wealthy and eminent people.[30]

By restricting the definition to penal situations, Seneca proposed a narrow notion of cruelty that excluded much of the violence in Roman society. Rome was an intensely violent place; it had developed elaborate and complex political and cultural techniques of violence. In the historian Donald Kyle's words, Rome "killed on an enormous scale, with efficiency, ingenuity, and delectation."[31] For Romans, taking life was not just a military or judicial operation. It took place in Rome's arenas, in its circuses, and in its amphitheaters. The killing of humans and animals was orchestrated for public consumption. It took the form of public spectacles, festivals, and sacrifices. Death, in short, was a "spectator sport."[32] Yet it was not the gratuitous forms of violence and the infliction of pain that Seneca and others understood by the term *crudelitas*. When first-century Stoics wrote about cruelty, they were by and large unconcerned with the cultural spectacularizations of violence, which a sixteenth- or twenty-first century reader might regard as instances of cruelty. Rather, they focused on cruelty as an individual vice, as a feature of moral psychology, and as a kind of irrational excess.

I emphasize these differences because Machiavelli adopts what I call a neo-Roman conception of cruelty. Writing amid burgeoning interest in

---

[28] Lintott, *Violence in Republican Rome*, xvii; Dowling, *Clemency and Cruelty in the Roman World*, 27.

[29] Andrew Lintott, "Cruelty in the Political Life of the Ancient World," in *Crudelitas: The Politics of Cruelty in the Ancient and Medieval World*, ed. Toivo Viljamaa, Asko Timonen, and Christian Krötzl (Krems: Medium Aevum Quotidianum, 1992), 9.

[30] Lintott, *Violence in Republican Rome*, 36.

[31] Donald G. Kyle, *Spectacles of Death in Ancient Rome* (London: Routledge, 1998), 2.

[32] Kyle, *Spectacles of Death in Ancient Rome*, 2.

Seneca, Machiavelli accepts the Roman criteria for cruelty but modifies them slightly. He narrows what counts as irrationality and excess. If, for Seneca, irrationality and excess in punishment establish an act as cruel, Machiavelli highlights the *apparent* irrationality and the excess. What he calls cruelty involves acts of physical violence that (1) seem to have no rational purpose and/or (2) defy the political status – typically that of belonging to an elite – of their target.

The appearance of *irrationality* is conspicuous in Remirro's execution. To Borgia's audience in Cesena, the display of Remirro's body would have looked irrational. By projecting irrationality, political actors mystify their intentions, and render their motives enigmatic and their actions unpredictable. Shrewd political actors must prevent their audience from anticipating their actions. To the extent that cruelty is an expression of such irrationality, it helps political actors seem capricious and unpredictable.

The defiance of *political status* becomes evident from a closer examination of the targets of Machiavellian cruelty. Most of the victims of cruelty Machiavelli describes were privileged elite citizens; they typically belonged to the nobility and exercised substantial political or administrative power prior to their assassination or were involved in conspiracies and intrigues against the public. They are sacrificed – like Jacopo Pazzi – to satisfy the people's anger and desire for revenge but also as notice and warning to discourage abuse of power. Like the Romans, Machiavelli regards *dignità* not as the universal basis of self-respect but as a class-specific status marker primarily of value to elites. Hence, he speaks frequently of the nobles' quest to uphold, defend, and restore their dignity (D 1.6; FH 2.14, 2.40, 3.1).

Dignitas could be violated in a variety of ways, among them the mode by which someone was executed. In Rome, the mechanisms of executions correlated with the status of the condemned. Honorable decapitation was generally reserved for citizens with claims to *dignitas*, whereas criminals of low social status could be subjected to a variety of torments, including exposure to wild beast, burning alive, or crucifixion.[33] Renaissance Italians similarly distinguished between decapitation, hanging, and executions that involved further forms of mutilation and dismemberment. Like the Romans, they generally viewed decapitation as the most honorable

---

[33] Kyle, *Spectacles of Death in Ancient Rome*, 53.

and hanging as a dishonorable form of death, with further mutilations and dismemberments, including defenestration, regarded as added insults.

Whereas, for the Romans, cruelty is rendered morally objectionable to the extent that it defaces the victim's *dignitas*, for Machiavelli, this is precisely what makes cruelty politically potent. Cruelty produces its effects by violating a social expectation, by breaching a certain presumption of privilege. By publicly invading presumptions of privilege, acts of cruelty address the political imagination, producing the phantasmatic images that evoke passionate responses.

Like Seneca, Machiavelli ties cruelty to punishment, but unlike Seneca he regards cruelty not only as a technique for tyrants but also for republics, rebels, and popular insurrections. If Seneca is primarily concerned with the moral psychology of cruelty's agents and if contemporary debates about cruelty focus on the moral psychology of victims, Machiavelli is interested in the moral psychology of a third party: the audience. What makes cruelty politically useful in his view is its theatrical and public dimension. For Machiavelli, then, cruelty constitutes a form of violence that deploys excess and apparent irrationality to address an audience beyond the immediate target.

JUSTIFYING CRUELTY

Machiavelli's theory of cruelty is laid out in three key sections of *The Prince*. Chapters 7–9 present cruelty as an important and even indispensable political strategy, especially for new princes; chapters 15–17 offer the outlines of a theoretical model of cruelty; and chapter 19 defends this theory of cruelty against Machiavelli's critics. The first section, chapters 7–9 of *The Prince*, forms the core of Machiavelli's theory that cruelty can establish a state's "foundations." Through a series of sometimes contradictory ancient and modern examples, featuring Cesare Borgia, Agathocles of Sicily, Liverotto of Fermo, and Nabis of Sparta, Machiavelli develops an account of how cruelty functions to found and consolidate political power, authority, and even popular legitimacy.

Both Cesare's and Remirro's acts serve as examples of an adroit application of cruelty in founding new states. Remirro's ruthlessness in the Romagna is described as giving rise to "peace and obedience," "peace and unity," and "peace and faith" (P 7, 17). The triple invocation of "peace" in the context of a brutal narrative of state-founding indicates that for Machiavelli, cruelty is not the opposite of peace but (at least here) its condition of possibility. Cruelty is depicted as a necessary instrument for the establishment of peace, but also of order and law.

Agathocles and Liverotto, by contrast, allow Machiavelli to theorize the criteria that justify the recourse to cruelty. Key among them is the replacement of conditions of disorder. That justification is laid out explicitly in chapter 8 of *The Prince*, where Machiavelli introduces the distinction between well-used and badly used cruelty:

Those cruelties can be called well-used (if it is permissible to speak well of evil) that are carried out at a stroke, out of necessity to secure oneself, and then are not persisted in but are turned into the greatest possible benefits for the subjects. Those cruelties are badly used which, though few in the beginning, increase rather than diminish with time.

(P 8, trans. mod.)

Here, three criteria differentiate well-used cruelties from badly used ones: First, they are necessary rather than gratuitous; second, they are exceptional rather than recurrent, conclusive rather than protracted; and third, they lead to long-term advantageous conditions for subjects. These criteria offer important constraints on the kinds of cruel actions that Machiavelli regards as justifiable. Everyday or habitual cruelty cannot be called well-used. To qualify, cruelty must be exceptional and deployed in moments of political transition ("out of necessity to secure oneself"). By specifying that justifiable cruelty should ultimately benefit subjects, Machiavelli condemns acts of cruelty that primarily advance a prince's self-interest. And finally, he suggests that there are conditions under which forms of violence that seem excessive and unreasonable in the moment in fact serve the long-term interests of a population.

As we know from Machiavelli's discussion of hatred, cruelty has its perils; yet significantly, it is not listed among the things from which princes must categorically abstain. Certain violations, especially pilfering one's subjects' property or assaulting "their" women, are of a kind that people will never forgive or forget (P 17). Machiavelli calls such acts of violence not cruelties but "rapaciousness" [*rapine*], as if to highlight the difference (P 17, 19). Preventing hatred is best achieved not by abjuring violence and cruelty but, as I argued in Chapter 1, by managing the passions. Such management might include mechanisms that allow princes to disavow cruelty while practicing it. Borgia's execution of Remirro is a case in point. Machiavelli underscores the importance of disavowals by way of a general maxim "that princes should have anything blameable administered by others, favors by themselves" (P 19). Hatred, in other words, is prevented not by omitting acts of cruelty but by finding ways to repudiate one's authorship.

This might seem like a cynical conclusion but isn't, if properly contextualized. Machiavelli's discussion of Cesare and his defense of "well-used" cruelty are part of a larger segment of chapters (7–9) that begins with Cesare's cruelty and ends with the civil principality. These three chapters form a thematic and theoretical unit. Chapters 7 and 8 both postulate that acts of cruelty are justifiable to the extent that they serve the long-term interests of the people. Chapter 9 then lays out the political form of a principality that prioritizes the people's interests. This is why the idea of the civil prince is key to Machiavelli's political vision in *The Prince*.[34] The cruel protagonists of chapters 7 to 9 – Remirro, Cesare, Agathocles, Liverotto, and Nabis – must thus be interpreted within the broader scope of this section, which ends with the civil principality.

The peculiarity of the civil prince is that he purportedly comes to power without "crime or other intolerable violence" [*non per sceleratezza o altra intollerabile violenza*] but by drawing on popular support. The example on offer is Nabis of Sparta, who is implicitly compared to Agathocles, labelled evil and criminal in the previous chapter. In contrast to Agathocles who held Syracuse "*con violenzia e sanza obligo di altri* " (P 8), the civil prince's apparent avoidance of "*sceleratezza o altra intollerabile violenza* " thus seems to mark an alternative course to power. By relying on popular support, the civil prince would appear to map out a peaceful alternative to violence.

Yet a closer look at Machiavelli's examples suggests that they challenge and contradict the theoretical points they are ostensibly adduced to corroborate. Agathocles and Liverotto are certainly illustrations for cruel princes, yet especially Agathocles also seems to be a case study for well-used cruelty. Even though Agathocles is said to lack virtue, Machiavelli refers to his virtue not once but three times in the very same chapter and also calls him a "most excellent captain." As interpreters have noted, there are, moreover, striking parallels between Agathocles and Cesare that undermine attempts to stringently dissociate the two.[35]

---

[34] Sasso, *Machiavelli e gli antichi e altri saggi*, 2:351. By declaring chapter 9 the center of the book, Sasso manages to synthesize the seemingly opposed political imaginations of *The Prince* and the *Discourses*. For a critique of Sasso's reading, see Peter Stacey, "Definition, Division, and Difference in Machiavelli's Political Philosophy," *Journal of the History of Ideas* 75, no. 2 (2014), 210.

[35] Strauss, *Thoughts on Machiavelli*, 309–10 n53; Kahn, "Virtù and the Example of Agathocles in Machiavelli's Prince"; McCormick, "Machiavelli's Inglorious Tyrants";

Similar questions arise with respect to the civil principality. As I suggested in the Introduction, the one example of a successful civil prince – Nabis – undermines the framing of the civil principality as an alternative to violence. Nabis accedes to the throne by executing the last two claimants of the Spartan royal dynasty. He is therefore not exactly an example of a peaceful prince who comes to power nonviolently. Both Polybius and Livy call Nabis a tyrant and note his brutal rule of terror.[36] Not only was Machiavelli well aware of the ancients' judgments, in *Discourses* 3.6 he seems to concur, also referring to Nabis as a tyrant. In sum, if Nabis qualifies as a civil prince, it is not because he represents a nonviolent alternative to Agathocles but for other reasons.

Looking at the examples of the three successive chapters together, it is hard to miss the irony: In chapter 7, Cesare, whose principate was remarkably short-lived, is treated as a virtuous albeit cruel founder; in chapter 8, Agathocles, who for the most part followed the steps Machiavelli maps out in the previous chapter and held on to power for decades, is labelled a cruel and evil usurper; and in chapter 9, Nabis, a brutal and hated tyrant who seized power through murder and intrigue and died in a conspiracy, is praised as a civil prince who came to power with the support of his fellow citizens. What then, is the relation between cruelty and Machiavelli's notion of the civil principality?

In his discussion, Sasso distinguishes between the civil prince's "formal" and "substantial" *civiltà*. Analogous to the two meanings of tyranny, formal *civiltà* refers to the manner by which a prince comes to power, and substantial *civiltà* concerns the way he rules. Building on this distinction, it makes sense to regard the civil prince not as a nonviolent alternative to the cruel prince but as a model for a politics of cruelty that is substantially civil to the extent that the cruelty is deployed not against but *in the service* of the people. The examples of Cesare, Agathocles, and Nabis make clear that popular support is frequently obtained precisely by means of cruelty.[37] The civil prince, then, does not abstain from cruelty

John P. McCormick, "Machiavelli's Greek Tyrant as Republican Reformer," in *The Radical Machiavelli: Politics, Philosophy, and Language*, ed. Filippo Del Lucchese, Fabio Frosini, and Vittorio Morfino (Leiden: Brill, 2015).

[36] Livy, 34.27; Polybius, *Histories*, 4.81, 13.6–8.

[37] This interpretation is also supported by Machiavelli's praise for Cleomenes's cruelty in the *Discourses*. There he praises Cleomenes's "very cruel enterprise," in which he eliminated the ephors as well as other ambitious men liable to challenge his reordering of the Spartan state (D 1.9, 1.18).

but uses it judiciously, targeting elites rather than the people.[38] He is characterized not by a peaceful rise to power – not, in other words, by the absence of violence and fraud – but by the fact that his violence is backed and endorsed by the population. His hallmark is that he is supported by and has the favor of, *"il favore delli altri sua cittadini"*, his fellow citizens.

The real significance of chapter 9 and of the civil principality is the implication that well-used cruelty is a political tactic deployed primarily against elites and that it serves to contain elite insolence and collusion and to generate popular support.[39] The emphasis is on *sua cittadini* not just *cittadini* in general.[40] Since "the few always behave in the mode of the few" (D1.7) and elites are always rivalrous and unreliable, the support a civil prince requires is to be found amid the people: *sua cittadini*, in other words, refers to the people as opposed to the oligarchs.

By discussing cruelty in terms of its effects on power and legitimacy, rather than by reference to the moral psychology of its authors, Machiavelli articulates a *political* conception of cruelty. What makes this conception distinctive is that Machiavelli redefines cruelty as a decidedly anti-oligarchic political tactic. Machiavelli's fascination with the ferocious and hyperbolic public displays of desecrated bodies is hence not the result of a perverse delight in brutality but an effort at theorizing a form of violence that specifically targets the social groups he regards as the principal threat to freedom: political and economic elites.

---

[38] Sasso, *Machiavelli e gli antichi e altri saggi*, 2:361; Mansfield, *Machiavelli's Virtue*, 187.

[39] What impressed Machiavelli about Nabis was that he managed to get the support of the people as a foundation for his power. In his discussion of the decemvirate (D 1.35; 1.40–41) Machiavelli compares Appius – qua failed prince – to Nabis, noting that while Nabis maintained the support of the people, Appius turned against them in his quest for tyranny. Having been elected by the plebs as a decemvir, Appius treated the plebs well during his first year in office. Yet immediately following his reappointment, which he secured by conspiring with the "noble youths," he showed his true nature as a "cruel persecutor of the plebs" (D 1.40), terrifying them and beating them down. Appius's insolence led him to break the golden rule of tyrants, not to touch their subjects' women. For Machiavelli, Appius's lesson is twofold: First, he shifts his power base from the plebs to the nobles, whereas what he should have done is the reverse, since "tyrants who have the collectivity as a friend and the great as an enemy are more secure." Second, Appius demonstrates the danger of a sudden about-face, from a humble and merciful friend of the plebs to a proud and cruel enemy. Nabis, by contrast, maintains popular support, which is why he can be called a civil prince.

[40] Contra Inglese, who juxtaposes the civil prince's *"favore dei cittadini"* to Agathocles's *"frode e violenza."* Giorgio Inglese, "Introduzione," in Niccolò Machiavelli, *Il principe* (Turin: Einaudi, 1995), xxi.

CRUELTY AND REPUTATION

Among the primary risks faced by princely perpetrators of cruelty is that they acquire a reputation for cruelty such as that attributed to Remirro. The question of reputation is central to the politics of cruelty, and it is treated in the second half of *The Prince*, beginning with chapter 15. That chapter opens with Machiavelli's claim to be a radical innovator (to "depart from the orders of others") by discussing the *verità effettuale* rather than the *immaginazione* of republics and principalities. Readers are asked to infer that truth and imagination can be distinguished, a point that Machiavelli later qualifies. The ostensible purpose of the chapter is not, however, to dwell on epistemology. Rather, Machiavelli's intent is "to write something useful," namely a critique of moralism. Given the distance that separates "how one lives to how one should live," readers ought to privilege historical reality over utopian thinking and focus on actual practices rather than abstract norms. The task of political theory, Machiavelli intimates, is to analyze actual, historically situated institutions and motivations rather than to design timeless and ideal templates for social organization.

Invited to dig beneath the moralism, the reader is asked to consider that moral goodness often leads to ruin rather than to political success. Hence the implication that princes who wish to preserve their states must learn "not to be good." The observation that unscrupulous and wicked actions are sometimes politically successful is not, however, Machiavelli's main point.[41] Neither is the principal claim of the chapter the tragic realization that politics requires people to sometimes act against virtue in the name of other values such as security, stability, patriotism, or the public good. The thrust of chapter 15 is about *appearance* and that princes ought not to worry about exposing themselves to a reputation of infamy:

one should not care about incurring the fame of those vices without which it is difficult to save one's state; for if one considers everything well, one will find something appears to be virtue, which if pursued would be one's ruin, and something else appears to be vice, which if pursued results in one's security and well-being.

(P 15)

---

[41] Berlin, "The Originality of Machiavelli," 26, 73–74.

It is common to interpret Machiavelli's critique of morality as an ostensibly more profound moralism.[42] According to this view, Machiavelli subordinates what is ordinarily regarded as virtuous action to the demands of politics. Against this moralist thesis, some authors have argued that Machiavelli redefines virtue by suggesting that wicked actions are only apparently evil and conceal true virtue. Both of these readings miss the crucial point, namely that virtue and vice are mediated by appearance. The claim of chapter 15 is that there is no such thing as an intrinsically virtuous or vicious action, but that these qualities are attached to what people see. Representation, in other words, emerges as a central dimension of state power.[43]

Appearances are important, Machiavelli insists elsewhere, for "men feed on what appears as much as on what is; indeed, many times they are moved more by things that appear than by things that are" (D 1.25). Managing and orchestrating the space of appearances thus constitutes a key political challenge. But how are readers to think about the relation between appearance and reality? The passage cited, that states that princes shouldn't be concerned about the reputation of infamy, suggests that appearances of virtue and vice may be false. A skilled political observer knows how to pierce the veil of appearances to access the reality they conceal. But this conventional schema of true/false aligned with real/phenomenal is quickly undone. In chapter 17, Machiavelli unravels the distinction between appearance and reality:

Cesare Borgia was *held to be cruel*; nonetheless *his cruelty* restored the Romagna, united it, and reduced it to peace and to faith. If one considers this well, one will see that *he was much more merciful* than the Florentine people, who so as to escape a name for cruelty, allowed Pistoia to be destroyed.

(P 17, my emphasis)

Cesare's appearance of cruelty obscures his clemency, while the Florentines' desire to treat Pistoia mercifully amplified violence. What are readers to make of Cesare's cruelty? Was he only "held to be cruel" but really merciful, or does "his cruelty" imply that the cruelty was real? Does

---

[42] Croce refers to the "sad necessity to have to soil one's hands" and to having to trade "the salvation of one's own soul" for the sake of the state. Croce, *Politics and Morals*, 62. Wolin describes Machiavelli as a "moralist" sensitive to the "anguishing elements in the political condition itself." Wolin, *Politics and Vision*, 186. Meinecke attributes to Machiavelli the discovery of "a virtù of a higher order," i.e. a political morality in conflict with conventional moral virtue. Meinecke, *Die Idee der Staatsräson*, 37.

[43] Althusser, *Machiavelli and Us*, 92.

Cesare's reputation for cruelty result from truly cruel actions, or does that reputation conceal his true mercy? Does Machiavelli invoke the standard metaphysical opposition between true reality and contrived appearance? Are cruelty and mercy opposites? The ambiguity of the text at this crucial juncture suggests that the conventional critical epistemic operation of stripping away the contrived appearance in order to recognize the underlying reality is not the most productive way of thinking about cruelty. If one takes seriously Machiavelli's claim, that it was Borgia's "cruelty" [*quella sua crudeltà*] that restored the Romagna, then cruelty is the cause of the outcome described as merciful. Both antitheses – the conventional Roman opposition between cruelty and mercy *and* the traditional epistemological opposition between appearance and reality – collapse.

In a well-known essay, Michael Walzer interprets this contradiction as the basic structure of the dirty hands dilemma. According to Walzer, the dilemma arises from the conflicting demands of morality and politics. A "good man" recognizes that a cruel action is morally wrong, yet he understands that he must do "terrible things to reach his goal."[44] To nonetheless label these acts "cruel" is important, Walzer asserts, because it indicates that moral principles have not simply been set aside or overridden. To claim that Cesare was cruel in order to be merciful both concedes the wrongfulness of Cesare's actions but suggests that the consequences vindicate the conduct. Thus, the dirty hand schema allows Walzer to describe Machiavelli as a political but not a moral consequentialist: "We know whether cruelty is used well or badly by its effects over time. But that it is bad to use cruelty we know in some other way."[45] Dirty hands theory thus rescues Machiavelli from the relativist peril at the price of saddling him with a moralistic agony.

Yet there is no textual warrant for burdening Machiavelli with abstract moral principles, such as "it is bad to use cruelty." To use a distinction cherished by moral philosophers, Machiavelli does not *excuse* cruelty; under certain conditions, he *justifies* it. The paradox of Cesare's cruelty – called cruel and merciful in the very same passage – is not a dilemma between moral and political consideration but an effect produced by appearances. Cesare was "held to be cruel," and if one considers his act carefully, this appearance will change and he will seem merciful. The evaluation of cruelty, in other words, is played out in the domain of appearances, in a world of phenomena as they are for human experience.

---

[44] Walzer, "Political Action: The Problem of Dirty Hands," 175.
[45] Walzer, "Political Action: The Problem of Dirty Hands," 175.

There is no opposition between the perception of cruelty and its objective reality, for the "effectual truth" of cruelty is its appearance. Appearances, readers learn as part of their education in political literacy, are not primarily to be judged in terms of how faithfully they reflect an underlying reality. Rather, appearances have their own effectiveness, images their own power and status, independent of their indexical quality. Appearances, readers can infer, are always specious and deceptive, but they are never merely true or false.

Remarkably, Machiavelli does not claim that the appearance of Cesare's cruelty is false or distorted; nor does he suggest that his reputation for cruelty is a political disadvantage. If his cruelty – that is to say, the appearance of his cruelty – is what makes the restoration of the Romagna possible, then it is incumbent upon the prince to seek out such appearances. By not absolving Borgia from the charge of cruelty, Machiavelli implies that such an appearance may be salutary.[46] In doing so, he complicates the earlier account, according to which Cesare's dexterity consists in his skillful disavowal of violence.

Sometimes, princes must be cruel and *deny* their responsibility for that cruelty. But according to chapter 17, such disavowals may not always be in the prince's best interest. Sometimes princes must be cruel and *acknowledge* that cruelty, perhaps even highlight it, to benefit from the "effect" such affirmation creates. This is the lesson readers can draw from the Medici response to the Pazzi conspiracy. Machiavelli emphasizes this point by counseling the prince not to care "about the infamy of cruelty." Indeed, a "name for cruelty" [*nome del crudele*] may be a useful resource, as evidenced by Hannibal, whose soldier respected him precisely on account of his "inhuman cruelty."

By collapsing the distinction between cruelty and the name-of-cruelty, Machiavelli undermines the idea (propagated, for example by Walzer) that cruelty is a time- and context-independent category that describes a particular class of deeds. If, as Machiavelli suggests, cruelty is a function of appearance and if an act is deemed cruel or merciful not on its own terms but mediated by its appearance, then cruelty is only what appears as such.

To recapitulate, Machiavelli's theory of cruelty can be summed up in five propositions: First, transitional moments require a spectacle, and the

---

[46] Contra Orwin, who writes that "Cesare was *thought* to be cruel. Machiavelli argues that he was not." Clifford Orwin, "Machiavelli's Unchristian Charity," *American Political Science Review* 72, no. 4 (1978), 1223.

public display of lethal violence is particularly well-suited for the purpose. Second, such cruelty is best understood not as the moral failure of tyrants but as a political tactic that ought to be evaluated in terms of its effects on the material and symbolic fields of power. Third, political cruelty is most effective when directed against privileged elites. In contrast to contemporary forms of terrorism, which distribute fear because everyone could become its targets, Machiavellian cruelty is an anti-oligarchic tactic aimed at conspiring elites.[47] Fourth, the reputation or appearance of cruelty is independent of its practice. Finally, depending on context, a reputation for cruelty can be politically advantageous or deleterious. These last two propositions have two further implications: First, a political analysis of cruelty cannot be generic or universal but is subordinated to an analysis of the conjuncture; and second, cruelty is always mediated by appearances and reputations. Cruelty's political effects materialize in the field of phenomena. An analysis of cruelty must therefore pay special attention to these circuits of mediation, that is, to the ways in which cruelty is performed, represented, interpreted, and narrated.

POPULAR CRUELTY

The emphasis on cruelty in *The Prince* and the comparable lack of discussion of cruelty in the *Discourses* may lead readers to consider cruelty a characteristic of principalities, but that is not so. As Machiavelli notes in *Discourses* 2.13, "What princes are necessitated to do at the beginning of their increase, republics also are necessitated to do until they have become powerful enough and force alone is enough." Until republics are strong enough that they can rely solely on force, they need to have recourse to the same kinds of controversial tactics as principalities, and those include cruelty. It follows that Machiavelli understands cruelty as a transitional strategy, a mode of violence that is of particular importance in moments of political crisis.

If *The Prince* theorizes cruelty from the point of view of princes, the *Discourses* and especially the *Florentine Histories* offer a perspective on cruelty from the point of view of the people. These texts emphasize that

---

[47] Historically, this has not always been the case. In the late nineteenth century, anarchist terrorist groups often targeted specific figures, monuments, or symbols associated with empire, the state, and the bourgeoisie. See Carola Dietze and Claudia Verhoeven, eds. *The Oxford Handbook of the History of Terrorism* (Oxford: Oxford University Press, 2014).

well-used cruelty is a form of violence directed against social superiors –
wealthy and ambitious elite citizens. In *Discourses* 1.16, Machiavelli writes:

> I judge unhappy those princes who have to hold to extraordinary ways to secure
> their states, since they have the multitude as enemies. For the one who has the few
> as enemies secures himself easily and without many scandals, but he who has the
> collectivity as enemy never secures himself; and the more cruelty he uses, the
> weaker his principality becomes. So the greatest remedy he has is to seek to make
> the people friendly to himself.

Unhappy are those princes who have to use "extraordinary ways,"
which in this context mean cruelty against the multitude. Happy, by
implication, are princes who can rely on "ordinary ways," in other
words, on the use of cruelty against the few. A prince who wishes to
follow Cesare's example and aims to "make and unmake men" thus
better align himself with the people and against the few.[48] Expanding
the point made in chapter 9 of *The Prince* concerning the popular and
anti-oligarchic dimension of cruelty, the *Discourses* and the *Florentine
Histories* relish in depictions of cruelty against the powerful and their
minions. As I argue in more detail in Chapter 6, cruelty is the name given
to modes of violence that target the particular class-dependent values
of the *grandi*, namely their conceptions of honor and privilege.[49]

Such punishments come in two forms: "extraordinary revenges"
taken by peoples "against those who have seized their freedom"
(D 2.2), and "excessive and notable" executions of powerful citizens
(D 3.1). As examples, Machiavelli cites the usurping nobles of Corcyra
who were apprehended, imprisoned, and killed "with many examples of
cruelty." When some attempted to resist their punishment, they were
suffocated by the people in the ruins of the prison (D 2.2). Other notable
examples include the brutal popular revenge against the agents of the
Duke of Athens who were cut to pieces, their flesh torn apart by hands
and teeth (FH 2.37); against the Bargello, the official in charge of
enforcing law and order, who during the Ciompi rebellion was hung
on the gallows by a foot and had pieces torn off his body "until there
was nothing left of him but his foot" (FH 3.16); as well as the decapitation of Giorgio Scali, a leading citizen (FH 3.20). In each of these

---

[48] Sasso, *Machiavelli e gli antichi e altri saggi*, 2:359.
[49] Sometimes, it also describes forms of violence deployed against the people – for instance
the war crimes committed by a Florentine commissioner against the people of the
Seravezza valley during the war against Lucca in 1429 (FH 4.20–21). But for the most
part, episodes of cruelty are directed against social superiors.

scenes, the multitude captures the political stage by means of a spectacular public deployment of anti-oligarchic cruelty. The hyperbolic depictions of popular cruelty emphasize bodily dismantlement and a shared collective practice of revenge. The examples of popular cruelty underscore Machiavelli's point that cruelty is by no means only available to princes. It is also a strategy at the disposal of rebels and one that is closely associated with the mobilization of popular and anti-oligarchic movements.

Throughout the *Discourses*, Machiavelli argues that cruelty is an ineffective and illegitimate way of governing the people. While he concedes that some ancient military commanders, especially Hannibal, successfully used cruelty to rule their armies (D 3.21), for the most part, Machiavelli defends the view that law, religion, and persuasion are more efficacious and advisable than cruelty. Hence he observes that Appius Claudius was "badly obeyed" because of his cruelty and "the Roman captains who made themselves loved by their armies" rather than hated were often more successful (D 3.19). Both Scipio and Camillus are mentioned as examples of how much more effective mercy and humanity can be than cruelty. By contrast, Machiavelli approvingly cites Manlius Torquatus, whose name became synonymous with severity and discipline after he executed his son for the latter's violation of military discipline (D 3.22). While Manlius was serving as consult in 340 BCE, his son contravened his father's order that no man leave his position under penalty of death, an act for which he paid with his life. Machiavelli endorses Manlius's "severity" (though he does not call it cruelty), as letting the violation go unpunished would have undermined political equality.

In early modern Italian cities, most interpersonal violence tended to be confined within social strata: Aggressors and victims were typically of the same social status. While there were occasional cases of assault on local officials, overall violence tended to occur "within rather than between social groups."[50] Violence that crossed such status boundaries was an unusual event and the forms of popular revenge that Machiavelli chronicles are notable precisely for violating the class-based *dignità* that his contemporaries would have taken for granted.

---

[50] Dean, *Crime and Justice in Late Medieval Italy*, 171.

CONCLUSION

Crudeltà is the concept most explicitly put forward by Machiavelli in his attempt to rethink the role of violence in politics; hence the distinction between well-used and badly used cruelty and the concern for reputation – *il nome del crudele*. Cruelty is a type of physical violence that traffics in appearances and deploys such appearances in a calculated manner: It is indissociable from the imagination, and it constitutes strategic acts of violence disguised as irrational and senseless. It attacks social rank by puncturing the façade of prestige and demonstrating the worthlessness and vanity of the elite's belief in their own inviolability. Machiavelli follows Roman convention in associating *crudeltà* with a kind of excess – the appearance of irrationality and attack on elite status.

In contrast to ancient and Renaissance authors, who associate cruelty with tyranny, and in contrast to modern authors, who often think of cruelty as equivalent to modern torture, Machiavelli theorizes it as a limited form of penal violence that functions politically through its publicity and theatricality. Rather than addressing the moral conditions that give rise to cruelty, Machiavelli focuses on cruelty's effects in terms of material and symbolic constellations of power. Machiavellian cruelty addresses the political imagination. Imbued with a peculiar logic – the rationality of irrationality – cruelty operates by producing appearances of irrationality and unpredictability. As such, this neo-Roman conception of cruelty is at once historically novel and political.

4

Beginnings

There exists in our political history one type of event for which the notion of
founding is decisive, and there is in our history of thought one political
thinker in whose work the concept of foundation is central, if not para-
mount. The events are the revolutions of the modern age, and the thinker is
Machiavelli, who stood at the threshold of this age and, though he never
used the word, was the first to conceive of a revolution.
   – Hannah Arendt, "What Is Authority?"

Machiavelli is perhaps one of the few witnesses to what I shall call *primitive
political accumulation*, one of the few theoreticians of the beginnings of the
national state. Instead of saying that the state is born of law and nature,
he tells us how a state has to be born if it is to last . . . He does not speak the
language of law, he speaks the language of the armed force indispensable to
the constitution of any state, he speaks the language of the necessary cruelty
of the beginnings of the state.
   – Louis Althusser, *Machiavelli and Us*

Beginnings are critically important in the lives of states. The problem
of beginning – of founding a political order – has been a central concern
in modern European political thought and is one of the defining characteristics of early modern political theory. The political theories of the
seventeenth and eighteenth century that bestowed so many of the concepts and images of modern constitutionalism largely conceived of
founding in terms of a historical and logical transition from a pre-political
to a political moment. Preoccupied by a concern with origins, many of
these theories imagine a pre-political world devoid of political and legal

institutions, a social or pre-social world governed by customary norms, natural law, or ravaged by war and chaos. Founding was thus frequently imagined as the *ex nihilo* creation of a state out of a pre-political condition. By contrast, ancient, medieval, and Renaissance authors understood founding as an immanent political act. Founders devise orders for the collective life of the city. They act not in a historical void but in concrete situations, harnessing the opportunities that present themselves in particular moments. For Machiavelli's predecessors and contemporaries, polities are founded on top of existing structures and traditions.[1] Beginnings, in other words, are never absolute. Any political change, Machiavelli notes, "leaves a dentation [*lascio lo addentellato*]" for the next (P 2). The metaphor of dentation refers to the walls of a building constructed in such a way that another wall can be attached to it. On such a wall, there is always a hook onto which another *mutazione* can be pegged. Every political transformation produces openings for future change. Working within a shifting political universe in which new states are continuously formed, acquired, and lost, Renaissance theorists had no theoretical motivation to understand founding as an *ex nihilo* act. Nonetheless, for Italian humanists, founding a political order was a creative act and one that was considered central to political life.[2] Founding is central, because it makes collective political life – *vivere politico* – possible. It establishes the institutions and norms that generate and sustain order, stability, and, at least potentially, freedom.

To found a state is not the same as to conquer or "acquire" it. Founders establish the form in which collective political life becomes possible. They author, as Wolin puts it, the "presuppositions" of political life.[3] These presuppositions are the conditions that make political life possible but that citizens normally take for granted. What distinguishes Machiavelli's "most excellent" princes, Moses, Cyrus, Romulus, and Theseus, is not that they conquered but that they established new frameworks of authority (P 6).[4] As such, they introduced "new orders and modes" [*nuovi ordini e modi*], a task Machiavelli describes as most

---

[1] Thus Machiavelli figures political transitions as transformations of the state, referring to *mutare, riformare, rimanere, assicurare, riprendere, pigliare,* and *socorrere* lo stato.

[2] Gilbert, *Machiavelli and Guicciardini: Politics and History*, 94.

[3] Sheldon Wolin, "Max Weber: Legitimation, Method, and the Politics of Theory," in *Fugitive Democracy and Other Essays*, ed. Nicholas Xenos (Princeton, NJ: Princeton University Press, 2016), 195.

[4] On the significance of the founder figure, see, for example, Pocock, *The Machiavellian Moment*, 156; Pitkin, *Fortune Is a Woman*, chap. 3; Wolin, *Politics and Vision*, 175–213.

difficult, uncertain, and dangerous. The problem of founding a polity is therefore not how to militarily defeat an enemy: The zero point of founding is set immediately following a military campaign or where such a campaign is not necessary. The military conquest itself is bracketed.[5]

Beginnings are vitally important in the lives of institutions, because they have a disproportionate influence in shaping their historical trajectories. A proper beginning, Machiavelli suggests, consists in laying foundations [*fare fondamenti*], an architectural metaphor common in ancient and medieval political thought. In the first book of the *Discourses*, he counsels states to create radically new foundations (D 1.26), while in *The Prince*, he warns that states that do not have good foundations from the outset must establish them later "with hardship" (P 6). The challenge of founding is to mold structures that can hold their own in the shifting quicksand of political life. Just as the foundations of a building bear and distribute the weight of the structure and the forces that batter it, so political institutions or *ordini* must sustain the pressures, swings, and tempests that shake a state. Since "all things of men are in motion and cannot stay steady," the problem is to establish institutions that last (D 1.6).

Yet founding is not merely a practical matter of creating stable institutions. Beginnings, Machiavelli insists, have an afterlife. They establish material sedimentations that continue to shape and affect states for their entire life cycle. It is not entirely clear what explains this continuing afterlife. At times, Machiavelli suggests that these repercussions are simply the material effects of institutional design – the way that institutions constrain the practices of political actors and the long-term development of a state. At other times, Machiavelli flirts with a more metaphysical language, according to which beginnings are mystical moments that breathe life into political institutions. In *Discourses* 3.1, for example, he writes that "[i]f one wishes a sect or republic to live long, it is necessary to draw it back often toward its beginning." Formulations such as these might suggest a mystified conception of origins, but as I will show over the course of this chapter, an immanent and materialist reading is more plausible.

Machiavelli sometimes figures political transitions in terms of giving form to matter (P 6, 26; D 1.18; FH DL, 1.7, 2.37, 7.18), an expression

---

[5] See Yves Winter, "Conquest," *Political Concepts: A Critical Lexicon* 1(2011).

that has conventionally been interpreted along Aristotelian lines.[6] Political actors find whatever *materia* fortune has provided and are faced with the challenge of imprinting a form upon it. Since they encounter not unformed matter but matter that always already has a form, the process of founding is one of *undoing* an existing form and impressing a new one. In Arendt's words,

> an element of violence is inevitably inherent in all activities of making, fabricating, and producing, that is, in all activities by which men confront nature directly, as distinguished from such activities as action and speech, which are primarily directed toward human beings. The building of a human artifice always involves some violence done to nature – we must kill a tree in order to have lumber, and we must violate this material in order to build a table.[7]

By conceiving political founding in terms of making or *poiesis* (rather than Arendt's preferred conception, which would be organized around speech and action or *praxis*), Machiavelli positions founding as never democratic and nearly always violent, except in rare situations of legendary lawgivers who bestow orders on new settlements. It is more complicated in cities that need to order themselves; indeed, it is "almost impossible" and never "without danger" (D 1.2). While not all political transitions are equally bloody, more often than not they involve significant violence, especially cruelty.

There are two different ways in which readers have thought about the Machiavellian assertion that founding is a violent event: either they have treated it as an empirical or as a transcendental claim. From an empirical perspective, founding violence describes a historical correlation. Early modern European state-making involved the concentration of power and resources along with the political and military subordination of rival magnates and noblemen. Typically, this process occurred through war and marriage but rarely without violence.[8] From a transcendental vantage

---

[6] See Pocock, *The Machiavellian Moment*, 175. By contrast, Stacey has argued for a rhetorical reading of the form–matter relation, while Gaille has questioned the primacy of form over matter. Stacey, *Roman Monarchy and the Renaissance Prince*, 226; Marie Gaille-Nikodimov, *Conflit civil et liberté: La politique machiavélienne entre histoire et médecine* (Paris: Honoré Champion, 2004), 119.

[7] Hannah Arendt, "What Is Authority?" in *Between Past and Future* (New York: Penguin, 1977), 111.

[8] On the historical sociology of state-making, see Weber, *The Vocation Lectures*; Charles Tilly, "War Making and State Making as Organized Crime," in *Bringing the State Back in*, ed. Peter B. Evans, Dietrich Rueschemeyer, and Theda Skocpol (Cambridge: Cambridge University Press, 1985); Charles Tilly, *Coercion, Capital, and European States, AD 990–1992* (Cambridge, MA: Blackwell, 1992).

point, founding violence asserts that violence is an essential factor in founding. This essential role derives either from attributing to violence a causal role in creating a new polity (based on cosmological or metaphysical schemas of founding) or from the impossibility of legitimating the founding moment within a juridical register. Arendt attributes such a causal conception of founding violence (replete with a tacit ontological schema) to Machiavelli. She argues that Machiavelli "saw that the whole of Roman history and mentality depended upon the experience of foundation, and he believed it should be possible to repeat the Roman experience through the foundation of a unified Italy."[9] By suggesting that Machiavelli thought it possible to "repeat" the foundation, Arendt imputes to Machiavelli a superficial idea of historical temporality, according to which historical experiences can simply be reinstantiated.[10] Contra Arendt, Miguel Vatter and Thomas Berns have proposed alternative transcendental interpretations of founding violence. Informed by the Derridean claim that law presupposes but cannot accommodate founding moments within its structure, Vatter and Berns highlight the impossibility of subsuming the founding moment within the normative categories of the law.

This chapter contests both the empirical and transcendental interpretations of Machiavellian founding. It proceeds by way of examining the origin stories of Rome through an analysis of its two founding moments – the establishment of the city by Romulus and the formation of the republic by Brutus. Comparing Machiavelli's portrayal of Romulus and Brutus to that of Philip of Macedon and the biblical David, I argue against the mystification of founding violence by ontological, cosmological, or deconstructive models. At the same time, the empirical reading fails to address the lasting political significance that Machiavelli ascribes to founding moments. Machiavellian founding violence, I contend, is political and immanent and is connected to issues of political memory and ideology. It has nothing to do with the ostensibly mystical foundations of political authority.

---

[9] Arendt, "What Is Authority?" 138. However, as Strauss rightly notes, the polity imagined by Machiavelli is "similar" yet not identical to Rome, for it must be "better than the Roman" republic. Strauss, *Thoughts on Machiavelli*, 116.

[10] For a critique of such a conception of historical temporality, see Pocock, *The Machiavellian Moment*; Vatter, *Between Form and Event*.

ROMULUS: REPUBLICAN FOUNDINGS

For the Renaissance, the paradigm of a well-founded city was Rome. As Arendt notes, "[a]t the heart of Roman politics … stands the conviction of the sacredness of foundation, in the sense that once something has been founded it remains binding for all future generations. To be engaged in politics meant first and foremost to preserve the founding of the city of Rome."[11] Rome's first founder – at least according to myth – was Aeneas, whom Machiavelli chooses to ignore in favor of Romulus. What makes Romulus a more interesting figure is that he was both Rome's first king and the (unsuspecting) founder of its republic.[12] Even though Romulus thought he was founding a monarchical state, he was in fact establishing the institutions for a republic. He was able to play both of these roles because he created a monarchy that was nonhereditary, an army staffed by the plebs, and a senate that comprised the nobility and balanced the power of the king.[13] He laid, in Cicero's words "excellent foundations for the commonwealth."[14]

But Romulus was not only a legendary institution-builder. He was also a domineering, combative, and bellicose figure, and his groundbreaking work in Rome has always been overshadowed by his killing of his brother, Remus. Livy renders the fratricide as the result of an unfortunate altercation – "a disgraceful quarrel" – in which blows were exchanged and Remus was accidentally killed.[15] Whereas Livy describes the murder as a crime of passion, most ancient and Renaissance commentators regarded it as more or less premeditated. The conventional view of this murder for over a thousand years prior to Machiavelli was that it had been a sinful crime that tainted Rome from its very origins.[16] In a famous

---

[11] Arendt, "What Is Authority?" 120.

[12] As Sasso notes, Machiavelli mentions Romulus only a handful of times, yet some of these occurrences are of an "extreme importance" and occur at "key points" in the theoretical reconstruction of Roman history. Sasso, *Machiavelli e gli antichi e altri saggi*, 1:119.

[13] McCormick, *Machiavellian Democracy*, 33; Catherine Zuckert, "Machiavelli's Democratic Republic," *History of Political Thought* 35, no. 2 (2014), 266.

[14] Cicero, *On the Commonwealth and on the Laws*, 2.17.

[15] In the process of founding the new city – all according to Livy – the twin brothers squabbled over who should govern the city and whose name it should bear. A brawl ensued, and "in the course of the affray Remus was killed" [*ibi in turba ictus Remus cecidit*]. Livy also offers a second version, according to which Remus jumped over the uncompleted wall of the new settlement "whereupon Romulus killed him in a fit of rage" (1.6–1.7).

[16] Augustine, *The City of God against the Pagans*, trans. R. W. Dyson (Cambridge: Cambridge University Press, 1998), 15.5.

passage of *De officiis*, Cicero impugns Romulus, insisting that he acted not out of political necessity and in the larger interests of the city, but out of purely self-serving motives: "when it seemed more beneficial to him to rule alone than with someone else, he killed his brother. He abandoned both familial obligation and humanity in order to secure something that seemed beneficial but was not ... He did wrong, then – and I speak with all the respect due to him."[17]

It is against precisely this line in Cicero's *De officiis* that Machiavelli writes *Discourses* 1.9. Rejecting conventional wisdom, this chapter praises Romulus not only for his successful wars and institution-building but also explicitly for his fratricide, which Machiavelli construes as an instance of founding violence. Against Cicero, Machiavelli insists that the fratricide was not discretionary but "necessary," because to found a republic, one must be alone.[18] Machiavelli offers the following rationale for Romulus's necessary solitude: While the many are good at *maintaining* states (in fact better than an individual prince), they are incapable of *founding* and *ordering* states because of the "diverse opinions among them." This diversity would not be an issue, were there binding decision-making procedures and institutions. But founding moments are characterized by the absence of precisely such procedures and institutions. In founding moments, so Machiavelli argues, one individual must claim a monopoly of decision-making. In such moments, the principle of unity of a state is embodied in the solitude of the founder. Hence states must be ordered by individuals, which means that founders must be princes and at the moment of their foundation, even republics must be principalities.[19]

Even if one accepts Machiavelli's assertion that founders must be solo, it remains a weak justification for murder.[20] The unapologetic vindication of what looks like gratuitous violence could be discounted as one of Machiavelli's eccentricities were it not so central to his entire account of founding. Romulus, for Machiavelli, is a paradigm case of a political founder, and the fact that he murdered his brother, rather than a nameless

---

[17] Cicero, *On Duties*, 3.41.
[18] Sullivan notes that Machiavelli may in fact even have exaggerated Romulus's crimes by pardoning him for a murder that, according to Livy, he did not commit, that of Titus Tatius. Sullivan, *Machiavelli's Three Romes*, 127.
[19] Lefort, *Machiavelli in the Making*, 245.
[20] Vatter argues that founders must be alone to insulate the many and to protect their authority from the taint of founding violence. But the founder's solitude cannot serve both as justification for violence and at the same time as instrument to protect the many from that very violence. Vatter, *Between Form and Event*, 69.

enemy, captures something central to transitional cruelty. Romulus's fratricide signals a transgression that cannot simply be justified by a schema of expediency. There is an incongruity between Machiavelli's insistence on exonerating Romulus and his refusal to fully account for the reasons.

As Machiavelli notes, "order[ing] a kingdom or constitut[ing] a republic" requires "extraordinary action" [*azione straordinaria*] (D 1.9). In this case, "extraordinary" has two contradictory meanings. On the one hand, it refers to the moral outrage of the founding act and to the violation of existing norms. On the other hand, it refers to the founding act's exceptional status, to its irreducibility to a normative order. As the shared morphology of *ordinare* and *straordinaria* indicates, what makes the founding act "extraordinary" is that it is not subsumable under the terms of the order it establishes. The moral outrage presupposes the existence of a normative order; yet the political irreducibility suggests that the founding act takes place in the absence of such an order.

Given the important role Romulus plays in Machiavelli's pantheon of founders, his ultimate rationalization of Romulean violence is anticlimactic. Ostensibly cutting through the Gordian knot, Machiavelli writes that Romulus is justified by the consequences: for "when the deed accuses him, the effect excuses him" [*accusandulo il fatto, lo effetto lo scusi*] (D 1.9). The rationale, readers are told, is that "he who is violent to spoil, not he who is violent to mend, should be reproved." According to this maxim, Romulus's absolution hinges on the "mending" consequences his murder produces. But the dilemma of evaluating founding violence is not so easily resolved. The seemingly unproblematic ranking of possible outcomes (in Machiavellian terms: it is better to "mend" [*racconciare*] than to "spoil" [*guastare*]) presupposes a standard of measurement that determines whether an outcome mends or spoils. If Romulus was Rome's first legislator and as Livy writes, gave his people "a body of law" in order to "unite them into one political body" (1.8), then readers must infer that the norms on which such reasoning relies are only established retroactively.[21] Founding, in other words, cannot be authorized by recourse to established legal or moral standards because its role is to establish the very conditions for new standards to emerge. Just as, according to modern constitutional theory, the constituent power of the people cannot be bound by the constitution because the former precedes the latter both

---

[21] See Jacques Derrida, "Force of Law: The Mystical Foundation of Authority," *Cardozo Law Review* 11, no. 5–6 (1990), 927.

logically and historically, so the founding moment is not susceptible to the rule or norm that it makes possible.[22]

In his influential reading of Thomas Jefferson's *Declaration of Independence*, Jacques Derrida examines the aporetic structure of the authority that undergirds such proclamations. The problem of the *Declaration* is that the subject that announces its independence – the people – is brought into being by the very act of the declaration. Even though the representatives that sign the declaration do so in the name of the people, that people does not formally exist in the instance it declares its independence. Strictly speaking, the signature on such a declaration "invents the signer" by "a sort of fabulous retroactivity."[23] Thus, the founding act by which a people declares independence, seizes power, and founds the law happens in a kind of void, lacking proper authorization. While Derrida does not label it violence – he calls it a *coup de force* – radical democratic political theorists have emphasized this undecidability at the heart of founding moments and identified it with a sort of violence.[24] In his late text "Force of Law: The Mystical Foundation of Authority," Derrida appears to authorize this terminology. There, he writes that the founding moment of law and justice consists of "a *coup de force*, of a performative and therefore interpretative violence that in itself is neither just nor unjust and that no justice and no previous law with its founding anterior moment could guarantee or contradict or invalidate."[25] Derrida calls this irreducibility of founding violence "mystical," because it is a form of violence that is presupposed by law yet cannot be accounted for within the law's terms. Instead, it interrupts and suspends the law in the name of a law yet to be founded.[26]

Commenting on Machiavelli, Vatter and Berns interpret this retroactive establishment of the law as the moment of founding violence. According to Vatter, "the violence of right ... which is directed against a pre- and non-rightful violence, itself presupposes the employment of such a pre-rightful violence in order to legitimate and institute itself. ...

---

[22] Ernst-Wolfgang Böckenförde, "Die verfassunggebende Gewalt des Volkes: Ein Grenzbegriff des Verfassungsrechts," in *Staat, Verfassung, Demokratie: Studien zur Verfassungstheorie und zum Verfassungsrecht* (Frankfurt a.M.: Suhrkamp, 1991), 99; Guillemain, *Machiavel: L'anthropologie politique*, 370.

[23] Jacques Derrida, "Declarations of Independence," *New Political Science* 7, no. 1 (1986), 10.

[24] Bonnie Honig, *Political Theory and the Displacement of Politics* (Ithaca, NY: Cornell University Press, 1993), 107–11.

[25] Derrida, "Force of Law," 941–43.

[26] Derrida, "Force of Law," 943, 991.

This trace of violence, anterior to the institution of modern right, both can and cannot be sublated in its theatre of well-used cruelty."[27] Berns refers to this aporetic structure as the "circularity" of founding violence. Examining Romulus's fratricide, Berns argues that the temporality of the act is out of sync with the temporality of its normative evaluation. A founding act cannot be justified in the present tense or in the future tense. Such justification, Berns argues, is only possible in the grammatical category of the future anterior.[28] Thus the foundation of legal authority is necessarily violent, insofar as it fills the gap between the ahistorical claim of the law and the historicity of its enactment. The figure of Romulus stands for the founding moment, which is, paradoxically, both historical and ahistorical: inscribed in a temporal continuum and yet the mark of a discontinuity, a moment that must be memorialized and commemorated as a beginning, yet also forgotten and repressed.

Derrida's reflections on the foundations of law and politics exhibit the aporetic structure of founding moments. Drawing on these insights as well as on Walter Benjamin's *Critique of Violence*, Vatter and Berns offer persuasive critiques of law and of the presumptive ahistoricity of juridical categories. Yet the problem with both arguments is that their category of violence is exceedingly underdetermined. By calling violence that which happens in the disavowed prehistory of law, in the interstitial moment of law's foundation, Vatter and Berns define violence in terms of its contradiction with law or right. In doing so, they invoke Benjamin's dialectical relation between *Recht* and *Gewalt*, which is itself a legacy of German idealism. As Vatter puts it, Machiavelli asks "under what conditions the law can assume its sovereign status, thereby taking the place of violence or force."[29] Violence, for these authors, is paradoxically both the mechanism of *Recht* and yet also that which is never entirely subsumable under it; hence violence's aporetic structure.[30]

The Benjaminian formulation of a dialectical relation between *Recht* and *Gewalt* makes sense only against the background of two historically particular ideas: the conception of the state that takes the form of right, most cogently expressed in Kant's political theory, and a linguistically

---

[27] Vatter, *Between Form and Event*, 119.
[28] Thomas Berns, *Violence de la loi à la Renaissance: l'originaire du politique chez Machiavel et Montaigne* (Paris: Kimé, 2000), 142–43.
[29] Vatter, *Between Form and Event*, 75.
[30] As Berns acknowledges, the baggage of the deconstructive approach is a broad notion of violence, one that includes not just physical but also literary and interpretive violence and ultimately converges with language as such. Berns, *Violence de la loi*, 137.

specific, German conception of *Gewalt* that confounds the ideas of *potestas* and *vis/violentia*.[31] In Kant's political theory, the role of right is to contain the undomesticated violence of the state of nature.[32] The deconstructive approach to founding violence is parasitic on the idea that the state takes the form of right and thus substitutes itself for the violence embodied in nature. Benjamin's claim that a cause becomes violent only "when it bears on moral issues" presupposes this *prima facie* opposition between violence and *Recht*.[33] Derrida's gloss is even more categorical: "There is no natural or physical violence." To refer to violence in nature is to "speak figuratively."[34]

While one might challenge the idealist philosophical schema on which this conception of violence depends, my aim here is narrower. To theorize violence in relation to the idea of right is one thing. But to deploy this category to interpret Machiavelli is misleading because his vocabulary of violence is shaped by the Roman tradition rather than by the Kantian problem of how to establish, by means of violence, a system of right that combines freedom with irresistible *Gewalt*.[35] That both this particular account of right and the ambiguity of the German word *Gewalt* could historically not have motivated Machiavelli's text is not my main concern. More important is that they are unsuited to capturing the political and theoretical substance of Machiavelli's concern, which has to do with theorizing the political presuppositions of a popular state.

Under Berns's pen, founding violence becomes a formal and dematerialized category. Because the founding act can, by definition, not be justified under an existing conception of right, it is ipso facto violent.[36] What this perspective overlooks is that, for Machiavelli, founding violence consists of cruel and memorable killings. Unlike the fantasies that

---

[31] See Étienne Balibar, "Gewalt," in *Historisch-kritisches Wörterbuch des Marxismus*, ed. Wolfgang Fritz Haug (Berlin: Argument Verlag, 2001).

[32] Immanuel Kant, "The Metaphysics of Morals," in *Practical Philosophy*, ed. Mary J. Gregor (Cambridge: Cambridge University Press, 1996), §42–44, 451–456.

[33] Walter Benjamin, "Critique of Violence," in *Reflections* (New York: Harcourt Brace, 1978), 277.

[34] Derrida, "Force of Law: The Mystical Foundation of Authority," 983.

[35] Immanuel Kant, "Idea for a Universal History With a Cosmopolitan Purpose," in *Political Writings*, ed. Hans Reiss (Cambridge: Cambridge University Press, 1991), 45.

[36] Bonnie Honig refers to the "violence and ambiguity that marked the original act of founding," and Jason Frank to the "violent arbitrariness of the exception." Honig, *Political Theory and the Displacement of Politics*, 109; Jason Frank, *Constituent Moments: Enacting the People in Postrevolutionary America* (Durham, NC: Duke University Press, 2010), 52.

informed later political theorists, Machiavelli did not conceive of founding as a transition from a pre-political to a political state but as a historical category: a transition that involves establishing a new political form. The reason violence is not a metaphor but a material category for Machiavelli is that his conception of founding is immanent and historical rather than ontological. Founding moments inaugurate a new polity, not the political as such. Founding violence, by extension, is targeted against the enemies of the new order. Central to the political function of these memorable killings is that they are directed against bodies, that they tear apart those bodies in ways that are theatrically staged. By reducing founding violence to an abstract ontological category, this important dimension of transitional cruelty is lost.

If the deconstructive interpretation of founding violence is inadequate, how are readers to make sense of Machiavelli's defense of Romulus and of the often cruel beginnings of states more generally? One potential explanation for the violent nature of such founding acts is to treat them simply as contingent empirical facts. On this reading, founders act violently in order to rid themselves of political rivals, or, to put it in contemporary terms, they act in accordance with security considerations.

CRUEL BEGINNINGS

Certain passages in the *Discourses* suggest that Machiavelli regards violence as a contingent aspect of founding. For instance, in D 3.7, he distinguishes, in typically hyperbolic terms, between transitions in which "infinite men have been put to death" and ones where "no one has been injured." He then goes on to list some examples of ostensibly nonviolent transitions, including the expulsion of the Tarquins from Rome, to which I will return later in this chapter, and that of the Medici from Florence in 1494. What distinguishes these transitions is that they were not triggered by revenge for injuries suffered at the hands of previous regimes. By contrast, transitions driven by revenge cause "the blood and death of men."

If founding can occur in bloodless ways, then the entire consideration of founding violence is beside the point. If violence is merely a contingent rather than a necessary component of states' beginnings, then to discuss it as if it were a constitutive feature is to hypostasize such violence. Yet, on reflection, neither of Machiavelli's examples is exactly peaceful. As regards 1494, we recall that Machiavelli considers the democratic republic introduced by Savonarola and reformed by Soderini as insufficiently founded.

Far from praising the absence of violence, he, in fact, reprimands both Savonarola and Soderini for failing to understand the role of violence in a political transition, a negligence that cost Savonarola his life, Soderini his job, and Florence its freedom. If only the expulsion of the Medici in 1494 had been accompanied by a memorable execution of some of their oligarchic *amici*, perhaps the Medici would not have been so easily restored in 1512. As regards the expulsion of the Tarquins and the establishment of the Roman republic, this political transition was triggered by the rape and suicide of Lucretia and sealed by the execution of the sons of Brutus, both of which I will discuss later in this chapter.

With the exception of the occasional reference to Venice, Machiavelli did not seriously entertain the possibility of founding moments devoid of at least some measure of staged cruelty.[37] In *Discourses* 1.26 Machiavelli formulates the challenge of founding a state in an existing territory most brazenly:

The best remedy ... is to make everything in that state anew ... to make in cities new governments with new names, new authorities, new men; to make the rich poor, the poor rich, as did David when he became king – 'who filled the hungry with good things and sent the rich away empty'; besides this, to build new cities, to take down those built, to exchange the inhabitants from one place to another, and, in sum, not to leave anything untouched in that province, so that there is no rank, no order, no state, no wealth there that [does not derive its claim from the prince] and to take as one's model Philip of Macedon, father of Alexander, who from a small king became prince of Greece with these modes.

Citing the biblical David and Philip of Macedon as examples, Machiavelli contends that such radical transformations are brutal, but they are the stuff of state-making. He quickly adds that this mode of proceeding is "very cruel" and inimical to "every way of life, not only Christian but human." Hence, he counsels his readers to avoid this evil by living "in private rather than as king." Yet whoever seeks to create new foundations "must enter into this evil if he wishes to maintain himself."

David and Philip are models of founding because they made everything anew. In doing so, they created not only new institutions but memories, myths, and traditions. Machiavelli explains the importance of this aspect of founding in the *Florentine Histories*, where he recounts the changes

---

[37] The archeological evidence in Rome suggests that he was right. Layers of burnt debris in the Forum that are dated to around 500 BCE may be signs that the change was less peaceful than narrated by Roman authors. Mary Beard, *SPQR: A History of Ancient Rome* (New York: Norton, 2015), 132.

brought to Italy by the barbarian invasions in the fifth century CE. The barbarians introduced new governments and princes, laws, customs, modes of life, religion, language, dress, and even names. Not only did the names of provinces change but "the names of lakes, rivers, seas, and men ... once Caesars and Pompeys, [men] are now called Piero, Giovanni, and Matteo" (FH 1.5, trans. mod.). There is no doubt that the populations must have experienced such changes as terrifying. Yet the destruction of some ancient cities whose names nobody remembers was also the condition for the growth and development of others, including Florence, Genoa, Pisa, Milan, Naples, and Bologna.

For political sociologists, the transformations that Philip of Macedon imposed on his conquered lands or the ones visited on Italy by the Barbarians can be understood in instrumental terms as effects of state-making. They are focused on incapacitating the new state's enemies. By remaking the entire social order, the new rulers remove resources from those most likely to harbor hostility toward them and instead create entire ranks of people who owe them their means and status. On this reading, the primary threat to the new state is imagined to come from the former rulers and elites who have been dispossessed of their power and status. That same concern is articulated in *Discourses* 3.4, where Machiavelli warns that a prince "never lives securely in his principality as long as those who have been despoiled of it are living." According to the state-making model, it is this insecurity that drives violence and that constrains the new state to deploy violence in order to consolidate power.

The empirical interpretation of founding violence can draw on *Discourses* 3.30, which explains founding violence as the elimination of envious rivals. Such adversaries tend to die either "by violence or by natural order." Ideally, they die naturally, because that forestalls "scandal," but sometimes it may be necessary to lend fate a hand. Machiavelli's notorious example is Moses, who was ready to "kill infinite men [*ammazzare infiniti uomini*]" among his own people "who ... were opposed to his plans" (D 3.30). If only Savonarola and Soderini had learnt from Moses, they might have forestalled their ruin. Yet neither of the two failed Florentine founders had understood founding violence: Savonarola lacked the authority to kill his rivals and Soderini was deluded by his belief that benefits and goodness could combat envy.

Moses is the prototype of a violent founder but a poor example for theorizing violence in terms of a logic of security. Moses was a master of staging violence to inspire fear of a supernatural being. Not only did he spectacularize violence for this purpose but he also disavowed it by ascribing the responsibility for such acts to God, his famous teacher. And, finally, as a military captain, Moses had a habit of entering "with violence [*con violenza*] into the countries of others" killing the inhabitants, seizing their possession, making "a new kingdom," and changing "the province's name" (D 2.8).[38] These acts of renewal foreshadow the forms of cruelty that Machiavelli associates with Philip of Macedon and with the Barbarians in Italy.

The trouble with the state-making model is not that is wrong but that it is incomplete. By depicting violence as narrowly instrumental and security-focused, it fails to address the symbolic dimensions of the particular exchange that is involved in founding. For founding to be effective it must be credible. That is to say, there is an audience who must believe that the founding act has been performed and accomplished in a competent and reliable way and that it has irreversibly changed the political status and conditions of a particular territorial space. Killing rivals or dislocating people does not, on its own, accomplish such a feat. There must be a symbolic exchange whereby a founder conveys intelligible signs that the violence that has been waged is not a force of chaos and disorder but a harbinger of a new order. In short, such violence must both perform for an audience and be performative as a creative act of *ordinare*, in creating the *ordini* and *modi* that structure and govern political life. As performance, violence exceeds the terms of the state-making framework, the premise of violence's instrumentality, and its orientation toward security.

Philip of Macedon and the biblical Moses and David deployed violence in more than strictly instrumental ways. For Machiavelli, what is interesting about Philip is that he turned a weak and divided kingdom with poorly organized armed forces into the leading military power of Greece. Philip achieved that feat in no small part through his reputation for cruelty, for which he is reviled by Justin, the third-century Roman historian, whose *Epitome* Machiavelli, like most educated Florentines, had read as a child.[39] What Justin in his revulsion against Philip does not consider, yet a reader

---

[38] Montag, "'Uno mero esecutore'."

[39] Marcus Junianus Justinus, *Epitome of the Philippic History of Pompeius Trogus*, trans. J. C. Yardley (Atlanta: Scholar's Press, 1994), 8.1–8.6; Ridolfi, *The Life of Niccolò Machiavelli*, 259n17. Both Plutarch and the Greek historian Diodorus Siculus focus on Philip's role as the architect of Macedonian expansion. Plutarch, "Alexander," in *Lives*, 11 vols, trans. Bernadotte Perrin (Cambridge, MA: Harvard University Press, 1914–1921), 7:223–51; Diodorus Siculus, *Library of History* (Cambridge, MA: Harvard University Press, 1952–1963), 16.1.1, 16.3.3, 16.8.2, 16.69.8.

trained by Machiavelli immediately sees, is that Philip's reputation for merciless savagery was carefully staged. Like Borgia or Moses, Philip exploited every opportunity to turn violence into a spectacle. In the battle against the Phocians at Crocus Field – a campaign that was instrumental in establishing Macedonian preeminence – Philip performed the role of divine avenger. Adorning his soldiers with crowns of laurel, the unmistakable sign of Apollo, he dressed them as the god's messengers. The laurel crowns inspired fear among the Phocians who had just desecrated Apollo's temple and thus mistook the Macedonian troops for divine warriors.[40] Writing about the battle, Diodorus refers to the ensuing slaughter of the Phocians as a "punishment visited by the gods" on those who had committed sacrilege.[41] The staged nature of Philip's warfare bespeaks the importance of theatrics both in battle and in founding moments.[42]

The reference to David is similarly more complicated than it appears. The biblical narrative is profoundly ambivalent. On the one hand, the books of Samuel present David as a brutal and ferocious figure whose cruelty in war was unsparing. Without counting any of the people David is described as having personally killed or betrayed, the Bible depicts David as having killed in battle tens of thousands of Philistines, over 60,000 Arameans, 18,000 Edomites, and 20,000 Israelites.[43] On the other hand, the biblical text goes to great lengths to insist that David was not only a man of God's heart but also greatly loved by all of Israel and Judah.[44] The love that the Israelites had for David suggests that, like Philip and Borgia, he was able to turn staged cruelty into a form that elicits awe and admiration among the people.

Most of Machiavelli's Florentine contemporaries would have associated David with virtue, courage, and glory.[45] A favorite motif of fifteenth-century art, David was cast in marble or bronze by three of the foremost Florentine sculptors of the time: Donatello, Verrochio, and Michelangelo. The young David was strongly associated with Florence's attachment to republican liberty. Even though his later career renders him an unlikely choice for such a symbol, the slaying of Goliath qualifies David as an

[40] Justinus, *Epitome of the Philippic History of Pompeius Trogus*, 8.2.
[41] Diodorus Siculus, *Library of History*, 16.61.1.
[42] For discussions of Machiavelli's theatrics of battle, see Spackman, "Politics on the Warpath"; Winter, "The Prince and His Art of War."
[43] 1 Samuel 18:7; 2 Samuel 8:5, 8:13, 10:18, 18:7.
[44] 1 Samuel 13:14, 18:16.
[45] Andrew Butterfield, "New Evidence for the Iconography of David in Quattrocento Florence," *I Tatti Studies in the Italian Renaissance* 6(1995).

unimpugnable tyrannicide. For example, Andrea del Castagno depicts the Youthful David as a vibrant and energetic giant-slayer, his lively wind-blown locks of red hair in sharp contrast to the detached head of Goliath that lies between his feet.[46] David's anti-tyrannical credentials also made him a favorite figure for would-be-princes. For a long time, the Medici family had Donatello's bronze David standing in the center courtyard of their palace on the via Larga, coopting the traditionally republican and anti-tyrannical symbolism.[47]

The contrast between Machiavelli's depiction of the biblical hero and his contemporaries is remarkable. Unlike Donatello, Verrochio, and Michelangelo, Machiavelli does not portray David as a pure and seductive adolescent; yet in contrast to David's detractors, he does not regard the Davidic body count as a discrediting factor. Highlighting the violent aspects of his rise to power, Machiavelli's "unsettling" David undermines the attempt to exonerate the biblical king for his killings.[48] Yet despite the blood on his hands, Machiavelli's David is not a villain but a model. Clearly, Machiavelli's aim is not to unmask David's crimes and taint his glory. Indeed, elsewhere in the *Discourses*, David is hailed as "without doubt" a "most excellent" prince, in a passage that emphasizes not only his military virtue but also his learning and judgment (1.19).[49] In refusing to choose between David-the-hero and David-the-tyrant, Machiavelli represents the warrior-king in a more complex light and insists that David's glory is tightly linked to his violence, and his cruelty to his political success.

RETURNS TO BEGINNINGS

Machiavelli's accounts of Romulus, Moses, David, Philip, and Valentino are origin stories of sorts. They narrate the beginnings of political order, form, and power; they tell a story about the emergence of a rudimentary state and its conditions. But what if a state is already there and it needs reform and reorganization? What are the prospects for a republic, such as

[46] Andrea del Castagno, *David with the Head of Goliath*, c. 1450, tempera on leather on wood, The National Gallery of Art, Washington DC, Widener Collection 1942.9.8.

[47] McHam, "Donatello's Bronze 'David' and 'Judith'." On the Medici's appropriation of the symbols of Florentine liberty, see Brown, "De-Masking Renaissance Republicanism," 189–94.

[48] Brown, *Medicean and Savonarolan Florence*, 241.

[49] In *The Prince*, David appears as the virtuous example of a prince who eschews the arms of others and confronts Goliath with his own arms (P 13).

Florence in the 1520s, that has lost its popular institutions or where the institutions serve only as a façade for oligarchic machinations?

Machiavelli addresses this issue in *Discourses* 1.16–18 and 3.1, where he discusses the problem of how to deal with corrupt states and how they can be reformed. The relation between violence and corruption is complicated. On the one hand, violence is a symptom of corruption: of the disintegration of public-spiritedness, the rise of ambition and insolence, especially among the few. On the other hand, violence is also a cause of corruption that contributed to the decline of republican political culture in Rome as well as in Florence. Finally, and it is in this capacity that I want to look at it in this section, violence is also a remedy or antidote for corruption, a therapeutic that if applied in the proper way at the appropriate time can be conducive to regenerating republican modes and orders.

Machiavelli's basic recipe is that corrupt states need to be refounded, that the persistence of structures of domination, myths and ideals is such that only a new foundation can turn around a state "where the matter is corrupt" (1.17). To order a state in such condition is very unlikely to succeed and requires one "to go to the extraordinary, such as violence and arms"; it demands "extreme force," a rebirth "with many dangers and much blood" (D 1.17–18). Corruption poses a serious limit on the possibility of regenerating a political order. Once too far progressed, it makes restoring freedom and republican government impossible, as was the case in Rome under Caesar. Once factionalized, the Roman republic could not be saved even by Caesar's assassination. Similarly, in modern times, there are cities, such as Naples and Milan, which are so corrupt that "no accident, even though grave and violent" could set them free (D 1.17).

Drawing on Renaissance medical theories and on Aristotelian natural philosophy, Machiavelli conceives of the state as a living and mortal body.[50] It is a "mixed body," that, like other bodies, goes through a life cycle that includes phases of growth, decline (corruption), and, ultimately, death. Just as simple bodies suffer disease, so in mixed bodies "many times infirmities arise that cannot be healed without fire and steel" [*sanza il fuoco o il ferro*] (FH 5.8). In such cases, politics must take on a therapeutic hue and a good citizen would do more wrong by letting such disorders fester than by "curing them." Because corruption

---

[50] Gaille-Nikodimov, *Conflit civil et liberté*, 33.

is an inevitable process that affects all political forms and institutions, mixed bodies, including states, "do not last if they do not renew themselves" (D 3.1).

The language of renewal, which is specific to republican political forms, draws on tropes from the medical fields that obliquely signify violence in a restorative and curative register. The medical references are part of a long-standing allegoric discourse that figures the polity as a body and the political actor as a physician.[51] As Machiavelli writes in *L'Asino*, "when evil [*il mal*] comes – for it always comes – take it down like a medicine" (OP 3:62; CW 2:759). In Machiavelli's text, the medical metaphors for violent regeneration come in three different forms, each of which has been a mainstay of political discourse since the Greeks: medication, surgical interventions, and purges.

The *pharmacological* metaphor figures political therapeutics as a prescription of medication, where "mild" medicine stands for minor corrective acts and "strong" medicine stands for severe forms of punishments, such as exile or the death penalty. Such forms of punishment are also metaphorized through *surgical* tropes. Just as the physician amputates in order to prevent a festering wound or a rotting limb from infecting the entire body, so political surgery involves the execution of conspirators or tyrants. *Purges*, finally, are based on the Hippocratic/Galenic theory of humors, according to which an imbalance of the four distinct bodily fluids – blood, phlegm, and yellow and black bile – causes disease. Here, the therapeutic intervention consists in bloodletting, which according to Galenic medicine balances the humors.[52]

Under Machiavelli's pen, the theory of the humors becomes a framework for theorizing the internal dynamics of a body politic. Unlike the human body, which according to Galenic medicine contains four humors, Machiavelli's state contains but two: that of the people versus that of the great (D 1.4, 5, 7). And whereas, for Galen, the four humors are equivalent and symmetric, Machiavelli regards one of them, that of the *grandi*,

---

[51] Dietmar Peil, *Untersuchungen zur Staats- und Herrschaftsmetaphorik in literarischen Zeugnissen von der Antike bis zur Gegenwart* (Munich: Fink, 1983), 430–65.

[52] As a political metaphor, bloodletting can point to a regrettable but restrained intervention, as for Seneca, who describes it as a merciful alternative to amputation. By contrast, Machiavelli's contemporary Pierio Valeriano, under the heading "The Healing of States," refers to bloodletting as the "violent purge" [*purgatione violenta*] appropriate to defend a republic against seditions and other political ailments. See Seneca, "On Mercy," 1.5.1; Pierio Valeriano Bolzani, *Hieroglyphicorum Collectanea, ex veteribus et recentioribus auctoribus descripta, et in sex libros ordine alphabetico digesta* (Frankfurt: 1678), 185.

as more harmful than the other. Moreover, for Galenic theory, a harmonious equilibrium between them keeps the body healthy, whereas excess or lack is the cause of illness and disease. Machiavelli's humors, by contrast, are dynamic – they keep the body politic in a constant state of disequilibrium, as is insinuated by the vocabulary of restlessness used to describe their movements.[53]

While these medical metaphors often seem to present as synonymous and equivalent, they actually convey slightly different valences of how therapeutic violence functions. Whereas the surgical metaphor presupposes the pathology to be concentrated in one part of the body politic, the pharmacological figure and the purge imply a more systemic conception of political illness. And if surgery suggests that a single act of abscission will swiftly cure the disease, the other metaphors intimate a duration and perhaps an iterative treatment plan to deal with the political malady. Finally, the surgical amputation of a limb leaves the political body permanently scarred, whereas a pharmacological intervention or a purge may return the body politic to health without lasting impairment.

Politically, these medical interventions into the life of a corrupt republic can happen either through domestic or foreign events ("intrinsic" and "extrinsic accidents"), and Machiavelli is primarily interested in the domestic ones, because they are the ones that can be deliberately shaped. Domestically, a return to beginnings can be triggered either through a virtuous individual (a "good man") or a virtuous order. By order, Machiavelli means, in this context, an institution that is organized to check the "ambition and insolence" of the few, and as examples he cites the Roman tribunes of the plebs and the censors.

In both cases (virtuous individuals and virtuous orders), Machiavelli's prescribed therapy involves an "excessive and notable" execution of elite citizens. *Discourses* 3.1 offers an entire list of examples that illustrate this practice: the executions of the sons of Brutus, of the Decemvirs, of Maelius, of Manlius Capitolinus, of Manlius Torquatus's son, and the indictment of the Scipios. These spectacular events drew the Romans "back toward the mark" and renewed "memory and fear." Machiavelli does not say why violence and blood are the only way that such recollections can be produced, but his reference to memory provides a clue that I will pursue in the next section.

---

[53] Gaille-Nikodimov, *Conflit civil et liberté*, 67, 83.

Just as founders have to be alone, so those who reorder a corrupt city through a notable execution must become "princes of that city" equipped with prerogative power. Machiavelli thinks such prerogative power is necessary because of the "insolence" of those who "cannot be corrected by the laws," in other words, the few. Under conditions of socioeconomic inequality, laws are insufficient to constrain elites, and violence is the only way to deal with the "corrupt" matter (D 1.55). Yet because such founding and refounding acts can only be performed by individuals, there is a political aporia that stands as an obstacle before the refounding act. Reorganizing a state for a "political way of life" [*vivere politico*] presupposes a good man, [but] becoming prince of a republic by violence presupposes a bad man," hence it is rare to find the right individual who combines exalted altruistic ambition with a callous readiness for autocratic power.

Assuming this problem has somehow been solved, Machiavelli discusses the particulars for how such a contradictory physician can reform a republic. Desire is not sufficient. There is no shortage of people who intend to restore a city to its old ways and to be known as "the new founder and second father" of a republic (FH 6.29). To effectively precipitate such a renewal, Machiavelli tells his readers, one must do more than have good intentions. One must act like Brutus: "there is no remedy more powerful, nor more valid, more secure, and more necessary, than to kill the sons of Brutus" (D 1.16). But what does it mean to "kill the sons of Brutus," and in what sense does Brutus's founding act differ from Romulus's, Philip's, or Borgia's?

Lucius Junius Brutus was the leader of the Roman revolt against the Tarquins that, according to Livy and legend, founded the Roman republic.[54] In 509 BCE, he led the uprising against the monarchy, which brought about the expulsion of the last king, Lucius Tarquinius Superbus, and the establishment of republican government. According to Roman historians, the king's son, Sextus, raped a Roman noblewoman, Lucretia. After she revealed the rape, Brutus rallied the people to overthrow the monarchy. He skillfully directs and manages the popular rage and exploits the moment to oust the king. Staging indignation,

---

[54] Though oddly enough, Machiavelli does not call Brutus a founder, but someone who renewed and revived the Roman republic. Machiavelli can discuss Brutus in this way because, on his telling, Rome had been an elective (rather than hereditary) monarchy, and the king's power had always been shared with the senate. See Zuckert, *Machiavelli's Politics*, 134, 212.

he forces the hands of his would-be conspirators, compelling them into an oath against the monarchy.

A year after the overthrow of the Tarquins – all according to Livy's report – while Brutus serves as Rome's first consul, his sons, along with other young aristocrats, are involved in a conspiracy against the republic. These young nobles "had found life under the monarchy very agreeable" because it had allowed them to "give a freer rein to their appetites." Because the republic restrained their ability to trade influence for honor and favors, they experienced the new political conditions as chains on their freedom. Whereas a king is susceptible to the power of the elites, they regarded the law as a threat to their prerogatives: "Law had no ears. An excellent thing, no doubt, for paupers, it was worse than useless" for the nobility (2.3). In order to return the public authority its ears, these young noblemen plotted to bring back the Tarquins. Yet, unbeknownst to the conspirators, the law had in fact ears albeit ones not well-disposed to treason. As Livy recounts, the conspirators were overheard by a slave and convicted of high treason. As consul, it was Brutus's task to execute his own sons. The prisoners were bound to the stake, stripped, flogged, and beheaded. Livy describes the scene as a collective tremor, with great anguish and pity for everyone involved. (Plutarch disagrees, portraying Brutus as unflinching and stern as he watches his sons' beheading, but Machiavelli ignores Plutarch's version as well as the Greek historian's ambivalence about whether Brutus's execution of his sons should incur praise or blame.)[55]

Since Machiavelli treats this execution as paradigmatic for renewing political orders, it is worth dwelling on some aspects of the event. A key trope in Livy's account of this majestic example [*exemplum nobile*] is the visual economy of the scene, in particular the gaze of the spectators. "It was a memorable scene," he writes, emphasizing the horror of a father who should not have been a spectator to this suffering. Brutus's children "drew all the eyes of the onlookers," while throughout the event, Brutus's face was a "spectacle" [*spectaculo*], his parental emotion on prominent display amid the performance of public punishment (2.5). These visual cues emphasize the spectacular dimension of the event, its effect as a public performance.[56]

---

[55] Plutarch, "Publicola," in *Lives*, 1:515.
[56] Andrew Feldherr persuasively argues that Livy intends his history to be a "visual artifact" placed at the "center of chain of visual images linking the past to the present and future." Andrew Feldherr, *Spectacle and Society in Livy's History* (Berkeley: University of California Press, 1998), 1.

Part of what makes Brutus's execution of his sons so grim and memorable is the asymmetry between the punishment of the Tarquins or the Medici – they were merely exiled – and that meted out to the young conspirators. Exile, Machiavelli intimates, perhaps reflecting Florence's long, and failed, experience with exiling conspirators and political antagonists – is not an adequate sanction for conspirators. Like the Medici, who between Cosimo's return in 1434 and the Pazzi conspiracy in 1478 expanded the role of capital punishment as a sanction for political crimes, Machiavelli argues that executions are more effective and more symbolically charged punishments than exile.

By executing the consul's children, the first act of the republic consists in undoing the very principles of monarchic political order. Roman monarchy was never formally hereditary, and so removing the conditions for the hereditary organization of power and authority was not the central symbolic aspect of this execution for Livy and his Roman readers. Yet for sixteenth-century Florence, dominated by a single family on their way to instituting a hereditary principate, "to kill the sons of Brutus" has an obviously anti-hereditary ring. "Brutus's sons" are no generic metaphor for conspiratorial enemies of the republic: They stand for the kind of corruption that comes with power and privilege passed through families and bloodlines, precisely the kind of power that had become so corrosive of Florentine politics. To kill Brutus's sons strikes at the heart of the principle of birthright, the monarchic and aristocratic notion that kinship is the rightful conveyor of authority and privilege.

Brutus's sons must bear the wrongdoings of the republic's citizens. The execution represents a purge, in which all offenses against the republican order are annulled. If the overthrow of the Tarquin kings produces not only satisfaction among Romans but also, as one would expect, fear and ambivalence, Brutus's dead sons provide a surface on which these ambivalences and animosities can be projected. One is tempted to conclude that the very category of the citizen is instantiated by the relation to this original murder.

POLITICAL MEMORY

In the midst of the French revolutionary fervor of 1792, days after the storming of the Tuileries, a bust of Lucius Junius Brutus was unveiled in the Jacobin club. Louis-Pierre Manuel, the Procureur of the Commune, declared to the club's members: "It is here that the fall of kings has been prepared, the fall of Louis XVI. Here must rest the image of the one who first wanted to purge the earth of kings. Gentlemen, this is Brutus, who will remind everyone that, in order to be a citizen, one must always be ready to sacrifice everything, even one's children, to the welfare of one's country."[57]

That Brutus's execution of his sons was material not only for the Roman republican mythology but also for the French Jacobins two millennia later suggests that it was successful at the level of establishing political memory. Narratives of founding are central not only to Rome but to the republican tradition more generally. As Arendt notes, it is through such stories that the authority of the past is harnessed for the political present.[58] According to Machiavelli, the political past lives on in the present in three modes: as institutions [*ordini*], as practices [*modi*], and as memory [*memoria*]. Founders create institutions; practices develop over time; but memories are inaugurated by theatrical performances of cruelty. The execution of Brutus's sons is a quintessential example of the latter.

Political memory can be regime-preserving or regime-subverting. It tends to sustain regimes when it is continuous with the present – thus republics benefit from an ensconced memory of political freedom, while princes profit from well-established memories of docility. While memories that are continuous with present practices reinforce regimes, republics and principalities differ with respect to discontinuous memories. Republics commemorate their founding moments as civic pageantry. A republic's non-republican prequel bolsters the legitimacy of present republican institutions and reinvigorates civic ideals. Forgetfulness about origins, by contrast, is one of the great dangers that republics face. Thus the ritualistic commemoration of political transitions forms an important part of the republican playbook.

As the example of Brutus's sons demonstrates, such transitions tend to generate a new political memory. Both Machiavelli and Livy emphasize the monstrosity of the act, in which a father stages the spectacular execution of his children for political reasons. Through the killing of his offspring, Brutus destroys the conditions for hereditary monarchy

---

[57] Philippe-Joseph-Benjamin Buchez and Pierre-Célestin Roux-Lavergne, eds. *Histoire parlementaire de la Révolution française, ou Journal des assemblées nationales depuis 1789 jusqu'en 1815* (Paris: Paulin, 1834–1838), 182.
[58] Arendt, "What Is Authority?"

and at the same time establishes himself as the rightful ancestor of the republic. Instead of a father of two sons, he becomes the father of republican liberty. It turns out that his biological sons are not his only or even his primary progeny since he, like Romulus, will be remembered by Romans as having fathered the republic. Thus, Machiavelli's solemn incantation of how one must "kill the sons of Brutus" is not a call for republican leaders to stage a frightful execution to inspire primeval terror in their citizens.[59] Nor is it a de-reification, whereby republics shed the accumulated institutional and conventional debris to rejuvenate themselves at the wellspring of unmediated collective action.[60] Rather, it indicates the transformation of these young men's deaths into narrative signifiers symbolizing the republican order. Republics, Machiavelli argues, are narrative constructs: They rely on recurring narrations and dramatic reenactments of stories about their origins and their history.

Principalities, by contrast, have a more complicated relation to their past. Dynastic states benefit from a certain amnesia about the "memories and causes of innovation" (P 2). Memories, especially of political transitions and rebellions, can be dangerous to principalities because they indicate that the question of a state's legitimacy has not been conclusively settled. Hereditary states are durable because people forget that usurpation and blood mark the cradle of the most illustrious princely dynasties. Yet the odor of illegitimacy and lawlessness clings to new princes and threatens to undermine them at every turn. In particular, principalities that are built on the ruin of republics are threatened by the memory of liberty, which according to Machiavelli is so robust that its "name" is "never forgotten" (P 5).

Unlike the bloodline of a prince, which can be extinguished, political memory constitutes a lasting source of political contestation. The best bet for princes is to hold out and wait for the passage of time to erode political memories. Some cultural techniques can help: Introducing new governments and laws, customs, modes of life, religion, language, dress, and even names tends to speed up the process. The cultural practices that Machiavelli ascribes to the Barbarian tribes that settled Italy in late antiquity and the early Middle Ages were aimed at establishing precisely such new memories. By renewing the nomenclature, they installed a

---

[59] Strauss, *Thoughts on Machiavelli*, 167.
[60] Pitkin, *Fortune Is a Woman*, 275–79.

cultural hegemony that pushed aside the cultural forms of late Roman and Latinate antiquity. Thus, the substitution of Pieros, Giovannis, and Matteos for Caesars and Pompeys was a critical part of the political transition. Memory, after all, is not simply a recording device that faithfully chronicles political events. Rather, it is a slice of the political imagination, marking a set of political possibilities as viable and imaginable because they circulate discursively and are articulated as experiences. Instead of thinking of political memory as annals of the political past, we should consider it to be shaped by mnemonic practices and cultural hegemony.

In contemporary radical democratic theory, inspired by Arendt, Derrida, Lefort, and Rancière, founding violence is sometimes figured as the constitutive division of the people. Thus, the impossibility of the demos to become whole, its split into parts that are uncounted and not fully accounted for, its paradoxical place between present and the future are the ostensible results of a primary tear and division. While I do not dispute the diagnosis, that "the people" is a divided, incomplete, and paradoxical category, I am unpersuaded by attempts to mystify that split by turning it into a historical engine that drives popular struggles. My point is that a material conception of political memory offers an alternative (and more compelling) way of theorizing the violence of founding moments.

Political memories are embodied in the practical consciousness of everyday life, in mentalities and dispositions. To analyze such memory, one must look at the representations of power and authority and at the mnemonic practices at work, including the ways in which political performances establish and reproduce structures of authority. From this vantage point, public executions and assassination can be understood as mnemopoietic practices that produce the "political presuppositions" that tacitly shape the conditions of political life. Such presuppositions include the republic as avenger of oligarchic conspiracies (Brutus) or the prince as ultimate arbiter, protector, and defender of the people (Borgia). By mnemopoiesis, I mean the cultural activity of creating memories, in this case by the unforgettable display of an executed body in the public square. Just as dynastic states rely for control not on military power but on everyday dispositions and memories that embody political subordination, so new states can marshal the powers of memory through appropriate mnemopoietic acts. By producing an aesthetic of power, law, and unity, the spectacle of public execution shapes the set of imaginable political possibilities.

THE GENDER OF FOUNDING VIOLENCE

In the cases of Romulus, Liverotto, and Brutus, founding a new state required the killing of a close relative – Romulus's brother, Liverotto's uncle and foster father, and Brutus's sons. Kinship and in particular male lineage becomes the scene of violence, the place where violence is staged. Being an immediate male relative is a resource, for one can be a "natural prince," an option not usually open to female next of kin. Natural princes, Machiavelli emphasizes in chapter 2 of *The Prince*, are in an advantaged position: They come to power without violence and thus benefit from the people's love and good will. Yet if the prospect of becoming a natural prince is an attractive privilege of male birthright, the nexus of male kinship is not only the point at which masculinity and power are reproduced. To the extent that it marks the "bloodline" of hereditary power and traditional legitimacy, male kinship is also a site of potential violence and thus precarious. As privileged sites for killing, kinship relations chart a social map of violent death and trace the gender code of Machiavellian political violence.

With a few exceptions, women neither inflict nor suffer the kind of lethal violence that Machiavelli stylizes as a metonym for political beginnings.[61] To some extent, this is the reflection of the marginal place of women as political agents in Machiavelli's universe, the patriarchal discourses in which the logics and practices of killing are embedded, and the myths of militarized masculinity they promote. Throughout Machiavelli's work, violence is coded as female only in the mythic and allegorical world of the dangerous and uncontrollable nonhuman forces *fortuna* and *necessità*, which are sometimes likened to violent actors and where femininity serves as a prop for nature. In the politico-historical narrative, violence by or against women is marginal.

This is all the more conspicuous because sexual violence and rape constitute an important subtext of Machiavelli's work. Indeed, rape is the neglected dimension of foundational violence in many of the episodes discussed in this and earlier chapters. The untold story of the Romulus

---

[61] There are exceptions. An important one is Caterina Sforza, the Countess of Forlì, whom Machiavelli mentions in all of his major political works (P 20; D 3.6; FH 8.34; AW 7.145). See Arlene W. Saxonhouse, *Women in the History of Political Thought: Ancient Greece to Machiavelli* (New York: Praeger, 1985), 164; Julia L. Hairston, "Skirting the Issue: Machiavelli's Caterina Sforza," *Renaissance Quarterly* 53, no. 3 (2000), 708; Michelle T. Clarke, "On the Woman Question in Machiavelli," *The Review of Politics* 67, no. 2 (2005), 254.

legend is that his conception was the result of a rape. According to Livy, Romulus's mother, Rhea Silvia, a priestess and vestal virgin, "was raped and gave birth to twin boys. Mars, she declared, was their father" (1.4). Similarly, the revolt against the Tarquins that led to the establishment of the Roman republic has at its origin the rape of Lucretia, the narrative of which, as celebrated by Livy, Ovid, Chaucer, and Shakespeare, is "one of the founding myths of patriarchy."[62]

According to Roman legend, Lucretia was raped by the king's son, Sextus Tarquinius, who desired her because of her exemplary chastity. Threatened at knifepoint, Lucretia rebuffs Sextus until the royal assailant threatens to not only kill her but soil her name by planting evidence that would compromise her honor. Lucretia surrenders, but in order to prove her sexual virtue, she later commits suicide. Brutus then goes on to instigate the popular uprising against the Tarquins who are forced out of the city.

While Machiavelli is full of praise for Brutus and treats the execution of his sons as paradigmatic for renewing political orders, he – in stark contrast – has little to say about Lucretia's rape and suicide. Yet according to Livy, it is over Lucretia's violated body that the fraternal bond between Brutus and his insurrectionary party is established. Brutus pulls the bloody knife from Lucretia's chest and passes it around, rallying the men present to swear an oath by her chaste blood to overthrow not only the Tarquins but the entire monarchical regime. Before he can become, as Machiavelli puts it, the "father of Roman liberty" (D 3.1), Brutus must pass the knife that inflicts the mortal wound on Lucretia from hand to hand in a morbid ceremony that concludes the conspiratorial bonds. Lucretia's blood seals the republican contract and establishes the brotherhood demanded by a republican political order.

Machiavelli's disavowal of Lucretia sits uneasily with his celebration of Brutus's filicide. I am not suggesting that representing Lucretia's rape and suicide as the founding moment of the Republic is a more progressive, egalitarian, and less patriarchal stance. Feminist critics have convincingly shown that such rape legends frequently inscribe a patriarchal logic of chastity into the founding narratives.[63] Nonetheless, the asymmetry

---

[62] Coppélia Kahn, "Lucrece: The Sexual Politics of Subjectivity," in *Rape and Representation*, ed. Lynn A. Higgins and Brenda R. Silver (New York: Columbia University Press, 1991), 141.

[63] See Stephanie H. Jed, *Chaste Thinking: The Rape of Lucretia and the Birth of Humanism* (Bloomington: Indiana University Press, 1989); Melissa M. Matthes, *The Rape of Lucretia and the Founding of Republics* (University Park: Pennsylvania State University

between the treatment of Lucretia and of Brutus is striking. Both defend virtue and freedom through heroic acts of sacrifice. In St. Jerome's words, Lucretia was "the equal of Brutus, if not her superior, since Brutus learnt from a woman the impossibility of being a slave."[64] Yet by extolling Brutus and marginalizing Lucretia, Machiavelli denies Lucretia's role in forcing Brutus's hand and in narrating her rape as a prelude to the overthrow of the Tarquins. In one case, the violence is accidental and contingent; in the other case, it is necessary and paradigmatic. Demurring to Roman and humanist traditions, Machiavelli denies the conventional republican emplotment of Lucretia's rape and substitutes the killing of Brutus's male children for the founding violence of the republic. While he does not challenge the premise that political change requires narratives of violence, he implies that some stories fulfill this role better than others and that narratives of rape and suicide are inadequate origin stories.

CONCLUSION

Arendt rightly notes that Machiavelli conceives of founding in terms of *poiesis*, that is, "in the image of making."[65] For Arendt, it is this poietic framework that leads Machiavelli to "speak the same language" as Robespierre. If only – and this is the punchline of Arendt's critique – Machiavelli had not confused the separate domains of *poiesis* and *praxis*, he might have come up with a conception of founding that emphasizes shared speech and action rather than violence. In this chapter, I have argued that Machiavelli does not in fact confound *poiesis* and *praxis*. Rather, he insists that there is no praxis that is not also poiesis. Arendt's abstract separation between the activities of *praxis* and *poiesis* insinuates that these are separate domains, but that is not so. By highlighting the symbolic and theatrical dimensions of founding violence, Machiavelli maps out a communicative practice that is irrevocably tied to cruelty. Memorable executions, such as Brutus's filicide, Cesare's assassination of Remirro, and Romulus's fratricide, fulfill important symbolic functions in the institution of a new order. By pushing beyond the limits of what is

---

Press, 2000); Barbara Baines, *Representing Rape in the English Early Modern Period* (Lewiston, NY: Edwin Mellen Press, 2003), 87–101.

[64] St. Jerome, *Against Jovinianus*, in *Letters and Select Works*, trans. W.H. Fremantle (Grand Rapids, MI: Eerdmans, 1989), 1.49.

[65] Arendt, "What Is Authority?" 139. It is this focus on making that Singleton has called the "perspective of art." Charles S. Singleton, "The Perspective of Art," *The Kenyon Review* 15, no. 2 (1953). See also Kahn, *The Future of Illusion*, 91–92.

thinkable and possible within a political field, this violence constitutes itself as extraordinary. The transgressive nature of these acts is what lends them their peculiar power; the excess renders them effective at reconfiguring the space of the political imagination. And in remaking the political imagination, these acts are incontrovertibly part of the practical field of sharing words and deeds. Machiavelli's poetics of cruelty is irreducible to Arendt's instrumental conception of "making."

Founding involves a wager on the inertia of time. By figuring founding as constructing the foundations of an edifice, Machiavelli signals the importance of the founding moment over the life cycle of a state. Founding moments have an afterlife; they continue to shape and condition political action throughout the life of the constitution or political form. Like most thinkers from classical antiquity through the Renaissance, Machiavelli believed that the past is never entirely past and continues to affect the present in a variety of ways. The concept of foundation allows Machiavelli to theorize the historicity of political order, the way in which a political order is constitutively shaped by the – typically bloody – history of its emergence. But to the extent that founding moments are exceptional rather than the norm, they point to a layered and uneven historicity of states. Founding moments, one might say, generate a ragged history and in doing so open up and close down political avenues and possibilities.

As Antonio Negri puts it, "the new Prince is not simply the author of the State: he is the author, rather, of logic and language, of ethics and the law."[66] The violence that Machiavelli regards as necessary for the creation and emergence of a new order is not simply the physical force that may be necessary to defeat, displace, or destroy the previous order and competing centers of power. The founding moment of a political order establishes its "political presuppositions," that is to say, the institutions, symbols, and memories that tacitly shape the conditions of political life. Put differently, at issue in the constitution of a political order is not only who controls the means of violence, but also how violence circulates symbolically.

---

[66] Negri, *Insurgencies*, 52.

5

Institutions

To cure the illness of the people words are enough, and for the prince's steel is needed.

– Niccolò Machiavelli, *Discourses on Livy*

Attentive readers of Cicero, fourteenth- and fifteenth-century humanists such as Salutati, Bruni, and Bracciolini regarded *concordia* or harmony as the preeminent condition for a durable republic. They viewed laws and civic concord as the sources of cohesion necessary for a civil way of life [*vivere civile*]. They expected the social harmony to result from a classical education, which was to train citizens in the principles and practices of civic virtue. For the Renaissance humanists, the use or threat of violence marked the breakdown of order and the collapse of the civic space. Machiavelli seems to follow this dominant humanist view at times. From Livy, Machiavelli learnt that cities cannot be founded on arms alone (D 1.18–1.20). Unlike the diseases of princes for which the only remedy is "steel," the illnesses of multitudes can be cured with words (D 1.58). He praises thirteenth-century Florence for maintaining its political freedom "inside by laws and outside by arms" [*dentro con le leggi e fuora con le armi*] (FH 2.10), suggesting that republics can successfully maintain arms outside the civic space. He applauds Rome for largely avoiding bloodshed for the first three centuries of its republican era. And he contrasts laws, order, and freedom with "violence unfavorable to the common good" (D 1.4). By providing "ordinary modes" for the resolution of social and political struggles, Roman institutions prevented the recourse to "extra-ordinary" remedies. Along similar lines, *Discourses* 1.34 warns republics against relying on "extraordinary modes," and the following chapter advises that "authority that is seized by violence ... harms republics."

The harm that forcible seizures of power inflict on republics has multiple dimensions, but, most importantly, it treats fellow citizens [*cittadini, compagni*] as if they were subjects [*sudditi*]. As Machiavelli notes, citizens deserve to be governed by agreement and consent (D 3.19). In contrast to principalities, where force can function as a temporary substitute for legitimacy, in republics such a substitution is not possible. Where popular support is lacking, force cannot create it (D 1.16). Whereas in principalities, force is the principal political technology that generates fear with religion in an auxiliary role, in republics the order is reversed. Republican citizens fear the divine just as monarchic subjects fear the prince. Hence the importance Machiavelli attributes to Rome's second king, Numa Pompilius, who succeeded Romulus and established the city's religious institutions. Celebrated as Rome's second founder, Numa stands for the "arts of peace" that complement the Romulean art of war (D 1.11). In short, republics seem to be prima facie incompatible with government by violence. To the extent that republics lay a claim to civic freedom and reciprocity, violence appears to be irreconcilable with the principles that animate their institutions.

In view of this presumptive incompatibility of republican life with force and cruelty, the *Discourses* surprise the reader with their in-depth treatment of republican violence. In his magnum opus, Machiavelli argues that republican freedom creates its own dynamics of violence, dynamics that in some respect overlap with those of principalities but are also importantly different. Whereas in *The Prince*, Machiavelli discusses force as a strategy for securing and stabilizing states that suffer from a lack of historical continuity, in the *Discourses*, the treatment of violence is more ambivalent. On the one hand, Machiavelli seems to accept the necessity of force as an instrument for republics in punishment, in war, and in emergencies. But on the other hand, he also worries about its long-term effects and about force's tendency to embed itself in institutions and practices.

A second contrast between principalities and republics has to do with political institutions. In principalities, the agency in charge of dispensing force and cruelty is the state (isomorphic with the prince), but in republics, violence is often the product of social conflict. Republican violence springs not only from the state but also from the structural conflict between social classes. Principalities are also riven by social antagonism between the few and many, but the political alliance between the prince and the people is meant to address precisely this problem. Republics, by contrast, face the additional problem of how to channel and contain violence that results from class struggle. These dynamics of violence create a number of political-theoretical problems: How can republican violence be made compatible with popular freedom? How can republics harness and institutionalize violence? How can they simultaneously prevent it from contaminating the entire political space? This chapter examines these questions through the lens of class conflict, punishment, and war. These dimensions give rise to a distinct republican account of political violence.

INSTITUTIONALIZING VIOLENCE

The *Discourses* are a book about political freedom, popular politics, and institutions. They are not simply a nostalgic recitation of Roman practices. In the preface, Machiavelli announces that he will discuss "ordering republics, maintaining states, governing kingdoms, ordering the military and administering war, judging subjects, and increasing empire." Ordering a state requires compulsion, typically involves internal or external threats, and is usually accompanied by manifest or latent force. Republics, in other words, are states, and as such they are subject to the same kinds of transitional problems faced by principalities. But republics differ from principalities in two key respects: First, they make possible political freedom [*vivere libero*], something that is by definition excluded in principalities; and second, they solve a structural problem of principalities: political reproduction.

The problem to which the *Discourses* respond is how to create and maintain freedom, especially once the people who first establish a republican constitution are no longer around. Rather than relying solely on individuals for political *virtù*, the *Discourses* focus on the people as a collective actor and on institutions that embody *virtù*. A people, Machiavelli notes in D 1.58, "is more prudent, more stable, and of better judgment than a prince" and it is "by far superior in goodness and in glory." Peoples surpass princes in many respects – they are better at anticipating political developments and have better political judgment. Most importantly, they can assure political continuity and durability. There is really only one task at which princes are superior, namely "ordering laws, forming civil lives, and ordering new statutes and orders." As soon as these orders are created, the people are "so much superior in maintaining things ordered" (D 1.58).

Individuals cannot assure the longevity of political forms and orders. Consider, for instance, what Machiavelli has to say about Romulus. Immediately following his apology for the Romulean fratricide, Machiavelli adds that one cannot rely on the virtue of individuals. A thing is "ordered to last long not if it remains on the shoulders of one individual but rather if it remains in the care of the many" (D 1.9). Principalities are so dependent on good rulers that they face a high risk of collapse under inferior leadership. Moreover, because successions are typically contested, principalities are prone to transition crises. Republican institutions mitigate both the problem of inferior leadership and that of succession by stipulating mechanisms of selecting governments, temporal and constitutional limits of power, and transition procedures. Founding, Machiavelli seems to say, is a necessary but insufficient metaphor for politics. If founding requires solitary agents, political reproduction is the province of the many.

By adjusting the focus from founding to maintaining, the *Discourses* raise the question of whether the problem of durability or political reproduction is analytically prior to that of foundation. In this vein, Althusser affirms that Machiavelli's "fundamental problem of the state ... is its duration."[1] From the perspective of reproducing the state, the problem of founding appears epiphenomenal. Founders are only founders if the states they establish endure. To paraphrase Weber, founders are not destined to see whether their struggles will bear fruit and whether posterity will recognize them as their forerunners.[2] For founders to be founders, they need their successors to celebrate them as such. Whether an act constitutes a founding moment can only be determined retrospectively. Thus founding presupposes political reproduction, and in order to inaugurate orders that last, founders must turn them over to the many.

The problem of the many is that they need to be coordinated in some way. They require forms of mediation, or as Machiavelli puts it, "modes" [*modi*] and "orders" [*ordini*], his terms for institutions and practices. Modes and orders make up the political structure and fabric of a state. They mediate between political form and matter. The political form is composed of countless *ordini*, which in turn are practiced, instantiated,

---

[1] Althusser, *Machiavelli and Us*, 40.
[2] Max Weber, *Political Writings*, trans. Peter Lassman and Ronald Speirs (Cambridge: Cambridge University Press, 1994), 27.

and actualized by *modi*.[3] Good orders, in other words, are a necessary but insufficient condition for political freedom. They must be supplemented by modes – practices – which are more or less regulated activities oriented by norms and customs.

By shifting from individuals to institutions, the *Discourses* introduce a different perspective on questions of political violence. How can certain forms of force be harnessed by political institutions without undermining the stability and freedom that these very institutions are designed to guarantee? In a principality, the use of violence is, of course, also subject to constraints. But the responsibility for balancing the constraints rests with the individual prince. In a republic, institutions have to be established that do this work. In the *Discourses* and the *Florentine Histories* Machiavelli introduces an important distinction between *private* and *public* force. The harm that befalls republics comes primarily from private violence [*privata violenza*]: force that is organized around "private ambition," oriented toward the "private good," contributes to the emergence of "private power," results from "private enmities," or other "private modes" (D 3.22; FH 3.2, 5.4, 7.1, 8.10). Whereas *The Prince* does not distinguish between public and private force (the two coincide, because the prince is both private individual and public authority), the *Discourses* and the *Florentine Histories* regard private means of violence – such as the armies recruited by Marius and Sulla in the prelude to Rome's First Civil War – as dangerous to the republic. Private force is associated with disintegrative impulses in a republic, with sects, and with political factionalism. If force is necessary, it should be public (D 1.7; FH 3.5). At their best, virtuous modes and orders take force out of the hands of individual political agents, transform private into public, and thus substitute public for private force.[4] In that substitution, the structure of force changes. It ceases to be an individual's means for political advancement and becomes a mechanism of public order and justice.

By conceptualizing public force as a replacement for private force, Machiavelli once again draws on and reformulates Roman sources. The distinction between public and private *vis* dates back to the Romans but emerged only after the fall of the republic. It is first mentioned in the

---

[3] Modes and orders are not the same as a written constitution. Modern constitutions are bodies of abstract rules and principles that define the nature, powers, procedures, and limits of state organs and offices. Modes and orders are much more concrete: Unlike constitutions, they do not stipulate principles but materialize political practices.

[4] Lefort, *Machiavelli in the Making*, 236.

Julian Law introduced by Augustus. Earlier, during the republic, *vis* had a much more protean character, and it was impossible to draw clear boundaries between private and public force. The Roman republic addressed the challenge of how to manage the constant threat of unabashedly self-interested violence through legal and political institutions. Against this background, Machiavelli's insistence on the publicness of violence can be understood as recognition of the inadequacy of Roman mechanisms to contain private violence.

Take for instance the Roman institution of the dictatorship. Machiavelli defends the Roman dictator as a constitutional means of dealing with emergencies.[5] Originally a short-term magistrate, the Roman dictator was endowed with special powers and named for the duration of a political crisis, either war or civil unrest. In Machiavelli's words, the Romans conferred power on "one man who could decide without any consultation and execute his decisions without any appeal" (D 1.33). Dictators had a limited term; they could suspend laws but not change them; they were endowed with the authority to act without consultation and to punish without appeal (D 1.34). Through these powers, the dictatorship solves a problem peculiar to republics: the slowness of their institutions. By sidestepping the consultation and decision mechanisms inherent in republican government, dictators speed up republican time.

The dictatorship contains republican violence by providing a limited institutional framework for the deployment of public force in emergency conditions. Yet even though Machiavelli defends the institution as an important constitutional mechanism, he does not regard it as a panacea for all kinds of crises.[6] The trouble with dictators is that they always risk becoming tyrants, as happened in Rome with the decemvirs (D 1.35). To the extent that the dictatorship involves a suspension of the law, it is always in danger of sliding into tyranny, constitutional provisions notwithstanding. Allowing a dictator to function in lieu of traditional executive authorities thus involves the nonnegligible risk of a coup d'état and a usurpation of public force. Laws are ultimately no match for a dictator who seizes legislative functions. The only way to deter magistrates from usurping power is for the people to "post a guard over [officials] to keep

---

[5] On Machiavelli's concept of the dictatorship, see Pedullà, *Machiavelli in tumulto*, 565–602; Marco Geuna, "Extraordinary Accidents in the Life of Republics: Machiavelli and Dictatorial Authority," in *Machiavelli on Liberty and Conflict*, ed. David Johnston, Nadia Urbinati, and Camila Vergara (Chicago: University of Chicago Press, 2017).

[6] Contra Negri who regards the chapters on the Roman dictatorship as the "central pivot" of the first book of the *Discourses*. Negri, *Insurgencies*, 67.

them good" (D 1.40). In short, it is not the law but the people's vigilance that ultimately resolves the fate of republics. The dictatorship is effective in temporarily forestalling the substitution of private for public force. But public force needs to be carefully surveilled, and the people must remain willing and capable to take up arms to prevent a seizure of public force by usurpers.

CLASS CONFLICT

A special case of private force is violence resulting from class conflict. Such conflict, Machiavelli avers, is a universal feature of states. All republics are structured by "[t]he grave and natural enmities that exist between the men of the people and the nobles, caused by the wish of the latter to command and the former not to obey ... This kept Rome disunited, and this, if it is permissible to compare little things with great, has kept Florence divided" (FH 3.1).[7] Social conflict is a structural component of all free forms of collective life; that it to say, it persists even if one of the two parties were to disappear and the other were to govern unopposed. Under such conditions, Machiavelli says, the governing party "must of necessity divide from within itself" (FH 3.5).

Unlike his contemporaries who tended to praise unity and consensus, Machiavelli considers conflict to be both a progressive and stabilizing force in free societies.[8] The language of unity has always been the language of tyrants, and conflict, while not a good in itself, sustains freedom. The tumults between the nobles and the plebs, Machiavelli famously declares, were the "first cause of keeping Rome free" (D 1.4). More generally, he argues that the conflicting humors between the *grandi* and the *popolo* make political freedom possible (P 9; D 1.5; FH 2.12).[9]

---

[7] Machiavelli uses an expansive vocabulary to depict class struggle: He writes of *disunione*, of *tumulti*, and of *disordini*. Cities engulfed in violent social struggle are described as having come "to blows," "to arms," or "to blood" [*venire alla zuffa, alle armi*, or *al sangue*]. He also speaks of injuries, persecutions, of revenge, and of the hatred between the *popolo* and the *grandi*.

[8] For contemporary commendations of unity and consensus, see Gilbert, "Florentine Political Assumptions"; Michelle T. Clarke, "Machiavelli and the Imagined Rome of Renaissance Humanism," *History of Political Thought* 36, no. 3 (2015).

[9] Numerous interpreters have highlighted the centrality of conflict for Machiavelli. See, for example, Alfredo Bonadeo, *Corruption, Conflict, and Power in the Works and Times of Niccolò Machiavelli* (Berkeley: University of California Press, 1973); Dotti, *Niccolò Machiavelli: La fenomenologia del potere*; Lefort, *Machiavelli in the Making*; Negri, *Insurgencies*; Gennaro Sasso, *Niccolo Machiavelli: Vol. 1, Il pensiero politico* (Bologna: Il Mulino, 1993);

As Kahn observes, disunion or class conflict "provides a structure or institution that constrains private interest to take the form of public good."[10]

Machiavelli justifies his unorthodox preference for conflict over consensus by claiming that good laws and institutions arise from the tumults "that many inconsiderately damn." He adds an important qualification, that for more than three hundred years, from the founding of the republic until the Gracchi, Roman tumults were "very rarely bloody."[11] Tumults that "killed very few" cannot be judged harmful (D 1.4). The virtue of class struggle, in other words, derives in part from the somewhat counterintuitive detachment of conflict from violence. Yet as McCormick has highlighted, the peaceful management of class conflict in Rome was made possible by very specific class-based institutions that Machiavelli identifies as central to the health of the Roman republic.[12] These include, in particular, the tribunes of the plebs, a magistracy created to protect plebeians from patrician abuse, and the mechanisms of public indictment, whereby charges could be brought against corrupt magistrates. Both are "modes" for the people to "vent its ambition" (D 1.4–1.7).

These institutions can be understood as technologies for ordering public violence. The power of the tribunes derived from their sacrosanct status, from the inviolability of their bodies. The tribune's privilege allowed him to physically intercede and protect citizens against arbitrary uses of power by magistrates. This exceptional status was consecrated in the *lex sacrata*, which granted impunity to anyone who, in the process of defending a tribune, killed the tribune's assailant. Established through a collective oath of the plebs on the *Mons Sacer*, the legal and religious codification of sacrosanctity shouldn't obscure the fact that, politically, the power and privilege of a tribune relied on collective self-defense: on the credible promise that any assault on a tribune would be avenged by the collective *vis* of the plebs.[13]

Del Lucchese, *Conflict, Power, and Multitude in Machiavelli and Spinoza*; McCormick, *Machiavellian Democracy*; Pedullà, *Machiavelli in tumulto*.

[10] Kahn, *Machiavellian Rhetoric*, 52.

[11] Plutarch writes that the murder of Tiberius Gracchus and the violence against his supporters marked "the first sedition at Rome, since the abolition of royal power, to end in bloodshed and the death of citizens." Plutarch, "Tiberius and Caius Gracchus," in *Lives*, 7:191.

[12] McCormick, *Machiavellian Democracy*, 30–34, 49, 92–97, 115–22.

[13] Lintott, *Violence in Republican Rome*, 24.

The institution of "accusations" created a public procedure for the plebs to prosecute corrupt magistrates for political crimes, thus preventing political antagonism from degenerating into slander and calumny (D 1.7–8). Such public trials provide avenues for holding officials accountable, even if these procedures are by no means perfect and will sometimes produce wrongs and injustice.[14] Yet by offering avenues to take action against former officeholders without recourse to extralegal force, the harm to the republic is minimized. "For if a citizen is crushed ordinarily in a republic, there follows little or no disorder in a republic, even though he has been done a wrong. For the execution is done without private forces and without foreign forces, which are the ones that ruin a free way of life; but it is done with public forces and orders" (D 1.7).

Rather than treating violence as the necessary consequence of social discord, Machiavelli deems it a result of corrupted forms of antagonism. Such corruption is introduced when the plebs or the patricians substitute private for public means. *Discourses* 1.37 clarifies the limits of virtuous and nonviolent conflicts by juxtaposing them to the struggle over the Agrarian law in the late republic. Following Roman sources, Machiavelli regards the conflict over the Agrarian Law as a political turning point. Motivated by the desire for a share in the nobility's "honors and belongings" [*gli onori e le sustanze*], the plebs sought a redistribution of land that ultimately led to civil war. In 133 BCE, a few weeks after taking office as a tribune of the plebs, Tiberius Gracchus introduced a *lex agraria*. The law strove to enforce the long-standing but ignored legal limit of five hundred *iugera* on any single land holding of the *ager publicus*. Any land held in excess of this limit would be reclaimed by the state and distributed in family-sized plots to the landless poor.[15] By threatening the interests of the large landowners in Italy, Tiberius provoked the hostility of the senatorial class and was massacred, along with hundreds of his supporters, by the *optimates* and their clients. A decade later, Tiberius's brother Gaius suffered the same fate when he proposed a series of even more sweeping social and political reforms. The Agrarian law, Machiavelli writes, "was the cause of the destruction of the republic" (D 1.37). The controversy around the law "altogether ruined Roman

---

[14] This does not, however, mean, as Zuckert infers, that the institution of accusation systematically sacrifices justice for the sake of releasing popular discontent. Zuckert, *Machiavelli's Politics*, 131.

[15] C. F. Konrad, "From the Gracchi to the First Civil War (133–170)," in *A Companion to the Roman Republic*, ed. Nathan Rosenstein and Robert Morstein-Marx (Malden, MA: Wiley-Blackwell, 2010).

freedom" because "it inflamed so much hatred between the plebs and the Senate that they came to arms and to bloodshed beyond every civil mode and custom" (D 1.37). The struggles that followed the controversy led to "recourse to private remedies," and ultimately to civil war.

The contrast between the nonviolent conflicts that gave rise to Roman freedom (D 1.4–5) and the violent conflicts that heralded its decay (D 1.37) appears to cast the presence of violence as the distinguishing feature between productive and destructive conflicts.[16] Yet a careful reading of the later books of the *Discourses* and the *Florentine Histories* challenges this common view. As Del Lucchese has shown, the neat juxtaposition of salutary and deleterious forms of conflicts is successively abandoned in these texts.[17] The more they develop the socioeconomic aspects of social struggle, the more they depict violence as a constitutive element of such conflicts.

Such a perspective is already implicit in Machiavelli's treatment of the Agrarian Law. There, he concludes that the Roman nobility was generally content to yield honors to the plebs but implacably opposed to relinquishing any of its "property" [*roba*]. As McCormick points out, the major flaw in the Gracchi's action was not the agrarian legislation but their failure to anticipate the brutal riposte by the senatorial plutocrats.[18] To an astute observer of the class politics in Rome, it should come as no surprise "how much more men esteem property than honors" (D 1.37). As Machiavelli remarks in *The Prince*, "men forget the death of a father more quickly than the loss of a patrimony" (P 17). Given the obstinacy of elites in defending their estates, violence is not the mark of degenerate (as opposed to salutary) conflict but sometimes the only effective means:

For such is the ambition of the great that it soon brings that city to its ruin if it is not beaten down [*sbattuta*] in a city by various ways and in various modes. So, if the contention over the Agrarian law took three hundred years to make Rome servile, it would perhaps have been led into servitude much sooner if the plebs had not always checked the ambition of the nobles.

(D 1.37, trans. mod.)

The verb *sbattere* – to beat or to slam – suggests that Machiavelli objects not to the use of violence per se but to the ambition and greed of the

---

[16] See Bock, "Civil Discord," 191.
[17] Filippo Del Lucchese, "'Disputare' e 'combattere': Modi del conflitto nel pensiero politico di Niccolò Machiavelli," *Filosofia Politica* 15, no. 1 (2001), 78–79, 94.
[18] See John P. McCormick, "Machiavelli and the Gracchi: Prudence, Violence, and Redistribution," *Global Crime* 10, no. 4 (2009).

patricians. If the Gracchi had prepared for the violent altercations and been as resolute in calling on armed support as they were in proposing legislation, perhaps their fate would have been different.

In sum, Machiavelli's analysis of the Agrarian law does not temper his defense of social conflict. He explicitly acknowledges that the antagonism between the Senate and the plebs was *both* the cause of Rome's freedom *and* the source of its downfall. This apparent paradox is resolved if social conflict is considered not an abstract symmetrical hostility between two commensurate adversaries but embedded in relations of social domination. The primary threat to freedom is not an abstract imbalance between humors that could flare up from any location on the social spectrum but rather the elite's obstinacy in defending their usurped privileges. While institutional design can mitigate, it cannot neutralize the immanent potential for class violence. Neither does Machiavelli regard such a neutralization as politically desirable. Freedom and violence, Machiavelli insists, are not opposites. While sometimes violence is detrimental to freedom, at other times it is generative of freedom.

Renaissance authors typically viewed republican violence as a continuum throughout Roman history, and they tended to use the Roman example to warn against the dangers and excesses of popular freedom. Aristocratic critics routinely pointed to the violence in Rome as evidence for the Roman state's instability and its moral failings. The fear of the masses is palpable in Bracciolini's panegyric on the Venetian constitution, penned in the 1450s. Having acknowledged the Roman republic's greatness, he proceeds to lambast its "quarrels and feuds, the uprisings of a fickle populace, the great and frequent struggles between the fatherland and the mob." He concludes that "it would be accurate to say that for many centuries Rome was not a republic at all but a den of thieves and a despotism of the cruellest sort."[19]

Machiavelli, by contrast, takes another route. Rather than interpreting Roman republican violence as a continuum, he postulates a distinction between certain forms of salutary violence, associated with the early republic, and the corrupt violence he ascribes to the late republic.[20] Had the plebeians not resisted the senatorial class, Rome would likely have

---

[19] Poggio Bracciolini, "In Praise of the Venetian Republic," in *Cambridge Translations of Renaissance Philosophical Texts. Vol. 2: Political Philosophy*, ed. Jill Kraye (Cambridge: Cambridge University Press, 1997), 138.

[20] On this distinction, see Andrew Lintott, "The Tradition of Violence in the Annals of the Early Roman Republic," *Historia: Zeitschrift für Alte Geschichte* 19, no. 1 (1970).

been "led into servitude much sooner" (D 1.37). The "few," Machiavelli insists, "always behave in the mode of the few," with no regard to the collective good (D 1.7, 1.49; FH 2.39). Popular violence, by contrast, tends to be more reactive in character, driven by the people's mistrust and fear that their freedom be taken away (D 1.28). Far from ascribing the fall of the republic merely to the conflagration of violence, Machiavelli highlights the asymmetries of wealth that resulted from imperial expansion, and the unrestrained ambition of the *optimates* as the principal causes for the escalation of violence in the late republic.

Even if their motivations are not necessarily stronger than those of the people, the structural privilege of elite citizens makes them far more likely to cause tumult. Because they are the principal cause for most disorders within a city, addressing the problem of social conflict means figuring out how to deal with "the few." The trouble with elites is that they are good at manipulating political institutions to their advantage, either by ensuring elite control of relevant offices or by getting non-elite citizens to do their bidding. The many, by contrast, are much harder to organize in a sustained manner. Because of this asymmetry, Machiavelli relegates the task of reforming institutions to individuals willing and able to deploy armed force against the *grandi*. Anyone who rises against the interests of the few is vulnerable to being neutralized by them. This is one of the important lessons Machiavelli draws from Roman and Florentine history: Irrespective of the institutional or discursive façades they put up, elites will use every instrument at their disposal to eliminate threats to their dominance. Hence whoever wishes to reorganize institutions in favor of the people must be prepared to use violence against usurping elites.

PUNISHMENT

Republican anti-oligarchic violence can to some degree be formalized in mechanisms of punishment, hence penal institutions are an important component of Machiavelli's conceptualization. Punishment is a thorny question for republics because it involves the "authority to shed blood against its own citizens" [*l'autorità del sangue*] (D 1.49). In liberal legal systems, punishment serves *criminal justice*: It sanctions violations of the law, based on the Roman legal principle *nulla poena sine lege* – no penalty without a law. For Machiavelli, by contrast, punishment also administers *political justice*, redressing political crimes. Republics, Machiavelli argues, need mechanisms for punishing not only regular but also political crimes, especially ones committed by powerful citizens. Political crimes are more difficult to punish than conventional criminal transgressions because they do not always involve the violation of a formal law.[21] In republican politics, punishment is sometimes appropriate even if no formal laws have been broken, because what are punished are not illegal acts per se but acts against collective freedom.

Authority for adjudicating such crimes and dispensing appropriate punishments should, Machiavelli insists, be accorded to the people. Because of the danger that powerful elites pose to political freedom, it is incumbent on the people to keep a vigilant eye on elite attempts to usurp freedom and punish such "ambition" and "insolence." The popular control over adjudication of crimes is an important element of Machiavelli's conception of the *vivere libero*.[22] It involves allowing citizens to challenge and indict magistrates, and it empowers popular assemblies – "very many judges" – to convict or acquit those indicted of political crimes. Such a democratic judicial authority is the only way to limit the ambition of powerful citizens. The "judges need to be very many," because the privilege and influence of the *grandi* can only be checked by numbers. By empowering the people to adjudicate and punish elites through "ordinary" channels, Rome offered an outlet for collective anger (D 1.7). Such outlets institutionalize the episodic anti-oligarchic violence necessary for restraining elite ambitions and maintaining political freedom.

Dispersing judicial authority among the multitude is not the only distinctly republican feature Machiavelli advocates in regard to penal violence. In book 3 of the *Discourses*, he also puts forward a preference for severity in punishment, which he justifies by juxtaposing two acclaimed military commanders and statesmen of the early Roman republic: Manlius Torquatus and Valerius Corvinus (D 3.22). Recall that Manlius executed his son for violating military discipline. Valerius, by contrast, was reported to be kind and amicable and popular with the soldiers. The chapter compares two strategies: Manlian "hardness" or severity and Valerian "kindness," and concludes that while both strategies can be effective, in republics, severity is "more praiseworthy and less dangerous, because this mode is wholly in favor of the public."[23]

---

[21] Harvey C. Mansfield, *Taming the Prince: The Ambivalence of Modern Executive Power* (New York: Free Press, 1989), 131.

[22] McCormick, *Machiavellian Democracy*, 67–73;

[23] Michelle T. Clarke, "The Virtues of Republican Citizenship in Machiavelli's Discourses on Livy," *The Journal of Politics* 75, no. 2 (2013), 326–27.

The problem with kindness is that it is liable to produce "partisans," that is to say patron–client relationships that have a corrosive effect on citizenship (D 1.16, 1.34, 1.43). If, by contrast, one demonstrates harshness to everyone, "one cannot acquire partisans" or "particular friends" and "there cannot be any suspicion of private power" (D 3.22). Manlian severity is not the same as Brutus's severity, which as we know, Machiavelli also praises as both "necessary and useful" (D 3.3). Whereas Brutus's severity is essential for founding a state, irrespective of whether it is a free state or a tyranny, Manlian severity is strictly republican and meaningless from a tyrannical perspective. In fact, Manlius serves to put forward what might be called a "Jacobin" rationalization of punishment, one that produces a republican argument for violence distinct from the argument for violence in principalities, where cruelty is preferred over mercy because it is safer to be feared than to be loved (P 17).

Florentine readers would have understood the topic of patronage as a reference to the strategy employed by the Medici to accumulate power and influence. When, in the 1430s, the Florentine elite belatedly grasped the full extent of the Medici patronage networks, the only remedy they could come up with was to send Cosimo into exile, a half-hearted and foolish scheme, whereas what they should have done is act with Manlian severity and execute him (FH 4.26–33). But by that time, material inequality and the political use of wealth had eroded the public ethos to such an extent that the Florentines had little appetite for a controversial execution of their most prominent citizen. When Cosimo returned from his exile, he, by contrast, made ample use of the death penalty, bloodily persecuting his enemies while the Mediceans plotted "without any hesitations ... how to secure the state for themselves" (FH 5.4).[24]

In contrast to the timid Florentines, the Romans knew how to punish influential citizens who failed to respect the commons. Rome was not above using "extraordinary" means to keep its ambitious elites in check. As I mentioned in Chapter 4, *Discourses* 3.1 includes a whole list of examples of "excessive and notable" executions that renew "memory

---

[24] As I noted in Chapter 3, under the Medici, the long-standing aversion of Florentine elites to the death penalty gradually lost steam. Political dissent was increasingly criminalized and the death penalty was used more frequently. The centralization of authority that took place under Cosimo's successors, especially under Lorenzo the Magnificent, led to increased political repression. Thus executions, especially by hanging and decapitation, became associated with political crimes such as treason and conspiracy.

and fear."[25] In discussing these various killings, Machiavelli also brings up the Medici, noting that they used to proclaim that the state had to be regained "every five years ... They called regaining the state putting that terror and that fear in men that had been put there in taking it." Republicans, Machiavelli implies, can learn both from the virtuous Roman precedent and from the tyrannical example of the Medici. Both knew how to deploy extraordinary public executions to maintain the state.

In the *Discourses*, Machiavelli dodges the question concerning the place of this violence in the institutional architecture of republics. Are such spectacular punishments part of *ordinary* republican life, in other words, do they belong to a republic's *ordini*? Or are they, by contrast, *extraordinary* events that shake up – refound – a state and revitalize a polity that has started its natural process of degeneration? Machiavelli seems to want to have it both ways, depicting dramatic punishments of elites as both ordinary and extraordinary events, thus confounding commentators.

Constitutionalist republican readers tend to identify ordinary modes as ones that conform to statutory or customary rules; extraordinary by contrast, are actions outside the legal framework.[26] Yet this schema fails to account for numerous examples of Roman executions that fall entirely within constitutional provisions yet are nonetheless described as extraordinary.[27] Populist interpreters, by contrast, identify ordinary with popular modes and extraordinary with oligarchic and antidemocratic ones.[28] But if that is so, then why does Machiavelli describe the popular revenge against the nobles of Corcyra or the execution of Brutus's sons as extraordinary? And what do we make of the instances when Machiavelli uses "the greatest extraordinary means" as a euphemism for violence against the *grandi* (D 1.17)? What both the constitutionalist and the populist perspectives have in common is that each is overly invested in

---

[25] Among them are the execution of Brutus's sons, the execution of the decemvirs, the killing of Spurius Maelius, the execution of M. Manlius Capitolinus, the execution of Titus Manlius, the planned execution of Q. Fabius Maximus by Papirius Cursor, and the accusation of the Scipios (D 3.1).

[26] John M. Najemy, "Machiavelli and the Medici: The Lessons of Florentine History," *Renaissance Quarterly* 35, no. 4 (1982), 560–61.

[27] *Discourses* 3.1 lists as extraordinary both executions that clearly violate Roman constitutional provisions (the decemvirs; Spurius Maelius) as well as ones within the bounds of magistrates' constitutional prerogatives (Brutus's sons, M. Manlius, and the Scipios). Similarly, both Titus Manlius and Q. Fabius Maximus were charged with violating military discipline, and in each case, it would have fallen under the authority of the dictator to impose an appropriate punishment.

[28] McCormick, *Machiavellian Democracy*, 132.

Machiavelli's ostensible preference for ordinary over extraordinary punishments. But this preference is highly contextual and applies only to
well-ordered and uncorrupted popular republics, in other words, prac-
tically never. On this point, Straussian readings are more compelling,
because they have no problem conceding Machiavelli's penchant for
extraordinary violence.[29]

That Machiavelli clearly relishes such violence, does not, however,
justify the Straussian inference that he collapses ordinary and extraordinary
and that he denies the difference between the two. There is an alternative
way to interpret Machiavelli's use of "extraordinary" that is much closer
to common usage: unexpected and exceptional. This sense is in play
when Machiavelli refers to Numa as an "orderer of extraordinary laws,"
implying – contra constitutionalists and populists – that laws are not
necessarily a subset of the "ordinary" (D 1.11). Extraordinary here takes
the sense of "unusual" (see also D 1.29). In the context of Numa's
religious institutions, "extraordinary law" refers to a law that regulates
rituals concerned with supernatural matters. Understood this way, extraordinary punishments are unconventional. It is this unexpected quality
that unites all of the examples Machiavelli mentions: the execution of a
consul's (Brutus's) sons; the capital punishment of patricians who pursue
populist social policies for ostensibly monarchic aspirations (Spurius
Maelius and Manlius Capitolinus); the execution (or prospect thereof)
of citizens for heroic but unauthorized military operations (Titus Manlius
and Q. Fabius Maximus); and the prosecution of renowned political and
military leaders for corruption and embezzlement (the Scipios). Even
though these cases raise important questions about how a constitutional
state ought to confront challenges to its power and authority, Machiavelli
refuses to engage them. Moreover, as Zuckert notes, Machiavelli exagger-
ates the number of death sentences that these trials yielded.[30] This is
because the examples are selected not to demonstrate the inherent justice
of the penalties but to analyze their *dramatic* effects.

By once again emphasizing the theatricality of violent executions,
Machiavelli highlights what many historians regard as a distinctive aspect
of Roman political culture. The ancient historian Donald Kyle argues that
spectacles of violence were not only a form of entertainment for Romans
but that the fascination with blood and death was also "intimately

[29] Sullivan, *Machiavelli's Three Romes*, 153–57; Coby, *Machiavelli's Romans*, 62–63, 156,
   160–61; Fischer, "Machiavelli's Rapacious Republicanism."
[30] Zuckert, "Machiavelli's Democratic Republic," 283n82.

associated with fertility and regeneration."[31] According to Kyle, public executions are best understood as ritualized killing, which is not quite the same as human sacrifice yet also involves the consecration of a victim for the sake of purifying and restoring the social order. As I argued in Chapters 1 and 4, this regenerative theme takes center stage in Machiavelli's account of extraordinary punishment. Juridico-political violence of this sort does not enforce laws but reorders a corrupt republic. Unlike ordinary punishment (whether for criminal or political offenses), extraordinary punishment enacts a political shock aimed at remaking political freedom.

This shock is expressed in an idiom of marks and signs. In *Discourses* 3.1, Machiavelli emphasizes the "excessive and notable" aspect of these executions, which "made men draw back toward the mark" [*ritirare verso il segno*]. The "mark" or "sign" [*segno*] to which men retreat is not the same as the law but more akin to the vital power that animates a *vivere politico*. Earlier in the same chapter, Machiavelli explains that mixed bodies tend to degenerate and become corrupt "unless something intervenes to lead [them] back to the mark [*riduca al segno*]." A similar expression, "return to the mark" [*ritornare dentro al segno*] occurs in a later chapter, where Machiavelli speaks of the punishment meted out to wealthy citizens for attempts to bribe the people (D 3.28). Elsewhere in the *Discourses*, Machiavelli uses the word *segno* to mean an index for something else, but also as emblem or symbol. As such, the signs inscribed by bloody executions partake in generating the political memory so central to republican longevity.

Executions and other forms of extraordinary punishment are effective in reordering a republic because violent signs can rekindle the "memory" of punishment and the resulting "terror" and "fear." Such penal violence serves, in other words, as a political mnemonic, assisting republican elites in establishing or recalling the *signs* of republican orders. In Chapter 4, I observed that the foundings rely on mnemopoiesis; analogously, punishment involves the creation of memories through signifying practices. In order to retain their efficacy, Machiavelli recommends that the penal spectacles be spaced out no more than ten years (although in *Discourses* 3.49 he seems to think that the intervention of a "physician" to deal with conspiratorial "accidents" may be a more quotidian operation). The ten-year cycle is apparently derived from a saying attributed to the Medici,

---

[31] Kyle, *Spectacles of Death in Ancient Rome*, 36. See also Dowling, *Clemency and Cruelty in the Roman World*.

"that it was necessary to regain the state every five years" (D 3.1). Periodic violence, then, allows a city to retain the *sign* of freedom, for the natural tendency to corruption will otherwise lead to decay that can only be remedied by a rebirth "with many dangers and much blood" (D 1.17).

WAR

Just as the *Discourses* present a distinctive republican logic of punishment different from the one that applies in principalities, in a similar way the work puts forward a particular republican dynamic of war. One of the central tenets of Machiavelli's political theory is that the people should be armed (P 14; D 2.30). The capacity for military violence, Machiavelli contends, is best distributed among the people rather than placed in an unaccountable professional army. While Machiavelli considers this lesson to be applicable to both principalities and republics, the implications are different for how armies are best governed. A republican army faces a danger analogous to the citizenry as a whole: how to avoid concentrations of private power and patronage. How can generals and commanders be prevented from turning the army into their "partisans" (D 3.22, 3.24)? Principalities encounter the inverse problem: how to bind an army to a prince? Thus, principalities must encourage the development of personal loyalties whereas republics must curb them. Conversely, republics must be vigilant in keeping an eye on their captains (and one way to do this is to promote harshness in command) whereas principalities need to promote kindness and distribute benefits. In *The Prince*, Machiavelli recounts that under the Empire, the Roman soldiers expected emperors to provide them with benefits, allow them to vent their "avarice and cruelty" against the people, and "double their pay" (P 19). The emperors who failed to secure such advantages for the soldiers were assassinated. Republican captains, by contrast, should model themselves on Manlius, who treated his soldiers with severity. A commander's kindness may prompt compliance in the short run (as shown by the successes of both Valerius and Scipio) but is ultimately pernicious because it may "prepare the way for tyranny" (D 3.22).

In addition to the problem of how to command armies, there are further imperatives that drive republican warfare. Unlike principalities, which need to engage in war to assure the defense of the state against external threats, republics face further political dynamics. Of these, Machiavelli identifies three. First, successful republics must fight wars not only for security but also for imperial expansion and to ensure domestic peace. In early sixteenth-century Florence, territorial expansion was much debated, as the city attempted to come to terms with increasing rebellions of the subject towns it had acquired over the course of the previous two centuries. Revolts and civil strife in Pisa in 1494, in Pistoia in 1500–1502, and in Arezzo and Val de Chiana in 1502 kept the question of how to manage an empire at the center of Florentine politics.

Machiavelli's view on the matter was that, in principle, a state could be organized along purely defensive lines. To do so, it would need strong military institutions and a credible commitment not to expand to the detriment of its neighbors. As long as it maintains these two policies, such a state should be both stable and secure, and if "held balanced in this mode, it would be the true political way of life" [*il vero vivere politico*] (D 1.6). Alas, maintaining this balance is tricky, for both internal and external reasons. Internally, the pursuit of peace and military prepared-ness are at odds. The longer peace lasts, the less a republic will arm itself; conversely, the more a republic builds up its military, the more likely it is to pursue an aggressive foreign policy. Externally, the balance is easily upset by events – "necessity" – that lead a state into offensive wars despite its best intentions. Once the pacific foreign policy is thrown overboard, the foundations of a self-contained republic are undone. For these reasons, Machiavelli argues, republics are unable to "maintain this middle way" and must pursue empire (D 1.6).

To this conceptual argument for the inevitability of imperial expan-sion, Machiavelli adds a second, conjunctural, one, connected to the geopolitical situation of Italy in the aftermath of the wars that began in 1494. The constellations introduced by the Italian Wars made the scale of the classical city-state no longer militarily feasible. The city-state model became untenable for both demographic and territorial reasons. To face adversaries such as the kingdoms of France and Spain, Italian states needed to draw both on larger populations to recruit armies and on a territorial base to secure their autonomy. The choice Machiavelli presents between expansionary and non-expansionary foreign policy, between Sparta or Venice on the one hand, and Rome on the other hand, is hence only apparent. In view of the changed historical circumstances after 1494, Machiavelli saw the Roman model of imperial expansion as the only one available to free states.[32]

---

[32] Romain Descendre, "Stato, imperio, dominio. Sur l'unité des notions d'État et d'empire au XVIe siècle," *Astérion* 10(2012), #7. On the use of the term *imperium* see Brown, "The Language of Empire," 46–47.

Third, Machiavelli views wars as effective outlets for the *grandi* to pursue their desire for domination and glory. Lacking public-spiritedness and thinking only "of their honor," the *grandi* can be coaxed into channeling their overbearing and self-absorbed ambitions into war (D 3.16). In this sense, war can be an outlet for class conflict, a way to deflect the glory-starved aspirations of elites away from the domestic political space. The pursuit of war provides aristocrats with opportunities to demonstrate their valor, serving as a safety valve for the republic. Rome's military institutions were maintained, Machiavelli explains, by the senatorial aristocracy's commitment to a martial culture that venerated war and empire as inherently glorious.

The senators' infatuation with war and the reputations it yields was also, however, their Achilles heel, one that the plebs were ready to exploit. By making its enlistment in the army conditional on widening political participation and eligibility for political office, the Roman plebs used the patricians' desire for imperial glory as leverage for instituting democratic political orders (D 1.4). Wielding the threat of a *secessio plebis*, a general strike in which the plebs would withdraw from the city and abandon the patricians, plebeians were able to exact political concessions and legal reform from the *patres* (D 1.40, 1.44, 1.57). By demonstrating to the nobles that their yearning for military glory and imperial conquest could not be fulfilled without popular enlistment, the people harnessed the patricians' desire for domination to advance domestic freedom. War, in other words, is a condition of possibility for republican freedom in more than one way. It yields not only the military power and the territorial and demographic resources necessary for republics in the face of the new powerful European territorial monarchies but it also provides important levers for the people to keep the *grandi* in check.

If these three characteristically republican political dynamics drive free city-states to imperial expansion and perpetual warfare, there are also pressures in the other direction.

War and empire bring not only benefits but also perils. In the Roman case, imperial expansion both made possible political freedom and charted its limits. Between 220 and 167 BCE, Rome defeated Carthage in the West and the Macedonian and Seleucid monarchies in the East, establishing an unparalleled dominance in the Mediterranean that covered, in Polybius's words, "almost the whole inhabited world."[33]

---

[33] Polybius, *Histories*, 1.1.

Rome's Mediterranean empire was unprecedented in antiquity, not solely because of its territorial span but also because of Rome's regime type. Whereas monarchies had amassed significant territorial empires, no republican city-state had ever dominated an empire even remotely similar in size to Rome's.[34] This uniqueness is noted not only by Polybius but also by Machiavelli, who thought that the success of Rome's imperial expansion had much to do with its reliance on "partners" rather than "subjects" (D 2.4). If in Polybius's time, the Roman *imperium* still included mostly independent states, over the following decades Rome increasingly relied on direct administration, which Machiavelli regards as one of the causes for republican decline. Other factors include the enormous wealth that flowed to Rome in the form of booty and levies from its imperial campaigns, the development of massive inequalities as a result of the slave economy in the Italian peninsula, and the increasing financial and military burdens of the empire that were shifted to Rome's provinces. For Machiavelli, once Rome proceeded to gain subjects rather than partners, the foundations of freedom were eroded.[35] Imperial expansion is only compatible with freedom as long as a republic remains egalitarian, avoids the emergence of a class of rentiers (D 1.55), leaves in imperial dominions no "sign of empire" [*segno d'imperio*], and keeps these dominions "in their state and dignity" (D 2.21).

In lieu of signs of empire, successful imperial republics incorporate new subject territories by means of spectacles. Such spectacles accelerate the mutation of political form by furnishing mnemopoietic impulses to the political imagination. In political bodies, growth and destruction are intimately related, a point Machiavelli stresses both in *Discourses* 2.3, where he cites Livy's adage "Meanwhile Rome grew from the ruin of Alba" and in *Florentine Histories* 1.4–1.7, where he indicates that modern Italy grew from the ruins of the Roman Empire. The ruin of one political form is the condition of possibility for the emergence of a new one; hence to build an empire, one must be willing and able to undo existing political forms. In practice, this means that victorious wars of conquest should be followed by rituals of subjection and incorporation, as was the case in Rome. Unlike Florence, Rome had understood the logic

---

[34] Arthur M. Eckstein, "Conceptualizing Roman Imperial Expansion under the Republic: An Introduction," in *A Companion to the Roman Republic*, ed. Nathan Rosenstein and Robert Morstein-Marx (Malden, MA: Wiley-Blackwell, 2010), 567.

[35] Contra Hulliung, who regards Machiavelli as praising the Romans for their resolute willingness to kill and destroy. Hulliung, *Citizen Machiavelli*, 53–54.

of imperial conquest. Aggressive wars to increase power must eventually lead either to incorporation or to some form of government of subject cities. This political transition, Machiavelli suggests, is most successful when people have been subjected to violence and fear because it is after such extreme experiences that they are most susceptible to being converted into citizens or subjects.[36]

The lesson of Alba may be aimed at Florence, more precisely at the Florentine failure to link military violence to spectacle in dealing with subject cities such as Pisa, Pistoia, and Arezzo. Machiavelli maintains that Florence had historically been unsuccessful at governing subject cities (D 3.27), and one way to interpret his thinking about empire is as counsel to a failed imperial power. Such a reading can draw on his early text *Del modo di trattare i popoli della Valdechiana ribellati*, where he theorizes Roman counterinsurgency techniques. Written in 1503, a year after the Arezzo rebellion, the text includes the speech to the Roman Senate attributed to Lucius Furius Camillus, who had led Roman troops to a resounding victory over the Latins in 338 BCE (Livy 8.13–14). After the military campaign was over, Camillus presented the senators with two options: to punish or to pardon. Rome could either destroy the rebellious cities and render Latium a desert or give the Latins citizenship and turn them into loyal allies and citizens. Facing the choice of punishment or reward, the Senate decided to consider each city separately, awarding citizenship to those with whom Rome could reconcile, while cruelly punishing [*gastigati crudelmente*] those who had previously rebelled. Machiavelli refers to cruel treatment [*incrudelire*], to cities that were ruined and destroyed, and to peoples forcibly relocated to Rome. Florence, he contends, could learn from the Roman example so as to avoid future revolts by subject cities like Arezzo. Instead of pursuing the middle way, Florence should either reconcile with the Aretine, reestablish their institutions, return the confiscated property, and withdraw its soldiers, or alternatively, punish the city by razing its walls and transferring settlers to Arezzo to stamp out any future rebellions. On this reading, the example of the Romans is supposed to steel the Florentines for enacting brutal measures in subject territories and to make credible threats to destroy mutinous subject cities.[37]

---

[36] Hörnqvist, *Machiavelli and Empire*, 275–77.

[37] See for instance Hulliung, *Citizen Machiavelli*, 65; Hörnqvist, *Machiavelli and Empire*, 103–6; Zuckert, *Machiavelli's Politics*, 201. On the Florentine rule over Arezzo, see Robert Black, "Arezzo, the Medici and the Florentine Regime," in *Florentine Tuscany: Structures and Practices of Power*, ed. William J. Connell and Andrea Zorzi (Cambridge: Cambridge University Press, 2000).

But a different interpretation is also possible. Here, as elsewhere, spectacular violence and cruelty function not as mechanisms of governance but as marks of a political transition. In addition to the instrumental interpretation, it is possible to read the cruelty deployed by the Romans in Alba and Latium as expressive. In the *Florentine Histories*, Machiavelli discusses the logic of ancient imperialism, praising the ancients for their willingness to rebuild and reconstruct cities. Lamenting the disappearance of this practice, Machiavelli contends that "unhealthy countries become healthy by means of a multitude of men that seizes them at a stroke; they cleanse the earth [*sanifichino la terra*] by cultivation and purge the air [*purghino l'aria*] with fires" (FH 2.1). The language of "purging" and "cleansing" indicates the ritualistic dimension of such transitional moments, pointing to the symbolic rather than the instrumental functions of violence.

Notwithstanding the praise for the Romans' virtue in subjugating towns and provinces near and far, Machiavelli displays some ambivalence about republican imperialism, especially when directed against other republics.[38] As he notes, a republic's worst lot is to be subjected to another republic because such domination tends to endure and because republics have a vampire-like quality. The "end of the republic is to enervate and to weaken all other bodies so as to increase its own bodies" (D 2.2). Imperial republics, Machiavelli concedes, destroy the freedom of surrounding republics more severely and rule them more oppressively than would a prince. While he is unconcerned with the normative contradictions raised by republican imperialism (they arise only from within an abstract universalism that Machiavelli eschews), his conclusions about imperial strategy are ultimately equivocal. Republics, he writes, expand in three modes: by building leagues; by incorporating other cities and granting their denizens citizenship; or by subjecting cities to direct domination. Of the three, Machiavelli recommends leagues and partnerships rather than a strategy of violent military conquest. Rule by force is "difficult and laborious" and even "entirely useless," hence republics are better off seeking allies rather than subjects (D 2.4).

The same ambivalent conclusion concerning imperial violence can be drawn from Machiavelli's treatment of Volterra, a Tuscan town about thirty miles south-west of Florence, which the Florentines conquered during the golden era of empire-building in the mid-thirteenth century (FH 2.4).

---

[38] See Erica Benner, *Machiavelli's Ethics* (Princeton, NJ: Princeton University Press, 2009), 481–82.

Volterra is an interesting case of imperial governance because it is a city that rebelled twice in the fifteenth century: once in 1429 over intrusive new levies and once in 1472 over the control of its alum mines, located on public lands but exploited by a private company without concession.[39] In response to the first rebellion, inspired by an elite conspiracy to sabotage the wealth tax, Florence reduced Volterra to a vicarate (FH 4.17). The second revolt was dealt with more brutally: furious at the Volterran people's demands that the alum profits be shared rather than privatized in the hands of a corporation, Lorenzo de'Medici decided to set a "memorable example" and "punish with arms the arrogance of the Volterrans" (FH 7.30).[40] Enlisting the Duke of Urbino as *condottiere*, Florence – under Lorenzo – amassed an enormous army and, despite the Volterrans' surrender, sacked the city. "For a whole day it was robbed and overrun; neither women nor holy places were spared" (FH 7.30). The city was reassigned to the *contado* instead of the Florentine *distritto*, cementing its subject status. Dozens of citizens were exiled or imprisoned, and a new prison, constructed on expropriated land, symbolized the town's conquered status.[41]

Given Machiavelli's fondness for dramatic punishments, we might expect him to endorse the war crimes against Volterra. Yet in the passages of the *Discourses* on the government of subject cities, Volterra is never mentioned despite its prominence in Florentine public discourse. In the *Florentine Histories*, his sympathies are clearly with the Volterrans, people whom he describes as "poor citizens attacked from outside by enemies and oppressed inside by friends" (FH 7.30). The leader of the first rebellion, a plebeian named Giusto, is portrayed by Machiavelli as an inspiring and courageous figure who is manipulated by the local nobility (FH 4.17). As to the second revolt, Machiavelli appears to agree with Tommaso Soderini, who regarded the violent punishment as both excessive and imprudent.[42] In a book, such as the *Florentine Histories*,

---

[39] On the Florentine rule of Volterra, see Lorenzo Fabbri, "Patronage and Its Role in Government: The Florentine Patriciate and Volterra," in *Florentine Tuscany: Structures and Practices of Power*, ed. William J. Connell and Andrea Zorzi (Cambridge: Cambridge University Press, 2000).

[40] On Lorenzo's Volterra massacre, see Najemy, *A History of Florence*, 348–52.

[41] Brown, "The Language of Empire," 42–43. The entire episode was chronicled in an epic poem by the late fifteenth-century Medicean, Naldo Naldi. Naldo Naldi, *Bucolica, Volaterrais, Hastiludium, Carmina Varia*, trans. William Leonard Grant (Florence: Leo S. Olschki, 1974).

[42] See Viroli, *Machiavelli*, 141–42; Benner, *Machiavelli's Ethics*, 345–47; Zuckert, *Machiavelli's Politics*, 444–45.

commissioned by and dedicated to the Medici family, there are obvious limits to how explicitly Machiavelli could declare his opposition to Medici policies. Princes such as the Medici are after all "always spoken of with a thousand fears and a thousand hesitations" (D 1.58). In the dedicatory letter, where Machiavelli defends himself against any suspicions of flattery, he urges readers to look at the "speeches" and "private reasonings" for a candid assessment (FH DL). As it happens, just such a quotation, ascribed to Tommaso Soderini, closes the relevant chapter on the sack of Volterra. Asked what he thought about the reconquest, Tommaso responds: "if you had received it by accord, you would have had advantage and security from it; but since you have to hold it by force, in adverse times it will bring you weakness and trouble and in peaceful times, loss and expense" (FH 7.30). Whether or not Machiavelli ultimately shares Tommaso's view, the assiduous construction of opposing viewpoints suggests that violent punishment is not an unambiguous strategy when dealing with subject populations.

Machiavelli's tactful disapproval of the brutal punishment meted out to the Volterrans reinforces the equivocal role attributed to violence in the government of empires. On the one hand, Machiavelli appears to vaunt the role of imperial violence, but on the other he seems to argue that successful empire is invisible – that it produces content subjects "under a dominion they do not see" (D 2.21). Invisible dominion surely is not built on violence and cruelty, for one of the latter's characteristics is precisely visibility. What, then, are the available courses of action for republics? If the Roman strategy of building an empire with partners may be difficult for modern republics to imitate, the option of associating with other states in a league remains open and preferable to the use of force. Given Florence's failure to hold its subject cities by violence, Machiavelli's message is clear: A Tuscan league would be a politically feasible and normatively superior arrangement over Florentine dominion.[43] To rule subject populations is to ensure that they "cannot or ought not to offend you" (D 2.23). This can be done by removing either the subjects' capacities to injure or their incentives to do so. Republics do best, Machiavelli seems to say, by focusing on the latter rather than the former.

---

[43] Zuckert, "Machiavelli's Democratic Republic," 274–75.

CONCLUSION

Republics, Machiavelli insists, are not the oases of peace and concord that Renaissance humanists had imagined them to be. Both force and cruelty are regular features of republican politics. Government by the many makes possible political freedom, but freedom is no antidote to violence. At their best, republics seek to institutionalize certain manifestations of state force and embed them within their orders. In doing so, they turn private into public force and invest it with a certain legitimacy. Yet republics also unleash forms of violence that are distinctive and of a considerable magnitude.

Because republics lack a strong executive power that can keep domineering elites in check, they are vulnerable to corruption by oligarchic factions. Such factions are liable to deploy violence to defend their wealth, power, and privileges. In virtue of this oligarchic pressure, institutions are a necessary but ultimately insufficient condition for political freedom. The struggle for freedom requires a vigilant people, willing and able to take recourse to arms to defend itself against domineering elites. While some forms of anti-oligarchic violence may be formalized in institutions of punishment, Machiavelli also envisions the deployment of extraordinary and unconventional sanctions against usurping elites. The purpose of such instances of cruelty is to punish but also to boost a republic's anti-oligarchic political memory.

Finally, and perhaps most problematically from a normative perspective, republics wage imperial wars against their neighbors near and far. Such wars are driven by geopolitical imperatives, dilemmas of military preparedness, and domestic considerations. Together, these factors generate a nearly insurmountable susceptibility to conduct an aggressive and expansionist foreign policy. And while Machiavelli regards the outgrowths of imperial domination with some apprehension, his republicanism remains indisputably imperial in character. That the obvious contradictions between civic freedom at home and imperial domination abroad do not preoccupy Machiavelli is testament to his anti-universalism, which, as we will see in the next chapter, is central to his thinking about insurrectionary politics.

6

Tumults

Everyone speaks ill of peoples without fear and freely, even while they reign; princes are always spoken of with a thousand fears and a thousand hesitations.

— Niccolò Machiavelli, *Discourses on Livy*

Hence I think not according to your perspective, wherein nothing but prudence is visible, but to the perspective of the many, which must see the ends, not the means of things.

— Niccolò Machiavelli, "Ghiribizzi"

In the *Florentine Histories*, Machiavelli offers a chronicle of conflict and civic strife. At the center of the historical narrative are the trials and tribulations of a divided city, which despite its manifold resources and opportunities fails to redeem the promise of historical greatness, betraying its destiny of becoming a modern-day Rome. Documenting Florence's consistent failure to overcome its divisions, the *Florentine Histories* announce a shift in Machiavelli's thinking about conflict. Whereas in the *Discourses*, Machiavelli makes a strong case for institutional solutions to political and social conflict, the *Histories* demonstrate the futility of Florence's incessant quest for constitutional solutions to its disunity.[1] Enfolded in this principal narrative is a series of discussions of popular revolts that centrally involve the part of the people that Machiavelli calls the "plebs." In contrast to the *Discourses*, where Machiavelli for the most

[1] Del Lucchese, "'Disputare' e 'combattere'," 82.

part discusses social conflict as a binary confrontation between the *popolo* and the *grandi*, in the *Florentine Histories* he introduces a third actor: the *infima plebe* or *popolo minuto*. By setting forth a tripartite division of the population of Florence, Machiavelli complicates the typology of the two humors set up in his earlier works.[2] In the *Florentine Histories*, Machiavelli highlights the *internal* division of the people, between those who count politically, that is, those who have public influence and access to political office, those who are excluded, that is, the liminal and unstable category of wage laborers, craftsmen, and petty merchants. The name *plebs* designates this latter group. It marks a counterpart to the *popolo*, just as *hoi polloi* is the counterpart to the *demos*. Denounced as "vile," "low," "base," "depraved," and "ignoble," the plebs stands for a politically marginalized, potentially dangerous, and insurgent part of the people.

Historically excluded from public life, through the fourteenth and fifteenth centuries the Florentine plebs rose to new prominence. The process whereby the plebs became a recognized, though by no means respectable, political actor involved a series of uprisings and revolts. This chapter reconstructs the political logic Machiavelli attributes to this periodic plebeian recourse to violence. Drawing on concepts and approaches developed in social history and contemporary political theory, I refer to the plebs' conduct as a "plebeian politics." By this I mean a more or less self-conscious collective agency in the pursuit of freedom that expresses itself in the form of agitation, tumults, and popular revolts. It is through such revolts, Machiavelli suggests, that the plebs become politically literate actors in their own right.

A central theme of the *Florentine Histories* is the elite's fear of the plebs, a fear so strong that in the 1450s the Florentine *grandi* came to Cosimo de'Medici "to beg him that he be so kind as to ... rescue them and himself from the hands of the plebs" (FH 7.3). The anxiety Machiavelli diagnoses among these elites raises a puzzle: Why would the Florentine establishment beg the Medici to deliver them from the threat of the rabble? If the plebs are excluded from political and economic power, lack access to office, and have no public authority, then why was the

---

[2] Even though in *The Prince* and the *Discourses* Machiavelli makes no conceptual distinction between the terms "people" [*popolo*] and "plebs" [*plebe*], there are already insinuations that "plebs" has a more restrictive meaning than "people," as well as a socioeconomic dimension. Jean-Claude Zancarini, "Les humeurs du corps politique," *Laboratoire Italien* 1 (2001).

Florentine aristocracy so afraid of them? How can a social group defined
by their powerlessness, poverty, and heterogeneity inspire such dread
among elites?

The answer to these questions lies in the historical transformation of
the Florentine plebs throughout the fourteenth and fifteenth centuries. As
a class, the Florentine *popolo minuto* was a crucial pillar of the gigantic
textile industry that drove economic growth and made possible the emergence of a new mercantile elite. Consisting of tens of thousands of low-
wage workers, employed in precarious jobs and subject to economic and
political domination, the Florentine plebs were no obvious political
actors. Yet by the early sixteenth century, when Machiavelli composes
the *Florentine Histories*, the Florentine plebs had lost their political
innocence. Through a series of riots, revolts, and uprisings over the course
of the past two centuries – most importantly the Ciompi revolt of 1378,
which Simone Weil dubbed the "earliest of all proletarian insurrections" –
the plebs demonstrated their capacity if not to effectively transform
political institutions or to govern the city, then at least to disrupt and
suspend customary Florentine politics.[3]

This penchant for episodic violence was, in the fifteenth century,
supplemented by a set of institutional developments that saw the plebs
take on a "distinctive role in communal representation."[4] At a time when
political participation became more restricted, with family lineage and
Medici patronage an ever more indispensable condition for political
status, the social groups excluded from political power and representation
developed a set of autonomous social, economic, and cultural institutions
that acquired increasing importance in the public life of the city. These
institutions included fraternal benefit societies and ceremonial associations, organized by neighborhoods and occupations. Set up as mutual
aid societies or "confraternities," these associations contributed to an
emerging self-consciousness about plebeian powerlessness and its causes.
Most confraternities were organized to provide assistance to their
members in case of illness, death, or poverty through distributing testa-
mentary bequests. They offered benefits, built hospitals, and established a
social and sometimes educational context for members and their families
to support each other. Pioneered by the scissors and knife makers and

---

[3] Simone Weil, "A Proletarian Uprising in Florence," in *Selected Essays, 1934–1943*, ed.
Richard Rees (Eugene, OR: Wipf and Stock, 2015), 55.
[4] Richard C. Trexler, *Public Life in Renaissance Florence* (Ithaca, NY: Cornell University
Press, 1991), 399.

soon followed by other vocations, these *compagnie* brought together occupational groups of so-called *sottoposti*, workers and subordinated craftspeople not eligible for guild membership.[5]

In addition to the confraternities, newly founded popular cultural associations seized ceremonial privileges traditionally limited to the optimates. These fifteenth-century ceremonial associations, so-called *potenze di plebi*, orchestrated plebeians for the festive life of the city. They provided avenues for the lower classes to participate in the parades, rituals, and spectacles so important in Florentine public life. They built ceremonial floats used during the processions of San Giovanni and choreographed the plebeian involvement in cultural performances that were the elites' traditional prerogatives. The *potenze* contributed to reorganizing the festive life of the city under Lorenzo de'Medici, when public celebrations, especially carnival, took on an increasingly important role. Given the amplified significance of spectacles in the city and the customary exclusion of the lower classes from public life, these festive associations marked a symbolic transformation. As if to highlight the inversion of the traditional hierarchy, the plebeian *potenze* organized the city into festive kingdoms, calling themselves "baronies, and their leaders ... kings, counts, dukes, and emperors."[6] In doing so, the plebs performed a dress rehearsal of taking over the city or, as Machiavelli puts it in the anonymous speech he attributes to a leader of the Ciompi, of becoming "princes of the city" (FH 3.13).

THE CIOMPI UPRISING

Machiavelli depicts the politicization of the plebs as a process that occurred in the latter half of the fourteenth century, a period bookended by the tyranny of the Duke of Athens in 1342 and the Ciompi revolt in 1378. The Duke of Athens, Walter of Brienne, was a French nobleman who in 1342 was solicited by the Florentine ruling class to govern the city. At the time, Florence was in the midst of a fiscal and banking crisis that resulted from crippling public debt incurred in the failed military campaigns to seize Lucca. Pronounced *signore* for life, Walter ruled tyrannically and quickly incurred the wrath of the elites by imposing new taxes

---

[5] Trexler, *Public Life in Renaissance Florence*, 404.

[6] According to Trexler, the division of the city into mock kingdoms [*reame di beffa*] had tradition in Florence, yet in the fifteenth century, with the increasing importance of public displays and festivities, especially around San Giovanni, these companies became more important. Trexler, *Public Life in Renaissance Florence*, 400, 406.

and forcing the city's creditors to accept new terms. Attempting to build a support base among the workers, Walter did, however, introduce new institutions to represent the plebs; he provided them with their own fellowship, insignia, and arms.[7] Thirty years later, in what became known as the Ciompi revolt, the Florentine plebs made their most extensive political bid. During the summer months of 1378, the lowest stratum of the Florentine working class overthrew the governing elites and instituted a revolutionary regime. For the first time in its history, Florence was ruled by a radical insurgent government that included artisans and manual laborers, drawn primarily from the textile industry.[8]

The wool workers, known as Ciompi, were the closest thing late medieval Florence had to an industrial proletariat.[9] A heterogeneous group, the Ciompi included workers as well as small artisans who owned their equipment and operated their own shops. Rallied by their subordinate position in the production process, they all depended on the merchants for their often unsteady employment. Their precarious living and working conditions, especially during economic downturns, meant that the cloth workers formed a significant portion (by some estimates up to half) of the *popolo minuto* – the Florentine poor.[10] Poverty rates of 50–70 percent maintained pressure on wages. The guilds further ensured that wages would rarely rise beyond subsistence levels by limiting production quotas and by facilitating loans to penniless workers that indentured them to labor under unfavorable conditions.[11]

Leading up to the revolt was an attempted coup by the upper echelon of the Florentine elites against the guild-based government. Riots broke out that mobilized the wool workers, and the elite power struggle was soon overshadowed by the wool workers, who a few weeks later escalated the protests. In late July, they overthrew the Florentine government and installed a revolutionary regime under the leadership of a wool carder, Michele di Lando. Several thousand armed workers besieged the Signoria;

[7] Najemy, *A History of Florence*, 136–37.
[8] John M. Najemy, "Audiant Omnes Artes: Corporate Origins of the Ciompi Revolution," in *Il tumulto dei Ciompi: Un momento di storia fiorentina ed europea*, ed. Istituto Nazionale di Studi sul Rinascimento (Florence: Leo S. Olschki, 1981), 59.
[9] On the condition of the wool workers, see Franco Franceschi, *Oltre il 'Tumulto': I lavoratori fiorentini dell'Arte della Lana fra Tre e Quattrocento* (Florence: Leo S. Olschki, 1993).
[10] Gene A. Brucker, "The Florentine *Popolo Minuto* and Its Political Role, 1350–1450," in *Violence and Civil Disorder in Italian Cities, 1200–1500*, ed. Lauro Martines (Berkeley: University of California Press, 1972), 157.
[11] Najemy, "Audiant omnes artes," 72–73.

the Palazzo del Podesta was seized; and the public executioner was hanged by his feet in front of the Palazzo Vecchio.

Despite the bold actions, the Ciompi's initial political and social demands were modest. They wanted the right to form a guild and demanded production increases for the wool industry to abate unemployment. On the whole, their petition remained well within the framework of the medieval corporatist system. It did not attempt to change or overthrow the regime or to institute a more egalitarian order.[12]

Yet the new Ciompi government was timid and remained deferential to the political and economic elites.[13] Instead of instituting reforms, it quickly compromised. Its leader, Michele di Lando, became a Thermidorian figure, clashing with the radical wing of the workers and thwarting their more radical demands. In response to this betrayal, the Ciompi continued their uprising. In late August thousands of workers assembled in the Piazza San Marco. Shouting: "Long live the *popolo minuto*," they demanded the resignation of Michele di Lando's government.[14] Pushing for a more egalitarian political and economic system and more power for

---

[12] The petition submitted to the Signoria on July 21 had six main components: (1) abolition of the tribunal of the *arte della lana*; (2) abolition of the penalty of amputating a hand for nonpayment of debts; (3) official recognition of and political representation for the *popolo minuto*; (4) two-year debt amnesty; (5) amnesty for everyone involved in the uprising; (6) change of the regressive tax system. Whether these demands were radical or moderate is subject to ongoing controversy. For Rodolico, Najemy, and Stella, they signal the revolutionary character of the movement. Niccolò Rodolico, *I Ciompi : Una pagina di storia del proletariato operaio* (Florence: Sansoni, 1980), 119ff; Najemy, "Audiant omnes artes," 60; Alessandro Stella, *La révolte des Ciompi : Les hommes, les lieux, le travail* (Paris : Éditions de l'École des Hautes Études en Sciences Sociales, 1993), 62–65. Rutenburg, Brucker, and de Roover consider these demands merely a call for recognition under a feudal system or for restoring the medieval corporation. Gene A. Brucker, *Renaissance Florence* (Berkeley: University of California Press, 1983); see also Gene A. Brucker, "The Ciompi Revolution," in *Florentine Studies: Politics and Society in Renaissance Florence*, ed. Nicolai Rubinstein (Evanston, IL: Northwestern University Press, 1968), 342, 345, 353; Victor Rutenburg, *Popolo e movimenti popolari nell'Italia del '300 e '400* (Bologna: Il Mulino, 1971), 198; Raymond de Roover, "Labour Conditions in Florence Around 1400: Theory, Policy, and Reality," in *Florentine Studies: Politics and Society in Renaissance Florence*, ed. Nicolai Rubinstein (London: Faber and Faber, 1968), 309. For Mollat and Wolff, these are relatively moderate demands, and Goldthwaite calls the event a "popular taxpayers' revolt." Michel Mollat and Philippe Wolff, *The Popular Revolutions of the Late Middle Ages*, trans. A. Lytton-Sells (London: George Allen & Unwin, 1973); Richard A. Goldthwaite, *The Economy of Renaissance Florence* (Baltimore: Johns Hopkins University Press, 2009), 328.

[13] Stella, *La révolte des Ciompi*, 53–59.

[14] See Stefani's chronicle in Louis Green, ed. *Chronicles of the Tumult of the Ciompi* (Clayton: Monash University, 1990), 90.

non-elite groups, they demanded redistribution and called for a suspension of political rights for the aristocracy and for worker involvement in industrial decision-making. On August 31, one of the bloodiest days in Florentine history, they were slaughtered by a reactionary coalition of guilds with the reformist forces under Michele di Lando.[15]

It may seem odd to appraise Machiavelli's analysis of plebeian politics by way of his depiction of the Ciompi revolt. But one must not underestimate the traumatic effects that the uprising had and the enduring spell its memory cast on Florentine politics.[16] As a class that did not own real estate, did not pay taxes and was not part of the guilds, the plebs had no institutional or symbolic political place.[17] Had it not been for this event, when the plebeians declared themselves political subjects, the plebs would not have been a recognizable part of Florentine political life.

Alarmed by the unprecedented mobilization of the plebs, the Florentine elites developed a lasting fear of the rabble manifest in successive generations of humanist writers. Florentine republicanism was, after all, a mercantile ideology; it was a political theory developed for the rising merchant class, affording that class political power against the feudal nobility and defending commerce and the virtue-inducing tendencies of private material wealth.[18] Machiavelli was unique among Florentine republicans in his attack on private wealth and his insistence that "well-ordered republics have to keep the public rich and their citizens poor" (D 1.37).

Most historians that preceded Machiavelli (and most that followed him, up until the nineteenth century) had little sympathy for the workers and described the uprising as instigated by the devil, a result of moral depravity, or as the work of a mob manipulated by intrigue and conspiracy.[19] Bruni considered the insurgents a bunch of violent and "impoverished criminals"

[15] Mollat and Wolff, *The Popular Revolutions*, 156.
[16] Brucker, *Renaissance Florence*, 46–47; Najemy, *A History of Florence*, 156–87.
[17] Zancarini, "Les humeurs du corps politique."
[18] Hans Baron, "Franciscan Poverty and Civic Wealth as Factors in the Rise of Humanistic Thought," *Speculum* 13(1938).
[19] It is not until the nineteenth century that liberal historians such as Corazzini and Falletti-Fossati began to look at the Ciompi in more sympathetic light. Giuseppe O. Corazzini, *I Ciompi: Cronache e documenti con notizie intorno alla vita di Michele di Lando* (Florence: Sansoni, 1887); Carlo Falletti-Fossati, *Il tumulto dei Ciompi: Studio storico-sociale* (Rome: Ermanno Loescher, 1882). See also Bock, "Civil Discord," 193–94.

whose "only goal was plunder [and] slaughter."[20] And Bracciolini thought the revolt was divine punishment for the sins of the city and of its citizens.[21] Machiavelli was the first historian who saw the causes and motivations for the uprising in the workers' social and political conditions. Unlike Bruni and Bracciolini, both of whom he criticizes for disavowing the role of civil discord in Florentine history, Machiavelli treats the Ciompi revolt as an unambiguously political movement (FH P).

In his extensive description of the uprising, Machiavelli includes a speech, ascribed to an anonymous leader of the revolt, that encapsulates the political positions he imputes to the plebs. Ostensibly delivered at a secret organizing meeting of the revolutionary Ciompi, the speech encourages the workers to pursue and escalate the uprising. Calling for the violent overthrow of plutocratic structures of power, the speech showcases a radical insurrectionary politics. Whether this speech expresses Machiavelli's views is subject to controversy in the literature. Elsewhere, I have defended the view that the speech should be read as a piece of serious political commentary, even though it is fictional and ascribed to an anonymous rabble-rouser. There are strong historical, literary, and rhetorical indications that the speech is more than merely a set piece and good reasons to be wary of treating the historical narrative in the *Florentine Histories* as a transparent reflection of Machiavelli's authorial intentions. Against the tendency of the secondary literature to accept at face value Machiavelli's self-presentation in the *Florentine Histories* as admiring compromise and moderation, I insist on the plurivocity of the work.[22]

---

[20] Leonardo Bruni, *History of the Florentine People*, trans. James Hankins (Cambridge, MA: Harvard University Press, 2007), IX, 9.

[21] Poggio Bracciolini, *Historia Florentina* (Venice: Johann Gabriel Hertz, 1715), 78. The idea of a divine punishment is taken from Alamanno Acciaiuoli's chronicle. See Donald J. Wilcox, *The Development of Florentine Humanist Historiography in the Fifteenth Century* (Cambridge, MA: Harvard University Press, 1969), 149–51.

[22] Yves Winter, "Plebeian Politics: Machiavelli and the Ciompi Uprising," *Political Theory* 40, no. 6 (2012), 743–44. For a more conventional but plausible alternative interpretation, see Gabriele Pedullà, "Il divieto di Platone. Niccolò Machiavelli e il discorso dell'anonimo plebeo," in *Storiografia repubblicana fiorentina: 1494–1570*, ed. Jean-Jacques Marchand and Jean-Claude Zancarini (Florence: F. Cesati, 2003), 233–34. A reader no less than Karl Marx interpreted the anonymous speech as Machiavelli's own views. His extensively annotated copy of the *Florentine Histories* contains the following marginalia: "Rede v. Machiavelli in d. Rolle eines tribuno dell'intima plebe (d. wahren Gründe d. Plünderungen d. populo minuto hat er oben selbst angegeben). Mach. macht einen Catilina aus d. Redner d. unzünftigen Prolétaires. D. Rede erinnert stellenweise an die d. Cat. im Sallust." Institut für Marxismus-Leninismus beim Zentralkomitee der SED, ed. *Ex Libris Karl Marx und Friedrich Engels: Schicksal und Verzeichnis einer Bibliothek* (Berlin: Dietz, 1967), 136–37.

A CALL FOR POPULAR VIOLENCE

As the medieval historian Trevor Dean notes, mob executions "*a furia del popolo*" are recorded throughout late medieval and early modern Italy.[23] Among the victims of reported lynchings are a number of tax officials, usurers, and others blamed for food shortages. Plebeian revolts that included these forms of popular violence were not uncommon. Chroniclers who report such instances of mob violence frequently explained them as divine judgments, relying on the idea that God intervenes in the course of the world in order to shape it and correct wickedness.

What differentiates the Ciompi revolt from such popular lynchings in Machiavelli's telling is its degree of political literacy. Rather than justifying the popular insurrection in terms of a political theology or a bread riot, Machiavelli's plebeian orator advocates violence in order to pursue two concrete objectives: to avoid punishment for the previous riots and "to live with more freedom and more satisfaction than we have in the past" (FH 3.13). To escape their condition of poverty and powerlessness, workers must rise up and take what is rightfully theirs. Figuring the privilege of wealthy elites as garments, the Ciompo calls on his fellow workers to "dress us in their clothes and them in ours, and without a doubt, we shall appear noble and they ignoble, for only poverty and riches make us unequal" (FH 3.13). Having rehearsed the inversion of social hierarchies through the *potenze di plebi* in the city's festivals, it is now time to put into practice what they trained for.

Forestalling objections to violence on moral grounds, the speaker urges his audience to refrain from evaluating violent action according to benchmarks of conscience and instead to apply a prudential standard:

> [W]e ought not to take conscience into account, for where there is, as with us, fear of hunger and prison, there cannot and should not be fear of hell. But if you will take note of the mode of proceeding of men, you will see that all those who come to great riches and great power have obtained them either by fraud or by force [o con frode o con forza]; and afterwards, to hide the ugliness of acquisition, they make it decent by applying the false title of earnings to things they have usurped by deceit or by violence [o con inganno o con violenza usurpate]. And those who, out of either little prudence or too much foolishness, shun these modes always suffocate in servitude or poverty.
>
> (FH 3.13)

---

[23] Dean, *Crime and Justice in Late Medieval Italy*, 57–58.

Rather than fearing otherworldly punishment, workers should focus on more mundane and temporal threats: hunger and prison. If, as the Ciompo plausibly argues, power and privilege are founded on usurpation, then the moralizing arguments against plebeian violence constitute an ideological conceit designed to maintain the workers in "servitude and poverty." For "faithful servants are always servants and good men are always poor" (FH 3.13). Painting the picture of a cannibalistic world in which "men devour one another," the speaker thus calls on the workers to seize the opportunity to become "princes of all the city":

> Now is the time not only to free ourselves from [our superiors] but to become so much their superiors that they will have more to lament and fear from you than you from them. The opportunity brought us by the occasion is fleeting, and when it has gone, it will be vain to try to recover it.
>
> (FH 3.13)

Like all political action, plebeian politics is about recognizing and seizing an *occasione* when one presents itself. The recourse to violence is a matter of "necessity," for there are no alternative courses of action available, if the workers wish to free themselves from their masters.

The plebeian speech is a remarkable rhetorical achievement, blending sophisticated techniques of argument with emotional appeals, vivid examples, and evocative figures. It emphasizes that political arguments are never disembodied ideas but rely on compelling communicative performances. The speech also exhibits a number of Machiavellian themes: the preference for conflict over harmony; the advice to the workers to seize the occasion; the insight that when many transgress, they will not be penalized and that small misdeeds are punished while great crimes are rewarded; the rejection of a Christian model of conscience as arbiter of political action; the claim that power and wealth often have their origins in violence and fraud, shrouded in tales of merit and entitlement; and the counsel that boldness is prudence, and that a failure to act decisively and if necessary violently may lead to greater violence and misery down the road.[24]

In short, the anonymous plebeian "speaks Machiavelli's language," which points to Machiavelli's recognition of the plebs as political actors, political subjects that assert their own claims and demands.[25] As

---

[24] Pitkin, *Fortune Is a Woman*, 311; Hulliung, *Citizen Machiavelli*, 89–92; Bock, "Civil Discord," 194.
[25] Del Lucchese, *Conflict, Power, and Multitude in Machiavelli and Spinoza*, 126.

Zancarini notes, in the wool worker's speech, we hear not the rage and the tumultuousness of the revolt but Machiavelli's thinking, above all his view that politics consists of confrontations, that it marks a battle-field where forces encounter one another. By lending the Ciompi his words, Machiavelli emphasizes that they must be recognized as political protagonists.[26]

In his pioneering article "The moral economy of the English crowd in the eighteenth century," E. P. Thompson contests as elitist the view that the common people do not become proper historical actors until the French Revolution.[27] The elite historiography against which Thompson (and other Marxist social historians such as Eric Hobsbawm and Georges Rudé) reacted tended to treat riots as driven by basic needs for food and shelter rather than by political aspirations to freedom, justice, or equality. On this view, early modern plebeian tumults are generally unpolitical. As resentful responses to physical depravations – especially hunger – such events lack political consciousness. Against this perspective, Thompson asserts that early modern riots were informed by a notion of legitimacy, and that popular grievances were based on a moral consensus concerning legitimate and illegitimate practices. "While this moral economy cannot be described as 'political' in any advanced sense, nevertheless it cannot be described as unpolitical either, since it supposed definite, and passionately held, notions of the common weal."[28]

On these criteria, Machiavelli's *popolo minuto* qualifies as "polit-ical," because the plebs' demands have undeniable normative content. Yet although the "moral economy" approach to insurgency allows us to conceptualize the plebs as political agents, one of its limitations is that it treats the crowd as motivated by communal and traditional norms rather than as contesting the authority of social and political institutions. If we look closely at the demands made by the plebeian insurgents and at the sustained deliberations in which they engage, the *popolo minuto* emerges as a political actor intent not only because they defend traditional entitlements but also because they articulate a set of

---

[26] Zancarini insists that this recognition exacts a price: the loss of the plebeian's own voice and aspirations. Yet this fetishization of authentic plebeian speech strikes me as wrong-headed and incompatible with any political pedagogy. After all, any learning process involves a "loss," and this one is no different. Zancarini, "Les humeurs du corps politique."

[27] Edward P. Thompson, "The Moral Economy of the English Crowd in the Eighteenth Century," *Past & Present* 50 (1971), 76.

[28] Thompson, "The Moral Economy of the English Crowd," 79.

counterhegemonic political norms, including claims about the nature of insurrectionary action, and the appropriateness of violence and destruction of property as their means. Writing against the oligarchic and republican biases of his time, Machiavelli regards the plebs as eminently capable of organized collective action to further their interests and freedom.[29]

Politically, one of the key issues raised by the speech is how to interpret its call for violence. Is the inclination to use violence a symptom of the plebs' political immaturity or moral corruption? Is the popular violence a consequence of the failure of the Florentine political system to provide avenues of participation? What distinguishes the people from the *grandi*, Machiavelli is fond of repeating, is that the latter desire to oppress whereas the former desire merely to avoid being oppressed. Is the plebeian desire to subjugate their masters therefore a cue that they are *grandi* in waiting, i.e. that they intend to merely invert relations of domination rather than transform them? Does the aspiration to crush and oppress their superiors, to dominate them and to loot their riches, signal that the workers are driven by the same impulses as the *ottimati* and that ambition is the fundamental human constant that shapes social hierarchies and relations of domination?

In the Ciompo's cannibalistic world, in which "men devour one another" and riches and power are obtained "either by fraud or by force," violence does indeed appear to have an anthropological rationale. Violence and fraud are what sustains the social order, an order in which the *popolo minuto* "suffocate in servitude and poverty." One might infer that violence here functions as a universal instrument for achieving political aims – what Machiavelli calls *forza* – or, alternatively, that Machiavelli laments the universal human capacity "for mindless, savage, unpredictable violence."[30] Yet, in the speech, the anthropological rationalization of violence is complemented by a conjunctural argument: Since the workers have already taken up arms, they are liable to be prosecuted unless they are victorious. The Ciompi must thus pursue a double-pronged strategy: the emancipatory struggle for "more freedom and more satisfaction [*più libertà e più sodisfazione*]" must be combined with the

---

[29] The oligarchic biases of the time are beautifully expressed, for example, in Guicciardini's *Considerations*. See Francesco Guicciardini, "Considerations of the Discourses of Niccolò Machiavelli," in *The Sweetness of Power: Machiavelli's Discourses and Guicciardini's Considerations*, ed. James B. Atkinson and David Sices (DeKalb: Northern Illinois University Library, 2007), 422.

[30] Rebhorn, *Foxes and Lions*, 99.

immediate tactical need to avoid punishment. This double aim is best attained not by a retreat but by a multiplication of violence.

Plebeian uprisings, Machiavelli intimates, are not just reactive events, driven by spontaneity and resentment. Rather, they are deliberate and coordinated practices and involve considerations of benefits and costs.[31] Just as acquiring and founding new states demands recourse to *forza* and *crudeltà*, so plebeian state-building cannot be accomplished by a pacifist commitment to nonviolence. Invoking the themes and tropes of *The Prince*, Machiavelli invites his readers to interpret the Ciompi's uprising in terms of the lessons dispensed there. Among the examples from *The Prince*, none seems as fitting to the plebeian's call to multiply violence as Duke Valentino, who turns violence into a cathartic moment by multiplying it and displaying the dismembered body of his deputy in the town piazza.[32]

THE LOGIC OF PLEBEIAN VIOLENCE

Commentators frequently insist that Machiavelli regarded as salutary only limited social conflicts, such as the ones in Rome that were resolved through speech and that yielded law, while rejecting as deleterious the conflicts in Florence that led to violence and murder. The conventional interpretations of the *Florentine Histories* depict Machiavelli as a disillusioned republican, disheartened by the Florentine inability to overcome the divisions and factions that defined the public life of the city over the course of the late fourteenth and fifteenth centuries.[33] While readers

---

[31] In the context of colonial historiography, Ranajit Guha observes that there is an often-repeated "myth … of peasant insurrections being purely spontaneous and unpremeditated affairs. The truth is quite to the contrary. It would be difficult to cite an uprising on any significant scale that was not in fact preceded either by less militant types of mobilization … or by parley among its principals seriously to weigh the pros and cons of any recourse to arms." Ranajit Guha, "The Prose of Counter-Insurgency," in *Selected Subaltern Studies*, ed. Ranajit Guha and Gayatri Chakravorty Spivak (Oxford: Oxford University Press, 1988), 45.

[32] See Nino Borsellino, "L'anonimo sovversivo," in *Letterature e critica: Studi in onore di Natalino Sapegno*, ed. Walter Binni, et al. (Rome: Bulzoni, 1974), 323.

[33] Gennaro Sasso, *Niccolò Machiavelli: Storia del suo pensiero politico* (Naples: Istituto italiano per gli studi storici, 1958), 494–95; Bausi, *Machiavelli*; Humfrey Butters, "Machiavelli and the Medici," in *The Cambridge Companion to Machiavelli*, ed. John M. Najemy (Cambridge: Cambridge University Press, 2010); Black, *Machiavelli*. For critiques of this view, see Jurdjevic, *A Great & Wretched City*; John P. McCormick, "On the Myth of a Conservative Turn in Machiavelli's *Florentine Histories*," in *Machiavelli on Liberty and Conflict: Commemorating the 500th Anniversary of* The Prince, ed.

disagree about the extent to which Machiavelli maintains or surrenders the anti-oligarchic stance he had laid out in his previous work, many interpreters converge on the view that he shared the Florentine anxieties about the *popolo minuto*, worried about the plebeian propensity for violence and tumult, and saw the "civil discords" and "enmities" as principal causes for the transformation of the Florentine republic to progressively more authoritarian forms. While a number of interpreters have noted Machiavelli's sympathies for the plebs' goals, most argue that they extend only to the moderates – those willing to compromise with their oppressors.[34]

Having attributed to Machiavelli a praise of moderation congenial to contemporary liberal sensibilities, commentators then consider the violence of the Ciompi revolt as the effect of pent-up grievances that lack institutional outlets.[35] In line with the conventional liberal script, such violence is interpreted as the pathological but predictable effect of a political system that offers no avenues for participation and denies the plebs adequate representative institutions that would allow their complaints to take a discursive form. Violence, on this reading, is the result of a denial of voice. And Machiavelli is seen as an advocate of moderation and compromise whose account of plebeian contestation is primarily of pedagogical value: It functions as a historical parable, instructing the reader that the absence of representative institutions results in radicalism and violence.[36] But the speech by the anonymous plebeian unlocks a different interpretive possibility, both more profound and more compelling than assimilating Machiavelli into the canon of early modern proto-liberals. It focuses on the logic of plebeian violence.

The peculiarity of the plebeian use of violence is that, at least in the case of the Ciompi revolt, it was quite limited. The workers' violence was remarkably restrained: The plebs burned down the houses of a few select elite citizens, especially ones that had previously treated them with contempt. They burnt the records of the wool guild, signifying their rebellion

---

Nadia Urbinati, David Johnston, and Camila Vergara (Chicago: University of Chicago Press, 2016).

[34] See Pitkin, *Fortune Is a Woman*, 310–14; Bock, "Civil Discord," 195; Martine Leibovici, "From Fight to Debate: Machiavelli and the Revolt of the Ciompi," *Philosophy & Social Criticism* 28, no. 6 (2002), 655–58; Benner, *Machiavelli's Ethics*, 304; Jurdjevic, *A Great & Wretched City*, 110–14. For a dissenting view, see Rodolico, *I Ciompi*.

[35] See, for example, Leibovici, "From Fight to Debate," 650.

[36] Maurizio Viroli goes so far as to call Machiavelli's narrative of plebeian mobilization a "radical critique of populism." Viroli, *Machiavelli's God*, 195.

against the oppressive administrative, judicial, and political power exercised by the guild. Looting was limited to a few palazzi, and the only physical violence against people Machiavelli describes is directed at Ser Nuto, the Bargello or police official appointed by the *grandi*, who was executed during the uprising:

> Ser Nuto was carried by the multitude to the piazza and hung on the gallows by one foot; and as whoever was around tore off a piece from him, at a stroke there was nothing left of him but his foot [*ser Nuto dalla moltitudine fu portato in piazza e a quelle forche per un piede impiccato; del quale avendone qualunque era intorno spiccato un pezzo, non rimase in uno tratto di lui altro che il piede*].
>
> (FH 3.16).

As the gleeful depiction of Ser Nuto's dismemberment makes clear, the modality of violence deployed by the Ciompi is cruelty. Recall that unlike *forza*, which requires what Machiavelli calls proportion, cruelty is the paradigmatic weapon of the weak. Unlike force, cruelty does not presuppose that one is the stronger party or that one has "proportion." In contrast to force, cruelty can be used not only by the state but also by those struggling against the state.

The mob execution of Ser Nuto is part of a string of similar acts of gruesome public vengeance that Machiavelli chronicles in the *Florentine Histories*. Giorgio Scali, another leader of the Ciompi who betrayed the *popolo minuto* and became so powerful that Machiavelli calls him almost a prince of the city (FH 3.18), was eventually decapitated, with "many of his closest friends ... killed and dragged about by the people" (FH 3.20). Earlier, the "fury of the multitude" cut to pieces the associates of the Duke of Athens, tearing them apart "with their hands and their teeth. And so that all their senses might be satisfied in revenge, having first heard their wails, seen their wounds, and handled their torn flesh, they still wanted their taste to relish them; so as all the parts outside were sated with them, they also sated the parts within" (FH 2.37).

As Rebhorn remarks, these killings "mount in a crescendo" through the course of the *Florentine Histories*.[37] Yet whereas Rebhorn attributes, on the basis of that observation, an aggressive and murderous view of human nature to Machiavelli, I think the lesson is a different one. The escalating instances of mob violence through the *Florentine Histories* suggest that plebeian violence is not arbitrary and that the narratives of cruelty are neither casual nor accidental. On the contrary: By placing

---

[37] Rebhorn, *Foxes and Lions*, 99.

these scenes of plebeian cruelty in an intensifying series, Machiavelli invites the reader to interpret the work as a *history of plebeian violence*. The interpretive question then is, what do readers learn from these illustrations about the nature of plebeian violence?

For one, popular vengeance needs to be relished with the senses. In the case of the killings following the fall of the Duke of Athens and in the Ciompo's speech, the objective of plebeian violence is framed in terms of "satisfaction" [*sodisfazione*]. Tearing apart body parts with hands and teeth enacts a form of revenge informed by a sensory need. The language of satisfaction evokes both Cesare's execution of Remirro that left the people "satisfied" [*satisfatti*] as well as the episode from the *Discourses* where Clearchus "cut to pieces all the aristocrats, to the extreme satisfaction [*sodisfazione*] of the people" (D 1.16). The "satisfaction" the Ciompi pursue is unlike that provided by Duke Valentino or by Clearchus; nevertheless, the terminological convergence is not coincidental. The emphasis on satisfaction in all three texts suggests that violence manifests a popular refusal of conventional forms of punishment. Not only is the retribution publicly performed but the hyperbolic imagery of bodies torn apart by hands and teeth also indicates that a kind of excess is central to the successful enactment of such revenge.

Plebeian politics, Machiavelli intimates, was performative even before the *potenze di plebi*, the groups that organized and channeled plebeian participation in the festive life of the city, came into being. Prior to being granted the formal privilege of participating in the parades, rituals, and spectacles so important in Florentine public life, plebeians seized the public space for performances of political violence. Appealing directly to popular demands for justice – i.e. redress against oppression – these performances were aimed at mobilizing political support by verging directly on the passions. It is this affective dimension of public cruelty that echoes through the worker's speech.

E. P. Thompson has emphasized the penchant of early modern crowds for theatricality. Writing about eighteenth-century England, Thompson observes that

Just as the rulers asserted their hegemony by a studied theatrical style, so the plebs asserted their presence by a theater of threat and sedition. ... the language of crowd symbolism is comparatively 'modern' and easy to read: effigy burning; the hanging of a boot from a gallows; the illumination of windows (or the breaking of those without illumination); the untiling of a house.[38]

---

[38] Edward P. Thompson, "Patrician Society, Plebeian Culture," *Journal of Social History* 7, no. 4 (1974), 399–401.

According to Thompson, the plebs used theater in lieu of violence, deploying performances that conjured fears of plebeian violence. Machiavelli, by contrast, suggests that in plebeian politics performance is no substitute for violence but its form. Just as princes and republics deploy diverse types of violence as forms of address, so the plebs have recourse to spectacular violence in order to appeal to an audience. Plebeian cruelty is not the fallback option of marginalized social groups who lack appropriate moral education and have no other avenue for political contestation. It is a deliberately staged address.

Throughout the *Florentine Histories*, Machiavelli frequently refers to the "rage" and "fury" of the multitude. Tumults and violence are driven, he suggests, by a mixture of political grievances and desires for revenge that he sometimes figures as "universal hatred [*odio universale*]" (FH 3.10). Rather than rebuking the plebs for their anger and hatred against their oppressors, Machiavelli treats these passions as indices of subordination and as sources of political mobilization. As he notes in *The Prince*, the hatred against the *grandi* has a cogent political explanation: The people hate the *grandi* because they fear them and because they aspire to secure themselves against domination (P 19). According to the *Florentine Histories*, the popular hostility against elites is both "grave and natural" (FH 3.1). And in the *Discourses*, he notes that the people "desires two things": revenge against their oppressors and recovery of their freedom (D 1.16). The people's hatred and their desire for revenge are, Machiavelli intimates, not pathologies but entirely sound responses to conditions of domination. As I have argued throughout this book, hatred is a resource for the people, and it is one that, unlike material wealth, is inexhaustible. To interpret plebeian violence and the pathos of the Ciompi speech as stoking the flames of dangerous unsociable passions is to miss the point that these passions are figured not as depraved desires lying dormant. What emerges clearly from the speech is that it is addressed to a frightened crowd, an audience whose debilitating "fear of hunger and prison" has to be transformed into a potential for collective action. The demand for *sodisfazione* thus indicates that the constitution of an insurrectionary political subjectivity takes place in the phantasmatic field of desire and affect, and that the strategies available to potential insurgents must take this into account.

Lest my intervention be misunderstood, my aim here is not to excuse plebeian violence, either by arguing that the plebs had no other means available to them or by suggesting that it is "merely" theater. On the contrary. I contend that Machiavelli treats plebeian violence as a legitimate strategy, and that he is right to do so. Machiavelli's point is that plebeian and elite actions cannot be measured by the same yardstick. Conduct that might be considered objectionable if undertaken by the *grandi* may be considered justifiable coming from the plebs.

In his recent defense of plebeian democracy, Jeffrey Green has emphasized the same point. Like Machiavelli, Green observes that plebeian indignation plays an important role in progressive politics.[39] Green's book vindicates not only indignation but also "principled vulgarity," by which he means deliberate violations of the norms of civility. Such norms of civility tend to uphold the idea that citizenship should be the same for everyone. Yet, to Green, actual conditions of inequality attest that equal citizenship is a fiction. Rather than defend the essential moral goodness, probity, and innocence of the plebs, Green argues that champions of plebeian democracy ought to embrace vulgarity. Embracing vulgarity is not the same as excusing plebeian indecency as exceptional, regrettable, but ultimately comprehensible acts by ignorant masses. Rather, it involves reclaiming epithets such as "vile," "low," "base," "depraved," and "ignoble" that are commonly attributed to the plebs. Among the practices Green defends as principled vulgarity are class-differentiated citizenship with special burdens for the wealthy; vindicating a certain arbitrariness in defining the category of "elite"; rehabilitating non-deliberative discourse, especially interruptive shouting and heckling; and defending rancorous sentiments like indignation, ingratitude, and vindictiveness.[40] Green – just like Machiavelli's anonymous Ciompo – proposes that a plebeian politics requires "overcoming the plebeian's good conscience."[41]

Even though Green mentions the anonymous Ciompo only in passing, his rejection of the norms of civility on grounds that they uphold a deceptive figment of universality might as well have come from the wool worker's speech.[42] By addressing what he somewhat chastely calls "morally ambiguous" practices, Green astutely challenges the reflex among theorists of plebeian politics to insist on the moral goodness of plebeian actions and to try to absolve plebeians of morally questionable behavior. Yet, like most contemporary champions of radical democracy

---

[39] Jeffrey Edward Green, *The Shadow of Unfairness: A Plebeian Theory of Liberal Democracy* (New York: Oxford University Press, 2016), 61.

[40] Green, *The Shadow of Unfairness*, 110–22.

[41] Green, *The Shadow of Unfairness*, 109–10.

[42] Green, *The Shadow of Unfairness*, 207n32.

and unlike the plebeian leader, Green studiously avoids the question of political violence. In fact, Green sidesteps not only violent forms of social action but also any illiberal form of organized collective action that mobilizes the power of the masses against elites. By restricting his discussion to what are ultimately minor breaches of the protocols of civility, Green appropriates the radical language of plebeianism to advance another version of political docility.

Machiavelli's defense of the plebs challenges such pious trust in constitutionalism. In stark contrast to his (and our) contemporaries' calls for reconciliation in response to oppression, Machiavelli analyzes plebeian violence, and the passions that sustain it – anger and hatred – as a form of popular resistance. As an insurrectionary political form, such popular resistance has more direction and focus than an isolated riot, yet it resists institutionalization. When the *popolo minuto* opens the prison and hangs the *bargello* by his feet, they strike not just individuals but the emblems of a public authority that is widely regarded as class-biased and as hostile to plebeian interests. When they attack and execute judicial officials, tax officials, and others who exercise administrative and political power over them, they revolt against institutions that reproduce social domination. And when they attack the palazzi of Florence's wealthiest families, they manifest a refusal to distinguish between perpetrators and beneficiaries of injustice.

These instances of popular resistance are responses to domination: incursions of the plebs into a political system that brands them as outsiders. The "lowest plebs" have a legitimate and well-founded fear of being abandoned in the political negotiations between powerful elites (FH 3.12). Plebeian revolts highlight the limitations of republican ideology, as plebeian demands cannot easily be folded into existing institutions or political discourses. Rather than dismissing these assaults as expressions of vengeful resentment, Machiavelli invites the reader to understand them as onslaughts against a state apparatus seen as an instrument of class power. It is not that plebeian violence is somehow a natural expression of popular justice, as if the plebs' conception of justice were limited to vengeance, but rather, that riots and popular executions convey a revolt against the judicial and fiscal apparatuses of the state and the symbols that epitomize them.

Elites will always frame plebeian violence as senseless and anti-political and as motivated by base instincts and resentment. This is one of the lessons Machiavelli draws from the second plebeian secession triggered by the abuses of the decemvirs (449 BCE). Livy reports that after having retreated to the Sacred Mount, the plebs, in their negotiations with the senatorial representatives, demanded not only the restoration of the tribunes but also custody over the decemvirs so that they could burn them alive (3.53). In response, the senatorial envoys, Valerius and Horatius, patronizingly explain to the angry multitude that their feelings of resentment and vindictiveness are excusable but unjust. Exhibiting a quintessentially elite attitude to demands for popular vengeance, the senators insist on the incompatibility of justice and cruelty and on the incoherence of the plebeian desire for retribution.

Whereas Livy's account highlights the naïveté, irresponsibility, and moral depravity of the plebs, Machiavelli's treatment of the episode emphasizes their strategic ineptitude. The plebs' mistake is not that they want their oppressors dead – it is that they foolishly advertise their cruel intentions (D 1.44). Misquoting Livy, Machiavelli has the senatorial representatives respond: "You damn cruelty, you rush into cruelty [*Crudelitatem damnatis, in crudelitatem ruitis*]," before advising the plebs that if they desire to execute the decemvirs, it would be prudent not to advertise it publicly until they actually have custody over them.[43] In Machiavelli's narrative, the senatorial representatives effectively become counsellors on cruelty. This is a good example of Machiavelli's political – rather than moral – conception of revenge. By altering the scene of reconciliation between the plebs and the patricians, he dismisses the oligarchic conceit of the patricians' moral authority and replaces the patronizing rationalization of plebeian resentment with concrete advice on how to pursue the decemvirs' punishment. Machiavelli does not yield to the aristocratic proclivity to dispense moral lessons to the people about cruelty. On the contrary: If he concurs with the patricians' counsel – a not improbable proposition – then he nonetheless regards the threat to burn tyrants alive as a justifiable part of a popular politics.

PARTISAN AND ANTI-UNIVERSAL

What do readers learn from the plebeian politics that the radical Ciompi enact? Not, I think, that the wool workers constituted themselves as the people, thereby contesting the representational politics of the Signoria.

---

[43] Livy's version reads: "Your anger is understandable but not to be indulged, for it is through hatred of cruelty that you rush to cruelty [*irae vestrae magis ignoscendum quam indulgendum est, quippe qui crudelitatis odio in crudelitatem ruitis*]." Livy 3.53, my trans.

Whereas the Marxist social historians in the 1970s responded to an elitist and paternalistic historiography that disregarded the crowd and denied the normative element of popular contestation, recent work by radical democrats tends, on the contrary, to glorify and romanticize the plebs. Among recent books on plebeian political mobilizations, there is a trend to attribute to the plebs unassailable democratic and revolutionary credentials.[44] Martin Breaugh, for instance, characterizes the "plebeian experience" as a desire for liberty, an urge to participate in the life of the city and to expand the public sphere. Informed by Lefort, Arendt, and Rancière, Breaugh understands plebeian politics as a transgressive assertion of radical equality and rejection of hierarchy: "'The plebs' is the name of an experience, that of achieving human dignity through political agency. The plebs designates neither a social category nor an identity but rather a fundamental political event: the passage from a subpolitical status to one of a full-fledged political subject. The plebeian experience signifies the metamorphosis of *animal laborans* into *zoon politikon*."[45]

Consistent with this Arendtian idiom, Breaugh understands plebeian politics as a coming-of-age story of the crowd. On his interpretation, plebeian status represents a purely political (rather than socioeconomic) category; plebeian political demands consist of claims to include previously disenfranchised groups; and plebeian actions paradigmatically take a nonviolent form.[46] A plebeian politics, for Breaugh, thus consists of demands by marginalized groups for full citizenship, political voice, and participation. It is fully compatible with progressivist narratives dear to political liberalism concerning the ongoing expansion of the franchise and the gradual extension of equal rights to formerly excluded groups.

Breaugh's is not the only recent tale in political theory that celebrates the plebs as the unsung heroes of liberal democracy. A less sanitized account is offered by Green, who in contrast to Breaugh puts forward an irreducibly antagonistic conception of plebeian politics. Like McCormick (who prefers the term "people"), Green takes seriously the

---

[44] Martin Breaugh, *The Plebeian Experience: A Discontinuous History of Political Freedom*, trans. Lazer Lederhendler (New York: Columbia University Press, 2013); Green, *The Shadow of Unfairness*; Joshua Clover, *Riot. Strike Riot: The New Era of Uprisings* (London: Verso, 2016).

[45] Breaugh, *The Plebeian Experience*, xv.

[46] At pains to show that economic domination functions only as a trigger for political action, Breaugh insists that the motives for the Ciompi uprising were political and that "it would be wrong to overstate the role of economic motives in triggering the events of 1378." Breaugh, *The Plebeian Experience*, 13.

social division between the few and the many and interprets plebeian politics not as an attempt to undo that division but to leverage it against the elites. Yet whereas for McCormick the second-class citizenship of ordinary people in liberal democracies is a scandal, Green proposes to embrace it. This sanguine approach to plebeianism has significant virtues, but it comes at a cost: the complete dissociation of the adjective "plebeian" from class and class struggle. Green's elite is so narrowly defined – the 1 percent – that the category of plebeian becomes amorphous, losing its conventional association with the rabble (and, as discussed earlier, with illiberal forms of social action such as riots that involve violence, looting, and destruction of property). For Green, we are all plebeians, at least those of us belonging to the 99 percent, insofar as our political voices do not carry the same weight as those of the 1 percent.[47] Despite the vindication of non-deliberative speech and of minor breaches of liberal etiquette, the plebeianism defended by authors such as Green and Breaugh is cleansed of blood and gore and hence of those features of historical plebeian movements that are incompatible with liberal democracy.[48]

There is, in short, a pattern in some contemporary efforts to rehabilitate plebeian politics: the disavowal of economic forces in the constitution of the plebs (along with the abandonment of the language of class) and the overstatement of the plebs' commitment to universal principles, to an ideal of social unity, and most importantly, to nonviolence.[49] From E. P. Thompson's claim that rioting is not just about bread and food prices but about normatively relevant disputes to the outright disavowal, by Breaugh and Green, of class as an attribute of what "plebeian" means, we have come a long way.

Machiavelli offers a useful corrective to this current trend. His theorization of the plebs avoids the pitfalls of elitist historiography that denies the political role of the plebs altogether. It conceives the plebs as motivated by both political and economic concerns. And it dodges the contemporary trend to glorify the plebs as a harbinger of democratic universality. Instead, Machiavelli puts forward an unapologetically

---

[47] Green, *The Shadow of Unfairness*, x.

[48] For a more nuanced perspective that acknowledges both unruliness of early modern crowds and their democratic aspirations without seeking to transform them into respectable political actors, see Frank, *Constituent Moments*, 67–100.

[49] On nonviolence, see for instance Howes's interpretation of the plebeian secession as nonviolent. Dustin E. Howes, *Freedom without Violence: Resisting the Western Political Tradition* (Oxford: Oxford University Press, 2016), 43-63.

partisan and antagonistic model of plebeian politics in which uprisings, secessions, and spectacular violence play a major role.

Such plebeian popular resistance is not universalizable. It functions by dismembering and mutilating the emblems of social and political domination, by piercing the deceitful veils of universality and by manifesting an unapologetically partisan political momentum. The Ciompo's speech deflates the presumptions of Florentine unity and stages the city's political divisions. While asserting a claim to embody popular voice, the speech dismisses the pretense to popular unity and instead defends a radically partisan perspective. Machiavelli's plebeian politics, in short, do not take the narrative form of a *Bildungsroman*, a becoming-political of the plebs, where the plebs progressively shed their partisan character and articulate their demands and objectives in universal terms. Machiavellian plebeian politics is a politics of struggle, not reducible to the quest for recognition or participation. Neither does it take the form of a transformation of pre-political plebeian ranting into proper political speech.

That this spontaneous form of insurrectionary politics has inherent limitations is obvious. Unless articulated as part of a comprehensive struggle, such acts remain isolated and episodic. The challenge for a plebeian political movement is to organize and develop political forms that go beyond conventional juridical categories yet do not fall back into an apparatus of domination. Indeed, the central unresolved question of Machiavelli's plebeian politics is that of organization and leadership. In *Discourses* 1.44 he calls a multitude without a head "useless," and in *Discourses* 1.57 he proclaims such a multitude weak. The problem that plebeian politics faces is how to organize the multitude, that is, how to share power in an effective way without coopting the plebeian leadership. One of the lessons of the Ciompi revolt is that plebeian leaders are highly susceptible to cooptation by elites.

To blame the plebeians for a corrupt understanding of justice is to ignore and disavow the conditions under which the desire to inflict violence on the powerful originates and the fear to which it testifies. It is also to disregard the phantasmatic structure of this desire and of the promise that animates it. By translating fear into vengefulness, the Ciompo's speech produces a reorganization of affect that is exactly the inverse of the one achieved by Borgia's *spettaculo*. Whereas Borgia purges hatred and generates love and loyalty among the Romagnol, the anonymous plebeian transforms fear into hatred.

Rather than sowing anxiety about plebeian violence, Machiavelli offers a political analysis, where popular violence manifests the refusal of dominated groups to internalize their oppression. Popular resistance repudiates a politics of reconciliation as well as the establishment of a state apparatus – for instance, in the form of a court. It neither seeks nor recognizes ostensibly neutral institutions standing between the people and their enemies, tasked with adjudicating true and false, arbitrating just and unjust, and determining guilty and innocent. On the contrary. This politics of resistance takes the form of public executions of those who have betrayed the people, just as revolutionary plebeians and peasants everywhere have, in C. L. R. James's words, always "aimed at the extermination of their masters."[50]

CONCLUSION

For Renaissance humanists, the alleged excesses of the Ciompi and the threat of plebeian politics frequently served as a motif to legitimate the oligarchic restoration and subsequent Medici rule.[51] At times, Machiavelli's language seems to support such a view. He repeatedly points to the unreliable and "inconstant spirit of the plebs" (FH 5.11, 7.34), judging it misguided for leaders to count and depend on the plebs for political support. He calls the plebs erratic and unpredictable, and complains about the "indecency" [*disonestà*] of the revolting multitude (FH 3.15). Identifying in the plebs a characteristic desire for revenge, he goes so far as to state that it is the "nature" of the plebs "to rejoice in evil" (FH 2.34, 2.41).

Yet a closer look at the *Florentine Histories* offers substantial evidence that Machiavelli's political sympathies were more ambiguous than presented by the anti-plebeian interpretation. While he describes the plebs as politically fickle, angry, hateful, and prone to violence, each of these attributes is, in the course of the *Florentine Histories*, explained in terms of particular political dynamics. The plebs' inconstancy turns out to be a refusal to be instrumentalized by elite forces. The plebs' anger and hatred turn out to be political responses to domination and motivating factors for collective mobilization. And the plebeian susceptibility to violence is the single political advantage that the politically excluded and economically disadvantaged classes have against the establishment.

---

[50] C. L. R. James, *A History of Pan-African Revolt* (Oakland, CA: PM Press, 2012), 40.
[51] John M. Najemy, "Civic Humanism and Florentine Politics," in *Renaissance Civic Humanism: Reappraisals and Reflections*, ed. James Hankins (Cambridge: Cambridge University Press, 2000), 83–85.

The plebs, Machiavelli concedes, are frequently instrumentalized by elite factions. They are, after all, a volatile and unpredictable force. Sometimes they will follow a seditious plot and sometimes they won't. Sometimes they stand up for popular interests, and sometimes they do the bidding of the elites. It is this mercurial and capricious nature that renders the plebs dangerous and sometimes undermines their own political projects and ambitions. Even if the plebs are sometimes used as a *strumento* or tool of the elites (FH 7.12), it is a subversive one. What, after all, is a reputation for inconstancy and fickleness, if not proof that the plebs will not loyally do the bidding that elites expect of them? To be capricious, in other words, is to be capable of acting, at least in some measure, autonomously and without following elite directives.

By depicting the Ciompi as pursuing a radical political project, Machiavelli challenges the oligarchic narrative and outlines the contours of a plebeian politics. At the center of this insurrectionary project is the *popolo minuto*'s claim to power and the defense of violence as a means to overthrow their oppressors. In order to free themselves from domination by the *grandi* and the wealthy *popolani*, the plebs must seize the state. Their task, then, is equivalent to that of the new prince: *acquistare lo stato*. In order to successfully acquire and maintain their state, plebeians – much like princes – need to learn how "not to be good" (P 15).

The plebeian politics that emerges from Machiavelli's account of the Ciompi revolt is a politics of struggle and of antagonism. It is no accident that this antagonism is preserved despite the plebeian assertion of equality in the worker's speech and that even this claim to equality is articulated in terms of the fundamental opposition between the plebeians and their *superiori*. By insisting on that opposition, the speech tacitly dismisses the republican pieties of order, social peace, and patriotic unity. At no point in the speech does the *popolo minuto* constitute itself as a universal and make the claim to represent the people as a whole. Rather than presenting the interests of the *popolo minuto* in universal terms or in the name of what is best for the collectivity as a whole, the speech remains resolutely partisan. At no point is the conflict between *popolani* and *plebe* resolved, nor does the orator give any indication that such a resolution may be on the horizon of emancipatory political action.[52] Dismissing the promise of social harmony as myth, the speech urges the reader to consider insurrectionary politics as a continuous and recurrent struggle with no guarantee for redemption.

---

[52] Contra Pedullà, "Il divieto di Platone," 230–32.

Conclusion

The cruelties of the multitude are against whoever they fear will seize the
common good; those of a prince are against whoever he fears will seize his
own good.

— Niccolò Machiavelli, *Discourses on Livy*

The dominant paradigm for theorizing violence in contemporary political
theory and philosophy is coercion. The language of coercion has allowed
recent generations of theorists to sanitize state violence, gradually divor-
cing it from physical force. One of the ways in which this dissociation has
been promoted is through the claim that coercion, properly understood,
involves not violence but communication: threat-making.[1] A prominent
article by Robert Nozick, published in 1969, defends this view, now
dominant in analytical political philosophy. Nozick's innovation consists
in defining coercion as a "proposal" – a conditional threat that excludes
physical force.[2] Coercion is thus turned into a communicative act and
cleansed of its association with violence. It takes the form of a transaction.
The coercer issues the "proposal," which in turn elicits a response by the
coercee. The entire exercise looks like a negotiation between two equal

---

[1] For excellent critical discussions, see Scott A. Anderson, "How Did There Come to Be Two
Kinds of Coercion?" in *Coercion and the State*, ed. David A. Reidy and Walter J. Riker
(Dordrecht: Springer, 2008); Scott A. Anderson, "Coercion." *The Stanford Encyclopedia
of Philosophy* Summer 2015 Edition: https://plato.stanford.edu/archives/sum2015/entries/
coercion/.

[2] Robert Nozick, "Coercion," in *Philosophy, Science, and Method: Essays in Honor of
Ernest Nagel*, ed. Sidney Morgenbesser, Patrick Suppes, and Morton White (New York:
St. Martin's Press, 1969).

parties, a bargain dickered at a market stall. The success or failure of coercion becomes contingent on how the "proposal" is taken up by the coercee. Rather than being forced, the coercee faces a "choice," and the relevant philosophical questions concern the psychology of that choice, the coercee's assessment of the consequences, her responsibility for the outcomes, and so on. By shifting attention entirely to the side of the coercee, this pastel account severs coercion from the coercer's repressive apparatus and from the material mechanisms by which the coercive "proposal" is communicated.[3]

Sheldon Wolin notes that political theorists in the Euro-Atlantic tradition have woven "ingenious veils of euphemism to conceal the ugly fact of violence."[4] The deodorized version of coercion instigated by Nozick and fashionable among analytical political philosophers falls under this heading. The dematerialization of coercion is one more iteration in a tradition that has long brandished concepts such as "authority," "law," or "justice" in a kind of vacuum, as if they were independent of the machinery of punishment that they tacitly presuppose. Wolin is no doubt right that euphemization has served to shroud violence, but veiling is not the only procedure whereby violence is mystified and depoliticized. Such depoliticization comes in various shapes, among which I have identified four as characteristic in contemporary political theory: marginalization, technicization, moralization, and ontologization. These four strategies dismiss, trivialize, displace, and dematerialize violence, contributing to the view that political theory has little to say about formations of violence and must restrict itself to normative considerations of when and under what conditions its use is justifiable.

Political violence is neither banal nor uniform. Hence to turn one particular mode of violence – say coercion – into its generic archetype is a mystification. Whatever its limitations may be, Machiavelli's political thought is attuned to this key point, something that sets his work apart from much contemporary theorizing about violence. Political violence, Machiavelli insists, includes not only the threat of harm whereby agents are coerced into compliance. It also involves the deployment of spectacular cruelty; the use of force directly against bodies; and the sometimes violent struggle for freedom from social and political domination. These formations of violence are not substitutes, and they are irreducible

---

[3] See Anderson, "How Did There Come to Be Two Kinds of Coercion?" 23.
[4] Wolin, *Politics and Vision*, 197.

to coercion. The conventional framework of coercion fails to get at these issues because it assigns violence the status of a residual product of nature.

* * *

"'It's a remarkable piece of apparatus,' said the officer to the explorer and surveyed with a certain air of admiration the apparatus which was after all quite familiar to him."[5] The apparatus, installed in Franz Kafka's penal colony, is a curious torture machine used for capital punishment. It functions with a set of needles that are elaborately designed to pierce the body of the condemned and use the skin as a canvas on which to inscribe the law. In Kafka's story, the machine is about to kill a prisoner who failed to obey his orders. The insubordinate convict will die by having the words "Honor Thy Superiors!" pigmented all over his body. In this way, the ingenious machine delivers justice with precision engineering: The punishment exacts the law to the letter. Word for word, it realizes the law by mercilessly inscribing it on the body of the condemned.

Kafka's story can be read as a parable for how legal violence operates. Michel de Certeau comments that law invariably writes itself on bodies and that it uses the skins of its subjects as the surfaces on which it signifies.[6] Law, on this reading, enacts its authority by marking the bodies of the subject, establishing its meaning in the process. Yet Kafka's insight applies not only to law but to formations of political violence more broadly. As Machiavelli highlights, political violence comprises a signifying dimension. Practices of violence do not speak for themselves. Like other political practices, they intervene in the political realm by signifying, and these significations are central to how violence functions. Like Kafka's parable of the penal colony, Machiavelli challenges the oft-repeated cliché that violence is crude. Violence, Machiavelli insists, generates signs that convey political meanings.

The heterogeneity of political violence should not obscure that violence's characteristic modus operandi has the structure of an address. As Machiavelli emphasizes time and time again, most formations of political violence are public performances. As such, they produce political effects not by physically compelling agents but by appealing to an audience. It is

[5] Franz Kafka, "In the Penal Colony," in *The Complete Stories* (New York: Schocken, 1971), 140.

[6] Michel de Certeau, "Tools for Body Writing," *Intervention* 21/22(1988), 7.

true that sometimes violence functions in transitive ways, taking a single direct object as its target, but for the most part, acts of political violence are designed to leave behind traces destined for an audience. Often elaborately staged, acts of political violence are intended to be perceived, experienced, remembered, and narrated. If Machiavelli is right about this point, then it follows that such acts of violence invoke cultural codes and aesthetic regimes and that their political valence depends on *la qualità de' tempi*. Dissecting these codes and regimes is an important analytical and critical task for political theorists.

Like Nozick, Machiavelli conceives of violence as a communicative act. Yet in emphasizing the aesthetic and theatrical aspects of violence, Machiavelli maps out an alternative way of conceptualizing the conventional dichotomy between coercion and consent or between force and deliberation. Unlike Nozick, who dissolves the power and the violence of coercion in the communicative act, Machiavelli retains the embodied materiality of coercive force. He accomplishes this by revising the concepts inherited from Roman political discourse and revived by Renaissance authors.

For the Roman taxonomy *vis/violentia*, Machiavelli substitutes *forza/crudeltà*. In doing so, he abandons the Roman category of *violentia*, because of its limited analytical value for political theorizing, and replaces it with *crudeltà*. The mark of cruelty is excess. It involves the use of typically lethal violence accompanied by dismembered bodies and upended status hierarchies. Politically, Machiavellian cruelty is a marker of transitions. It is common, among some interpretive strands, to regard Machiavelli as an unrestrained advocate of violence, but such readings are, as I have argued throughout, implausible. Cruelty, for Machiavelli, is not a mechanism of governance but represents an exceptional intervention once normal modalities of political life have broken down. It can serve to consolidate authority, build political support, generate legitimacy, and reduce bloodshed in the long run. Machiavelli thus theorizes cruelty as a productive rather than a repressive strategy; cruelty generates political effects by stimulating the political passions and by producing political memories.

Forza, by contrast, describes the more common use of armed violence, by the state or by non-state actors, in the pursuit of political objectives. In contrast to the dazzling spectacles of violence staged by cruelty, *forza* marks the prosaic appeal to the concrete physical vectors directed against bodies in order to move or destroy them. Machiavelli's theory of *forza* comprises two original claims: First, force is inherently unstable, and second, force can create belief. The instability of force means that it requires, as supplements, legal and ideological apparatuses. Bodies of armed men are insufficient to guarantee political reproduction. Force's capacity to generate belief suggests, conversely, that, like cruelty, force has a productive dimension.

The aesthetic and performative dimension of political violence is conspicuous in the case of cruelty. The transgression and scandal are constitutive of this particular mode of violence, what endows it with its particular political valence. Machiavellian cruelty is incontrovertibly triadic, in the sense that it is designed to be experienced, observed, and remembered by an audience. Less obvious, perhaps, is that force – the more disciplined and less lurid modality of political violence – similarly relies on the triadic structure. Force is not self-sustaining. It always yields to a greater force, which means that it is unstable, unless it can rely on external supports, such as law, religion, and ideology. It is only when force can credibly generate the belief that it operates in the name of something larger than itself that it becomes politically sustainable. As such, force – like cruelty – relies on assiduous choreographies that provoke such beliefs.

Unlike the means of violence, which at least in theory can be centralized and monopolized by states, the significations of violence necessarily escape state control. Hobbes was well aware of this problem, which is why he was convinced that the sovereign must be master not only of the sword but also of the word. Historically, states have developed numerous ways to manipulate the appearances of violence so as to mask their inability to conclusively master these meanings. This, incidentally, is why the idea that violence has no meaning or that its meaning is identical with its function is so pernicious. Not only does it subvert a better understanding of how modes of political violence operate; it also misjudges the interest of states, as principal modern purveyors of violence, in representing violence as purely technical. States have a vested interest in presenting their violence as "neutral" and therefore as free of any meaning, precisely because interpretations of violence are always potentially subversive.

I have argued for interpreting Machiavelli as a popular realist, a category I take from Gramsci. The framework of popular realism I have proposed in this book captures the conflictual, materialist, historicist, and radical populist dimensions of Machiavelli's political thought. This framework sheds light on Machiavelli's theory of violence, because it enables readers to grasp violence as material and as a heterogenous set of tactics embedded in the political strategies of concrete social actors. In each case, the different capacities and objectives of social actors shape the dynamics of violence, as do the vectors of material forces that make up the unstable equilibria that constitute every political moment.

Yet while political reality is unstable, it is not unstructured. In contrast to the Hobbesian paradigm of natural war – where every man is enemy to every man – for Machiavelli, the structure of political conflict is based on class struggle, whether framed in binary terms as the contradictions of the two humors or in the ternary model introduced in the *Florentine Histories*. This configuration of conflict directly translates into the modes and orders of political violence. Elites have inherently different resources available to them than the people or the plebs. While elite actors can frequently mobilize significant forces to pursue their objectives, popular actors must rely on numbers and on tactics that specifically target elite properties: their privileges, wealth, reputation, and social standing, Analyzed through the lens of popular realism, violence is not an abstract constitutive dimension of politics but has social and historical determinations.

Against the tendencies in some strands of contemporary political theory to treat violence as a constitutive but abstract feature of the political, I have insisted on a material and embodied interpretation. On my reading, Machiavelli's category of founding violence is neither ontological nor transcendental but immanent and political. Founding moments inaugurate a new political order, not the political as such. As a correlate, founding violence denotes not an abstract split constitutive of the people or the simultaneous condition of possibility and impossibility of politics as such, but it targets the enemies of a new order, typically disaffected elites, and creates political memories.

Popular realism offers not only criteria for differentiating historical manifestations of violence; it also provides a rationale for Machiavelli's extensive depiction of and investigation into various forms of violence. That rationale, I have argued, is pedagogical: It is aimed at strengthening popular political literacy. Acquiring a more sophisticated understanding of violence is important, not least because political actors must appraise the situations they face and make decisions about the use of violent means. This is obviously true for the agency of the state but also, as Machiavelli notes, in popular insurgencies. If violence produces political effects by appealing to an audience, and if this performative dimension is central rather than peripheral to its function, then understanding these mechanisms is crucial for actors who seek to advance popular and democratic political projects.

The plebs – *il vulgo* – tend to judge actions by their outcomes (P 18). In other words, they treat violence in purely consequentialist and utilitarian terms, as justified by the results. Such a stance is a good starting point: It is more politically compelling than the deontological position, which adjudicates the means irrespective of the ends pursued. However, it is only a starting point. Consequentialism is ultimately insufficient for evaluating political violence because it fails to attend to the aesthetics of violence, which Machiavelli regards as fundamental to its political operations. That violence cannot simply be judged by its immediate outcomes is clear from his choice of Duke Valentino as the most prominent example in *The Prince*. If Machiavelli's objective were merely to highlight the expediency of using violence, he might have chosen a more successful role model. By employing the example of a political actor who ultimately failed, Machiavelli suggests to his readers that the appropriate criteria by which to evaluate violence are not reducible to efficacy. Facing a complex tableau, readers are invited to consider the structure of the address and the significations of violence rather than just the ends. In short, the portrayal of violence functions as a lesson in political literacy. Anti-oligarchic projects require such literacy both to assess performances of violence in which the people are implicated as participant audiences and to deploy violence for their own objectives.

Revolts against oligarchic power require, Machiavelli stresses, "steel" or *ferro*. Along with most modern theorists of revolution, Machiavelli doubts that nonviolent means can bring about emancipatory social change. Yet unlike some twentieth-century theorists of revolutionary violence, such as Georges Sorel or Frantz Fanon, Machiavelli does not associate violence with inherently emancipatory or redemptive qualities.[7] Fanon and Machiavelli both consider the productive, aesthetic, and spectacular dimensions of popular, insurrectionary violence and both thinkers draw on the metaphors of rejuvenation and regeneration for theorizing violence's productivity. Yet whereas Fanon attributes to anticolonial violence cathartic effects on the perpetrators, Machiavelli locates the catharsis within the audience.

Moreover, whereas for Fanon violence plays a decisive role in the process of subject formation, liberating the colonized from the psychic sedimentations of colonialism, Machiavelli accords violence no subjective dimension.

---

[7] Georges Sorel, *Reflections on Violence*, trans. Jennifer Jennings (Cambridge: Cambridge University Press, 1999), 165–73; Frantz Fanon, *The Wretched of the Earth*, trans. Richard Philcox (New York: Grove Press, 2004), 2, 21, 44, 50–52.

In the tumultuous history of plebeian revolts, violence plays an important part in the emergence of a collective political subject with a determinate class identity and political bonds. Yet unlike Fanon's, this collective subject has no interiority and no psychic life at all. Neither glorifying nor vilifying the plebs, Machiavelli offers a sober assessment of plebeian violence as a legitimate albeit limited political strategy. The work that violence performs in the production of a collective political subject is pedagogical. Episodic insurgency creates political bonds. The bonds established through the shared experience of insurgency shape political subjectivity. While violence may well be a necessary component of such struggles, its role is tactical and didactic rather than redemptive.

Bibliography

Agamben, Giorgio. *The Kingdom and the Glory: For a Theological Genealogy of Economy and Government.* Translated by Lorenzo Chiesa and Matteo Mandarini. Stanford, CA: Stanford University Press, 2011.

Alberti, Leon Battista. *The Albertis of Florence: Leon Battista Alberti's Della Famiglia.* Lewisburg, PA: Bucknell University Press, 1971.

Albertini, Rudolf von. *Das florentinische Staatsbewußtsein im Übergang von der Republik zum Prinzipat.* Bern: Francke Verlag, 1955.

Alighieri, Dante. *The Divine Comedy: Inferno, Vol. 1 Part 1.* Translated by Charles S. Singleton. Princeton, NJ: Princeton University Press, 1990.

Althusser, Louis. *Machiavelli and Us.* Translated by Gregory Elliott. London: Verso, 1999.

For Marx. Translated by Ben Brewster. London: Verso, 2005.

Althusser, Louis and Étienne Balibar. *Reading Capital.* Translated by Ben Brewster. London: New Left Books, 1970.

Alvisi, Edoardo. *Cesare Borgia: Duca di Romagna.* Imola: Ignazio Galeati, 1878.

Anderson, Scott A. "How Did There Come to Be Two Kinds of Coercion?" In *Coercion and the State.* Edited by David A. Reidy and Walter J. Riker. Dordrecht: Springer, 2008.

"Coercion." *The Stanford Encyclopedia of Philosophy* Summer 2015 Edition: https://plato.stanford.edu/archives/sum2015/entries/coercion/.

Anglo, Sydney. *Machiavelli – The First Century: Studies in Enthusiasm, Hostility, and Irrelevance.* Oxford: Oxford University Press, 2005.

Antoninus Florentinus, *Summa Theologica in Quattuor Partes Distributa.* Verona: Ex Typographia Seminarii, Apud Augustinum Carattonium, 1740.

Aquinas, Thomas. *The Summa Theologica.* Translated by Fathers of the English Dominican Province. London: Burns Oates and Washbourne, 1920.

Ardito, Alissa M. *Machiavelli and the Modern State: The Prince, the Discourses on Livy, and the Extended Territorial Republic.* Cambridge: Cambridge University Press, 2015.

Arendt, Hannah. *The Origins of Totalitarianism*. New York: Harcourt Brace, 1973.
"What Is Authority?" In *Between Past and Future*. New York: Penguin, 1977.
On Revolution. London: Penguin, 1990.
Aristotle. *The Complete Works*: The Revised Oxford Translation. 2 Vols. Princeton, NJ: Princeton University Press, 1984.
The Politics and the Constitution of Athens. Translated by Steven Everson. Cambridge: Cambridge University Press, 1996.
Aron, Raymond. *Machiavel et les tyrannies modernes*. Paris: Editions de Fallois, 1993.
Atkinson, James B. and David Sices, eds. *Machiavelli and His Friends: Their Personal Correspondence*. DeKalb: Northern Illinois University Press, 1996.
Augustine. *The City of God against the Pagans*. Translated by R. W. Dyson. Cambridge: Cambridge University Press, 1998.
Austin, John. *The Province of Jurisprudence Determined*. Edited by Wilfrid E. Rumble. Cambridge: Cambridge University Press, 2007.
Baines, Barbara. *Representing Rape in the English Early Modern Period*. Lewiston, NY: Edwin Mellen Press, 2003.
Balibar, Étienne. "Gewalt." In *Historisch-kritisches Wörterbuch des Marxismus*. Edited by Wolfgang Fritz Haug. Vol. 5. Berlin: Argument Verlag, 2001.
Violence and Civility: On the Limits of Political Philosophy. Translated by G. M. Goshgarian. New York: Columbia University Press, 2015.
Baraz, Daniel. "Seneca, Ethics, and the Body: The Treatment of Cruelty in Medieval Thought." *Journal of the History of Ideas* 59, no. 2 (1998): 195–215.
Medieval Cruelty: Changing Perceptions, Late Antiquity to the Early Modern Period. Ithaca, NY: Cornell University Press, 2003.
Barberi-Squarotti, Giorgio. *La forma tragica del 'Principe' e altri saggi sul Machiavelli*. Florence: Leo S. Olschki, 1966.
Barlow, J. J. "The Fox and the Lion: Machiavelli's Reply to Cicero." *History of Political Thought* 20, no. 4 (1999): 627–45.
Baron, Hans. "Franciscan Poverty and Civic Wealth as Factors in the Rise of Humanistic Thought." *Speculum* 13 (1938): 1–37.
"Machiavelli: The Republican Citizen and the Author of 'the Prince'." *English Historical Review* 76 (1961): 217–53.
The Crisis of the Early Italian Renaissance. Princeton, NJ: Princeton University Press, 1966.
In Search of Florentine Civic Humanism: Essays on the Transition from Medieval to Modern Thought. 2 Vols. Princeton, NJ: Princeton University Press, 1988.
Bausi, Francesco. *Machiavelli*. Rome: Salerno, 2005.
Beard, Mary. *SPQR: A History of Ancient Rome*. New York: Norton, 2015.
Beiner, Ronald. *Civil Religion: A Dialogue in the History of Political Philosophy*. Cambridge: Cambridge University Press, 2011.
Bell, Duncan, ed. *Political Thought and International Relations: Variations on a Realist Theme*. Oxford: Oxford University Press, 2009.
Bellamy, Richard. "Dirty Hands and Clean Gloves: Liberal Ideals and Real Politics." *European Journal of Political Theory* 9, no. 4 (2010): 412–30.

Bendix, Reinhard. *Max Weber: An Intellectual Portrait*. Garden City, NY: Doubleday, 1960.

Benjamin, Walter. "Critique of Violence." In *Reflections*. Translated by Edmund Jephcott. New York: Harcourt Brace, 1978.

Benner, Erica. *Machiavelli's Ethics*. Princeton, NJ: Princeton University Press, 2009.

Machiavelli's Prince: A New Reading. Oxford: Oxford University Press, 2013.

Berlin, Isaiah. "The Originality of Machiavelli." In *Against the Current: Essays in the History of Ideas*. London: Pimlico, 1979.

Berns, Thomas. *Violence de la loi à la Renaissance: l'originaire du politique chez Machiavel et Montaigne*. Paris: Kimé, 2000.

Black, Robert. "Arezzo, the Medici and the Florentine Regime." In *Florentine Tuscany: Structures and Practices of Power*. Edited by William J. Connell and Andrea Zorzi. Cambridge: Cambridge University Press, 2000.

Machiavelli. London: Routledge, 2013.

Bock, Gisela. "Civil Discord in Machiavelli's Istorie Fiorentine." In *Machiavelli and Republicanism*. Edited by Gisela Bock, Quentin Skinner, and Maurizio Viroli. Cambridge: Cambridge University Press, 1990.

Böckenförde, Ernst-Wolfgang. "Die verfassunggebende Gewalt des Volkes: Ein Grenzbegriff des Verfassungsrechts." In *Staat, Verfassung, Demokratie: Studien zur Verfassungstheorie und zum Verfassungsrecht*. Frankfurt a.M.: Suhrkamp, 1991.

Bolzani, Pierio Valeriano. *Hieroglyphicorum Collectanea, ex veteribus et recentioribus auctoribus descripta, et in sex libros ordine alphabetico digesta*. Frankfurt: 1678. www.uni-mannheim.de/mateo/camenaref/valeriano/valeriano1/Valeriano_hieroglyphica_4.html.

Bonadeo, Alfredo. "The Role of the 'Grandi' in the Political World of Machiavelli." *Studies in the Renaissance* 16 (1969): 9–30.

Corruption, Conflict, and Power in the Works and Times of Niccolò Machiavelli. Berkeley: University of California Press, 1973.

Bondanella, Peter E. *Francesco Guicciardini*. Boston: Twayne, 1976.

Borsellino, Nino. "L'anonimo sovversivo." In *Letterature e critica: Studi in onore di Natalino Sapegno*. Edited by Walter Binni et. al. Vol. 1. Rome: Bulzoni, 1974.

Bracciolini, Poggio. *Historia Florentina*. Venice: Johann Gabriel Hertz, 1715.

"In Praise of the Venetian Republic." In *Cambridge Translations of Renaissance Philosophical Texts. Vol. 2: Political Philosophy*. Translated by Martin Davies. Edited by Jill Kraye. Cambridge: Cambridge University Press, 1997.

Breaugh, Martin. *The Plebeian Experience: A Discontinuous History of Political Freedom*. Translated by Lazer Lederhendler. New York: Columbia University Press, 2013.

Breiner, Peter. "Machiavelli's 'New Prince' and the Primordial Moment of Acquisition." *Political Theory* 36, no. 1 (2008): 66–92.

Brown, Alison. "De-Masking Renaissance Republicanism." In *Renaissance Civic Humanism*. Edited by James Hankins. Cambridge: Cambridge University Press, 2000.

"The Language of Empire." In *Florentine Tuscany: Structures and Practices of Power*. Edited by William J. Connell and Andrea Zorzi. Cambridge: Cambridge University Press, 2000.

"Lorenzo de' Medici's New Men and Their Mores: The Changing Lifestyle of Quattrocento Florence." *Renaissance Studies* 16, no. 2 (2002): 113–42.

The Return of Lucretius to Renaissance Florence. Cambridge, MA: Harvard University Press, 2010.

Medicean and Savonarolan Florence: The Interplay of Politics, Humanism, and Religion. Turnhout: Brepols, 2011.

Brown, Robert McAfee, ed. *The Essential Reinhold Niebuhr: Selected Essays and Addresses.* New Haven, CT: Yale University Press, 1987.

Brown, Wendy. *Manhood and Politics: A Feminist Reading in Political Theory.* Totowa, NJ: Rowman & Littlefield, 1988.

Brucker, Gene A. "The Ciompi Revolution." In *Florentine Studies: Politics and Society in Renaissance Florence.* Edited by Nicolai Rubinstein. Evanston, IL: Northwestern University Press, 1968.

"The Florentine *Popolo Minuto* and Its Political Role, 1350–1450." In *Violence and Civil Disorder in Italian Cities, 1200–1500.* Edited by Lauro Martines. Berkeley: University of California Press, 1972.

Renaissance Florence. Berkeley: University of California Press, 1983.

Bruni, Leonardo. *History of the Florentine People.* 3 Vols. Translated by James Hankins. Cambridge, MA: Harvard University Press, 2007.

Buchez, Philippe-Joseph-Benjamin and Pierre-Célestin Roux-Lavergne, eds. *Histoire parlementaire de la Révolution française, ou Journal des assemblées nationales depuis 1789 jusqu'en 1815.* Paris: Paulin, 1834–1838.

Bullard, Melissa Meriam. "Adumbrations of Power and the Politics of Appearances in Medicean Florence." *Renaissance Studies* 12, no. 3 (1998): 341–56.

Burckhardt, Jacob. *The Civilization of the Renaissance in Italy.* Translated by S. G. C. Middlemore. London: Penguin, 1990.

Burrill, Alexander M. *A Law Dictionary and Glossary: Containing Full Definitions of the Principal Terms of the Common and Civil Law.* New York: Baker, Voorhis & Co., 1867.

Butterfield, Andrew. "New Evidence for the Iconography of David in Quattrocento Florence." *I Tatti Studies in the Italian Renaissance* 6 (1995): 115–33.

Butterfield, Herbert. *The Statecraft of Machiavelli.* London: G. Bell and Sons Ltd., 1940.

Butters, Humfrey. "Machiavelli and the Medici." In *The Cambridge Companion to Machiavelli.* Edited by John M. Najemy. Cambridge: Cambridge University Press, 2010.

Cadoni, Giorgio. "Libertà, repubblica e governo misto in Machiavelli." *Rivista internazionale di filosofia del diritto.* Series III 39 (1962): 462–84.

Carocci, Sandro. "The Papal State." In *The Italian Renaissance State.* Edited by Andrea Gamberini and Isabella Lazzarini. Cambridge: Cambridge University Press, 2012.

Carr, E. H. *The Twenty Years' Crisis 1919–1939.* London: Macmillan, 1958.

Cassirer, Ernst. *The Myth of the State.* New Haven, CT: Yale University Press, 1946.

Chabod, Federico. *Machiavelli and the Renaissance.* Translated by David Moore. New York: Harper & Row, 1958.

Scritti su Machiavelli. Turin: Einaudi, 1964.

Chiapelli, Fredi. *Studi sul linguaggio del Machiavelli*. Florence: Felice Le Monnier, 1952.

Cicero, Marcus Tullius. *On Duties*. Translated by M. T. Griffin and E. M. Atkins. Cambridge: Cambridge University Press, 1991.

On the Commonwealth and on the Laws. Translated by James E. G. Zetzel. Cambridge: Cambridge University Press, 1999.

Philippics. 2 Vols. Translated by D. R. Shackleton Bailey, John T. Ramsey, and Gesine Manuwald. Cambridge, MA: Harvard University Press, 2010.

Clarke, Michelle T. "On the Woman Question in Machiavelli." *The Review of Politics* 67, no. 2 (2005): 229–55.

"The Virtues of Republican Citizenship in Machiavelli's Discourses on Livy." *The Journal of Politics* 75, no. 2 (2013): 317–29.

"Machiavelli and the Imagined Rome of Renaissance Humanism." *History of Political Thought* 36, no. 3 (2015): 452–70.

Clausewitz, Carl von. *On War*. Translated by Michael Howard and Peter Paret. Princeton, NJ: Princeton University Press, 1984.

Clover, Joshua. *Riot. Strike Riot: The New Era of Uprisings*. London: Verso, 2016.

Coady, C. A. J. "The Problem of Dirty Hands." *The Stanford Encyclopedia of Philosophy* Spring 2014 Edition: https://plato.stanford.edu/archives/spr2014/entries/dirty-hands/.

Coates, Ta-Nehisi. *Between the World and Me*. New York: Spiegel and Grau, 2015.

Coby, J. Patrick. *Machiavelli's Romans: Liberty and Greatness in the Discourses on Livy*. Lanham, MD: Lexington Books, 1999.

Cochrane, Eric W. "Machiavelli: 1940–1960." *The Journal of Modern History* 33, no. 2 (1961): 114–36.

Colish, Marcia L. "The Idea of Liberty in Machiavelli." *Journal of the History of Ideas* 32, no. 3 (1971): 323–50.

"Cicero's De Officiis and Machiavelli's Prince." *The Sixteenth Century Journal* (1978): 81–93.

"Machiavelli's Art of War: A Reconsideration." *Renaissance Quarterly* 51, no. 4 (1998): 1151–68.

Corazzini, Giuseppe O. *I Ciompi: Cronache e documenti con notizie intorno alla vita di Michele di Lando*. Florence: Sansoni, 1887.

Croce, Benedetto. *Politics and Morals*. Translated by Salvatore J. Castiglione. New York: Philosophical Library, 1945.

Davidsohn, Robert. *Geschichte von Florenz: Vierter Band. Die Frühzeit der Florentiner Kultur*. Berlin: E.S. Mittler & Sohn, 1922.

de Certeau, Michel. "Tools for Body Writing." *Intervention* 21/22 (1988): 7–11.

de Grazia, Sebastian. *Machiavelli in Hell*. New York: Vintage, 1989.

de Roover, Raymond. "Labour Conditions in Florence Around 1400: Theory, Policy, and Reality." In *Florentine Studies: Politics and Society in Renaissance Florence*. Edited by Nicolai Rubinstein. London: Faber and Faber, 1968.

de Vries, Hent. *Religion and Violence: Philosophical Perspectives from Kant to Derrida*. Baltimore: Johns Hopkins University Press, 2001.

Dean, Trevor. *Crime and Justice in Late Medieval Italy*. Cambridge: Cambridge University Press, 2007.

Del Lucchese, Filippo. "'Disputare' e 'combattere': Modi del conflitto nel pensiero politico di Niccolò Machiavelli." *Filosofia Politica* 15, no. 1 (2001): 71–95.

Conflict, Power, and Multitude in Machiavelli and Spinoza. London: Continuum, 2009.

"Machiavelli and Constituent Power: The Revolutionary Foundation of Modern Political Thought." *European Journal of Political Theory* 16, no. 1 (2014): 3–23

The Political Philosophy of Niccolò Machiavelli. Edinburgh: Edinburgh University Press, 2015.

dell'Oro, Ignazio. *Il segreto dei Borgia*. Milan: Ceschina, 1938.

Derrida, Jacques. *Of Grammatology*. Translated by Gayatri Chakravorty Spivak. Baltimore: Johns Hopkins University Press, 1976.

Writing and Difference. Translated by Alan Bass. London: Routledge, 1978.

"Declarations of Independence." *New Political Science* 7, no. 1 (1986): 7–15.

"Force of Law: The Mystical Foundation of Authority." *Cardozo Law Review* 11, no. 5–6 (1990): 920–1045.

Descendre, Romain. "Stato, imperio, dominio. Sur l'unité des notions d'État et d'empire au XVIe siècle." *Astérion* 10 (2012): http://asterion.revues.org/2243.

Dietze, Carola and Claudia Verhoeven, eds. *The Oxford Handbook of the History of Terrorism*. Oxford: Oxford University Press, 2014.

Diodorus Siculus. *Library of History*. Cambridge, MA: Harvard University Press, 1952–1963.

Dorini, Umberto. *Il diritto penale e la delinquenza in Firenze nel sec. XIV*. Lucca: Domenico Corsi, 1916.

Dotti, Ugo. *Niccolò Machiavelli: La fenomenologia del potere*. Milan: Feltrinelli, 1979.

Douglass, Frederick. *My Bondage and My Freedom*. New York: Penguin, 2003.

Dowling, Melissa Barden. *Clemency and Cruelty in the Roman World*. Ann Arbor: University of Michigan Press, 2006.

Eckstein, Arthur M. "Conceptualizing Roman Imperial Expansion Under the Republic: An Introduction." In *A Companion to the Roman Republic*. Edited by Nathan Rosenstein and Robert Morstein-Marx. Malden, MA: Wiley-Blackwell, 2010.

Edgerton, Samuel Y., Jr. *Pictures and Punishment: Art and Criminal Prosecution During the Florentine Renaissance*. Ithaca, NY: Cornell University Press, 1985.

Enders, Jody. *The Medieval Theater of Cruelty: Rhetoric, Memory, Violence*. Ithaca, NY: Cornell University Press, 1999.

Ercole, Francesco. "Introduzione." In Coluccio Salutati, *Il trattato 'De tyranno' e lettere scelte*. Bologna: Nicola Zanichelli, 1942.

Euben, Peter J. "Justice and the Oresteia." *The American Political Science Review* 76, no. 1 (1982): 22–33.

The Tragedy of Political Theory. Princeton, NJ: Princeton University Press, 1990.

Evans, Richard. *Rituals of Retribution: Capital Punishment in Germany 1600–1987*. Oxford: Oxford University Press, 1996.

Fabbri, Lorenzo. "Patronage and Its Role in Government: The Florentine Patriciate and Volterra." In *Florentine Tuscany: Structures and Practices of Power*. Edited by William J. Connell and Andrea Zorzi. Cambridge: Cambridge University Press, 2000.

Falletti-Fossati, Carlo. *Il tumulto dei Ciompi: Studio storico-sociale*. Rome: Ermanno Loescher, 1882.

Fanon, Frantz. *The Wretched of the Earth*. Translated by Richard Philcox. New York: Grove Press, 2004.

Feldherr, Andrew. *Spectacle and Society in Livy's History*. Berkeley: University of California Press, 1998.

Femia, Joseph. "Gramsci, Machiavelli and International Relations." *The Political Quarterly* 76, no. 3 (2005): 341–49.

Fischer, Markus. "Machiavelli's Rapacious Republicanism." In *Machiavelli's Liberal Republican Legacy*. Edited by Paul A. Rahe. Cambridge: Cambridge University Press, 2006.

Forde, Steven. "Varieties of Realism: Thucydides and Machiavelli." *The Journal of Politics* 54, no. 2 (1992): 372–93.

Foucault, Michel. *Discipline and Punish: The Birth of the Prison*. Translated by Alan Sheridan. London: Penguin, 1991.

Fournel, Jean-Louis. "La connaissance de l'ennemi comme forme nécessaire de la politique dans la Florence des guerres d'Italie." In *L'Italie menacée: Figures de l'ennemi*. Edited by Laura Fournier-Finocchiaro. Paris: L'Harmattan, 2004.

Franceschi, Franco. *Oltre il 'Tumulto': I lavoratori fiorentini dell'Arte della Lana fra Tre e Quattrocento*. Florence: Leo S. Olschki, 1993.

Frank, Jason. *Constituent Moments: Enacting the People in Postrevolutionary America*. Durham, NC: Duke University Press, 2010.

Frazer, Elizabeth and Kimberly Hutchings. "Avowing Violence: Foucault and Derrida on Politics, Discourse and Meaning." *Philosophy & Social Criticism* 37, no. 1 (2011): 3–23.

"Virtuous Violence and the Politics of Statecraft in Machiavelli, Clausewitz and Weber." *Political Studies* 59, no. 1 (2011): 56–73.

Fredona, Robert. "*Liberate Diuturna Cura Italiam*: Hannibal in the Thought of Niccolò Machiavelli." In *Florence and Beyond: Culture, Society and Politics in Renaissance Italy: Essays in Honour of John M. Najemy*. Edited by David S. Peterson and Daniel E. Bornstein. Toronto: Centre for Reformation and Renaissance Studies, 2008.

Fusero, Clemente. *Cesare Borgia*. Milan: Dall'Oglio, 1963.

Gaille-Nikodimov, Marie. *Conflit civil et liberté: La politique machiavélienne entre histoire et médecine*. Paris: Honoré Champion, 2004.

Gasché, Rodolphe. *Deconstruction: Its Force, Its Violence*. Albany: State University of New York Press, 2016.

Geerken, John H. "Machiavelli's Moses and Renaissance Politics." *Journal of the History of Ideas*, 60, no. 4 (1999): 579–95.

Gentili, Alberico. *De legationibus libri tres*. Translated by Gordon J. Laing. New York: Oxford University Press, 1924.

Germino, Dante. "Machiavelli's Thoughts on the Psyche and Society." In *The Political Calculus: Essays on Machiavelli's Philosophy*. Edited by Anthony Parel. Toronto: University of Toronto Press, 1972.

Geuna, Marco. "Extraordinary Accidents in the Life of Republics: Machiavelli and Dictatorial Authority." In *Machiavelli on Liberty and Conflict*. Edited by David Johnston, Nadia Urbinati, and Camila Vergara. Chicago: University of Chicago Press, 2017.

Geuss, Raymond. *Philosophy and Real Politics*. Princeton, NJ: Princeton University Press, 2008.

Gilbert, Felix. "Bernardo Rucellai and the Orti Oricellari: A Study of the Origins of Modern Political Thought." *Journal of the Warburg and Courtauld Institutes* 12 (1949): 101–31.

"Florentine Political Assumptions in the Period of Savonarola and Soderini." *Journal of the Warburg and Courtauld Institutes* 20, no. 3/4 (1957): 187–214.

Machiavelli and Guicciardini: Politics and History in Sixteenth-Century Florence. Princeton, NJ: Princeton University Press, 1965.

"Machiavelli: The Renaissance of the Art of War." In *Makers of Modern Strategy. From Machiavelli to the Nuclear Age*. Edited by Peter Paret. Princeton, NJ: Princeton University Press, 1986.

Gillespie, Michael Allen. *The Theological Origins of Modernity*. Chicago: University of Chicago Press, 2008.

Giorgini, Giovanni. "The Place of the Tyrant in Machiavelli's Political Thought and the Literary Genre of *The Prince*." *History of Political Thought* 29, no. 2 (2008): 230–56.

Girard, René. "Mimesis and Violence: Perspectives in Cultural Criticism." *Berkshire Review* 14 (1979): 9–19.

Violence and the Sacred. Translated by Patrick Gregory. London: Continuum, 2005.

Goldhammer, Jesse. *The Headless Republic: Sacrificial Violence in Modern French Thought*. Ithaca, NY: Cornell University Press, 2005.

Goldhill, Simon. *Aeschylus, the Oresteia*. Cambridge: Cambridge University Press, 1992.

Goldthwaite, Richard A. *The Economy of Renaissance Florence*. Baltimore: Johns Hopkins University Press, 2009.

Gorgias. "Encomium of Helen." In *The Older Sophists: A Complete Translation by Several Hands of the Fragments*. Edited by Rosamond Kent Sprague. Indianapolis: Hackett, 2001.

Gramsci, Antonio. *Selections from the Prison Notebooks*. Translated by Quintin Hoare and Geoffrey Nowell Smith. New York: International Publishers, 1971.

Quaderni del carcere. 4 Vols. Edited by Valentino Gerratana. Turin: Einaudi, 2007.

Green, Jeffrey Edward. *The Shadow of Unfairness: A Plebeian Theory of Liberal Democracy*. New York: Oxford University Press, 2016.

Green, Louis, ed. *Chronicles of the Tumult of the Ciompi*. Clayton: Monash University, 1990.

Grosz, Elizabeth. "The Time of Violence: Deconstruction and Value." *Cultural Values* 2, no. 2/3 (1998): 190–205.

Guarini, Elena Fasano. "Machiavelli and the Crisis of the Italian Republics." In *Machiavelli and Republicanism*. Edited by Gisela Bock, Quentin Skinner, and Maurizio Viroli. Cambridge: Cambridge University Press, 1990.

Guha, Ranajit. "The Prose of Counter-Insurgency." In *Selected Subaltern Studies*. Edited by Ranajit Guha and Gayatri Chakravorty Spivak. Oxford: Oxford University Press, 1988.

Guicciardini, Francesco. *The History of Florence*. Translated by Mario Dommandi. New York: Harper & Row, 1970.

Dialogue on the Government of Florence. Translated by Alison Brown. Cambridge: Cambridge University Press, 1994.

"How the Popular Government Should Be Reformed [Discorso Di Logrogno]." In *Cambridge Translations of Renaissance Philosophical Texts*. Translated by Russell Price. Edited by Jill Kraye. Cambridge: Cambridge University Press, 1997.

"Considerations of the Discourses of Niccolò Machiavelli." In *The Sweetness of Power: Machiavelli's Discourses and Guicciardini's Considerations*. Edited by James B. Atkinson and David Sices. DeKalb: Northern Illinois University Library, 2007.

Guillemain, Bernard. *Machiavel: L'anthropologie politique*. Geneva: Librairie Droz, 1977.

Habermas, Jürgen. *Between Facts and Norms: Contributions to a Discourse Theory of Law*. Translated by William Rehg. Cambridge: Polity, 1996.

Hairston, Julia L. "Skirting the Issue: Machiavelli's Caterina Sforza." *Renaissance Quarterly* 53, no. 3 (2000): 687–712.

Hammill, Graham and Julia Reinhard Lupton, eds. *Political Theology and Early Modernity*. Chicago: University of Chicago Press, 2012.

Hammill, Graham L. *The Mosaic Constitution: Political Theology and Imagination from Machiavelli to Milton*. Chicago: University of Chicago Press, 2012.

Harrington, James. "A System of Politics." In *"The Commonwealth of Oceana" and "A System of Politics."* Cambridge: Cambridge University Press, 1992.

Hart, H. L. A. *The Concept of Law*. Oxford: Oxford University Press, 1994.

Hartman, Saidiya V. *Scenes of Subjection: Terror, Slavery, and Self-Making in Nineteenth-Century America*. New York: Oxford University Press, 1997.

Haslam, Jonathan. *No Virtue Like Necessity: Realist Thought in International Relations Since Machiavelli*. New Haven: Yale University Press, 2002.

Hellegouarc'h, Joseph. *Le vocabulaire latin des relations et des partis politiques sous la république*. Paris: Les belles lettres, 1972.

Hexter, J. H. "*Il principe* and *lo stato*." *Studies in the Renaissance* 4 (1957): 113–38.

Holman, Christopher J. *Machiavelli and the Politics of Democratic Innovation*. Toronto: University of Toronto Press, forthcoming.

Honig, Bonnie. *Political Theory and the Displacement of Politics*. Ithaca, NY: Cornell University Press, 1993.

Hörnqvist, Mikael. "The Two Myths of Civic Humanism." In *Renaissance Civic Humanism*. Edited by James Hankins. Cambridge: Cambridge University Press, 2000.

"Perché non si usa allegare i Romani: Machiavelli and the Florentine Militia of 1506." *Renaissance Quarterly* 55, no. 1 (2002): 148–91.

Machiavelli and Empire. Cambridge: Cambridge University Press, 2004.

"Machiavelli's Military Project and the *Art of War*." In *The Cambridge Companion to Machiavelli*. Edited by John M. Najemy. Cambridge: Cambridge University Press, 2010.

Howes, Dustin E. *Toward a Credible Pacifism: Violence and the Possibilities of Politics*. Albany: State University of New York Press, 2009.

Freedom without Violence: Resisting the Western Political Tradition. Oxford: Oxford University Press, 2016.

Hulliung, Mark. *Citizen Machiavelli*. Princeton, NJ: Princeton University Press, 1983.

Hyde, J. K. "Contemporary Views on Faction and Civil Strife in Thirteenth- and Fourteenth-Century Italy." In *Violence and Civil Disorders in Italian Cities, 1200-1500*. Edited by Lauro Martines. Berkeley: University of California Press, 1972.

Inglese, Giorgio. "Introduzione," in Niccolò Machiavelli, *Il principe*. Turin: Einaudi, 1995.

Per Machiavelli. Rome: Carocci, 2007.

Institut für Marxismus-Leninismus beim Zentralkomitee der SED, ed. *Ex Libris Karl Marx und Friedrich Engels: Schicksal und Verzeichnis einer Bibliothek*. Berlin: Dietz, 1967.

Isocrates. *Isocrates I*. Translated by David C. Mirhady and Yun Lee Too. Austin: University of Texas Press, 2000.

Jacobson, Norman. *Pride & Solace: The Functions and Limits of Political Theory*. New York: Methuen, 1986.

James, C. L. R. *A History of Pan-African Revolt*. Oakland, CA: PM Press, 2012.

Janni, Ettore. *Machiavelli*. Translated by Marion Enthoven. London: George G. Harrap, 1930.

Jed, Stephanie H. *Chaste Thinking: The Rape of Lucretia and the Birth of Humanism*. Bloomington: Indiana University Press, 1989.

Jerome. *Letters and Select Works*. Trans. W. H. Fremantle. Grand Rapids, MI: Eerdmans, 1989.

Jurdjevic, Mark. *A Great & Wretched City: Promise and Failure in Machiavelli's Florentine Political Thought*. Cambridge, MA: Harvard University Press, 2014.

Justinus, Marcus Junianus. *Epitome of the Philippic History of Pompeius Trogus*. Translated by J. C. Yardley. Atlanta: Scholar's Press, 1994.

Jütte, Daniel. "Defenestration as Ritual Punishment: Windows, Power, and Political Culture in Early Modern Europe." *The Journal of Modern History* 89, no. 1 (2017): 1–38.

Kafka, Franz. "In the Penal Colony." In *The Complete Stories*. Translated by Willa Muir and Edwin Muir. New York: Schocken, 1971.

Kahn, Coppélia. "Lucrece: The Sexual Politics of Subjectivity." In *Rape and Representation*. Edited by Lynn A. Higgins and Brenda R. Silver. New York: Columbia University Press, 1991.

Kahn, Victoria. "Virtù and the Example of Agathocles in Machiavelli's Prince." *Representations* 13 (1986): 63–83.

Machiavellian Rhetoric: From the Counter-Reformation to Milton. Princeton, NJ: Princeton University Press, 1994.

"Machiavelli's Reputation to the Eighteenth Century." In *The Cambridge Companion to Machiavelli*. Edited by John M. Najemy. Cambridge: Cambridge University Press, 2010.

"Revisiting Agathocles." *The Review of Politics* 75, no. 4 (2013): 557–72.

The Future of Illusion: Political Theology and Early Modern Texts. Chicago: University of Chicago Press, 2014.

Kalyvas, Andreas. *Democracy and the Politics of the Extraordinary: Max Weber, Carl Schmitt, and Hannah Arendt*. Cambridge: Cambridge University Press, 2008.

Kamm, Frances. "Terrorism and Severe Moral Distinctions." *Legal Theory* 12, no. 1 (2006): 19–69.

Kant, Immanuel. "Idea for a Universal History with a Cosmopolitan Purpose." In *Political Writings*. Edited by Hans Reiss. Cambridge: Cambridge University Press, 1991.

"The Metaphysics of Morals." In *Practical Philosophy*. Edited by Mary J. Gregor. Cambridge: Cambridge University Press, 1996.

Kelsen, Hans. *The Pure Theory of Law*. Translated by Max Knight. Berkeley: University of California Press, 1967.

Kent, Dale V. *The Rise of the Medici: Faction in Florence, 1426–1434*. Oxford: Oxford University Press, 1978.

Kern, Fritz. *Gottesgnadentum und Widerstandsrecht im früheren Mittelalter: Zur Entwicklungsgeschichte der Monarchie*. Munster: Böhlau, 1954.

Kingston, Rebecca. *Public Passion: Rethinking the Grounds for Political Justice*. Montreal: McGill-Queen's University Press, 2011.

Konrad, C. F. "From the Gracchi to the First Civil War (133–170)." In *A Companion to the Roman Republic*. Edited by Nathan Rosenstein and Robert Morstein-Marx. Malden, MA: Wiley-Blackwell, 2010.

Kristeller, Paul Oskar. "The Philosophy of Man in the Italian Renaissance." *Italica* 24, no. 2 (1947): 93–112.

Kyle, Donald G. *Spectacles of Death in Ancient Rome*. London: Routledge, 1998.

Lahtinen, Mikko. *Politics and Philosophy: Niccolò Machiavelli and Louis Althusser's Aleatory Materialism*. Translated by Gareth Griffiths and Kristina Kölhi. Leiden: Brill, 2009.

Landucci, Luca. *A Florentine Diary from 1450 to 1516*. Edited by Iodoco Del Badia. Translated by Alice de Rosen Jervis. New York: E.P. Dutton, 1927.

Larner, John. *The Lords of Romagna*. London: Macmillan, 1965.

"Order and Disorder in Romagna, 1450–1500." In *Violence and Civil Disorders in Italian Cities, 1200–1500*. Edited by Lauro Martines. Berkeley: University of California Press, 1972.

Lefort, Claude. "The Permanence of the Theologico-Political?" In *Democracy and Political Theory*. Translated by David Macey. Cambridge: Polity, 1988.

Machiavelli in the Making. Translated by Michael B. Smith. Evanston, IL: Northwestern University Press, 2012.

Leibovici, Martine. "From Fight to Debate: Machiavelli and the Revolt of the Ciompi." *Philosophy & Social Criticism* 28, no. 6 (2002): 647–60.

Lintott, Andrew. "The Tradition of Violence in the Annals of the Early Roman Republic." *Historia: Zeitschrift für Alte Geschichte* 19, no. 1 (1970): 12–29.

"Cruelty in the Political Life of the Ancient World." In *Crudelitas: The Politics of Cruelty in the Ancient and Medieval World*. Edited by Toivo Viljamaa, Asko Timonen, and Christian Krötzl. Krems: Medium Aevum Quotidianum, 1992.

Violence in Republican Rome. Oxford: Oxford University Press, 1999.

Lorenz, Konrad. *On Aggression*. Translated by Marjorie Kerr Wilson. New York: Harcourt Brace Jovanovich, 1974.

Löwith, Karl. *Meaning in History*. Chicago: University of Chicago Press, 1949.

Lukes, Timothy J. "Lionizing Machiavelli." *American Political Science Review* 95, no. 3 (2001): 561–75.

"Martialing Machiavelli: Reassessing the Military Reflections." *The Journal of Politics* 66, no. 4 (2004): 1089–1108.

Lynch, Christopher. "Interpretive Essay." In Niccolò Machiavelli, *Art of War*. Chicago: University of Chicago Press, 2003.

MacKinnon, Catharine A. *Toward a Feminist Theory of the State*. Cambridge, MA: Harvard University Press, 1989.

Maher, Amanda. "What Skinner Misses About Machiavelli's Freedom: Inequality, Corruption, and the Institutional Origins of Civic Virtue." *The Journal of Politics* 78, no. 4 (2016): 1003–15.

Mahlow, G. "Lateinisches 'odi'." *Zeitschrift für vergleichende Sprachforschung auf dem Gebiete der indogermanischen Sprachen* 56, no. 1/2 (1929): 117–20.

Mallet, Michael. *The Borgias: The Rise and Fall of a Renaissance Dynasty*. London: Bodley Head, 1969.

"The Theory and Practice of Warfare in Machiavelli's Republic." In *Machiavelli and Republicanism*. Edited by Gisela Bock, Quentin Skinner, and Maurizio Viroli. Cambridge: Cambridge University Press, 1990.

Mansfield, Harvey C. *Taming the Prince: The Ambivalence of Modern Executive Power*. New York: Free Press, 1989.

Machiavelli's Virtue. Chicago: University of Chicago Press, 1996.

Marasco, Robyn. *The Highway of Despair: Critical Theory after Hegel*. New York: Columbia University Press, 2015.

Marchand, Jean-Jacques. "L'évolution de la figure de César Borgia dans la pensée de Machiavel." *Schweizerische Zeitschrift für Geschichte / Revue suisse d'histoire* 19, no. 2 (1969): 327–55.

Niccolò Machiavelli. I primi scritti politici (1499–1512): Nascita di un pensiero e di uno stile. Padua: Antenore, 1975.

"Da Livio a Machiavelli. Annibale e Scipione in *Principe*, XVII." *Parole Rubate: Rivista Internazionale di Studi sulla Citazione* 7, no. 13 (2016): 33–49.

Maritain, Jacques. "The End of Machiavellianism." In *The Range of Reason*. New York: Scribner, 1952.

Martelli, Mario. "Introduzione," in Niccolò Machiavelli, *Il principe*. Rome: Salerno, 2006.

Martines, Lauro. *April Blood: Florence and the Plot against the Medici*. Oxford: Oxford University Press, 2003.

Martinez, Ronald L. "Machiavelli and Traditions of Renaissance Theater." In *The Cambridge Companion to Machiavelli*. Edited by John M. Najemy. Cambridge: Cambridge University Press, 2010.

Matthes, Melissa M. *The Rape of Lucretia and the Founding of Republics*. University Park: Pennsylvania State University Press, 2000.

Mattingly, Garrett. "The Prince: Political Science or Political Satire?" *The American Scholar* 27 (1958): 482–91.

McCanles, Michael. "Machiavelli's 'Principe' and the Textualization of History." *MLN* 97, no. 1 (1982): 1–18.

McCormick, John P. "Machiavelli and the Gracchi: Prudence, Violence, and Redistribution." *Global Crime* 10, no. 4 (2009): 298–305.

Machiavellian Democracy. Cambridge: Cambridge University Press, 2011.

"Prophetic Statebuilding: Machiavelli and the Passion of the Duke." *Representations* 115, no. 1 (2011): 1–19.

"Machiavelli's Greek Tyrant as Republican Reformer." In *The Radical Machiavelli: Politics, Philosophy, and Language*. Edited by Filippo Del Lucchese, Fabio Frosini, and Vittorio Morfino. Leiden: Brill, 2015.

"Machiavelli's Agathocles: From Criminal Example to Princely Exemplum." In *Exemplarity and Singularity: Thinking through Particulars in Philosophy, Literature, and Law*. Edited by Michèle Lowrie and Susanne Lüdemann. London: Routledge, 2015.

"Machiavelli's Inglorious Tyrants: On Agathocles, Scipio and Unmerited Glory." *History of Political Thought* 36, no. 1 (2015): 29–52.

"On the Myth of a Conservative Turn in Machiavelli's *Florentine Histories*." In *Machiavelli on Liberty and Conflict: Commemorating the 500th Anniversary of The Prince*. Edited by Nadia Urbinati, David Johnston, and Camila Vergara. Chicago: University of Chicago Press, 2016.

McHam, Sarah Blake. "Donatello's Bronze 'David' and 'Judith' as Metaphors of Medici Rule in Florence." *The Art Bulletin* 83, no. 1 (2001): 32–47.

McMahan, Jeff. "Innocence, Self-Defense and Killing in War." *Journal of Political Philosophy* 2, no. 3 (1994): 193–221.

"Torture in Principle and in Practice." *Public Affairs Quarterly* 22, no. 2 (2008): 91–108.

McQueen, Alison. "Politics in Apocalyptic Times: Machiavelli's Savonarolan Moment." *The Journal of Politics* 78, no. 3 (2016): 909–24.

Meinecke, Friedrich. *Die Idee der Staatsräson in der neueren Geschichte*. Edited by Walther Hofer. Munich: Oldenbourg, 1957.

Merback, Mitchell B. *The Thief, the Cross and the Wheel: Pain and the Spectacle of Punishment in Medieval and Renaissance Europe*. London: Reaktion, 1999.

Merleau-Ponty, Maurice. "Note sur Machiavel." In *Signes*. Paris: Gallimard, 1960.

Humanism and Terror: The Communist Problem. Translated by John O'Neill. Boston: Beacon Press, 1969.

Mindle, Grant B. "Machiavelli's Realism." *The Review of Politics* 47, no. 2 (1985): 212–30.

Minogue, Kenneth Robert. "Theatricality and Politics: Machiavelli's Concept of Fantasia." In *The Morality of Politics.* Edited by Bikhu Parekh and Robert Nandor Berki. London: Allen & Unwin, 1972.

Mollat, Michel and Philippe Wolff. *The Popular Revolutions of the Late Middle Ages.* Translated by A. Lytton-Sells. London: George Allen & Unwin, 1973.

Montag, Warren. "'Uno mero esecutore': Moses, *fortuna,* and occasione in *The Prince.*" In *The Radical Machiavelli: Politics, Philosophy, and Language.* Edited by Filippo Del Lucchese, Fabio Frosini, and Vittorio Morfino. Leiden: Brill, 2015.

Moore, Barrington Jr. "Thoughts on Violence and Democracy." *Proceedings of the Academy of Political Science* 29, no. 1 (1968): 1–12.

Morgenthau, Hans J. "The Machiavellian Utopia." *Ethics* 55, no. 2 (1945): 145–47.

Politics among Nations: The Struggle for Power and Peace. New York: Knopf, 1954.

Mouffe, Chantal. *On the Political.* London: Routledge, 2005.

Münkler, Herfried. *Machiavelli: Die Begründung des politischen Denkens der Neuzeit aus der Krise der Republik Florenz.* Frankfurt a.M.: Fischer, 2004.

Nadeau, Christian. "Machiavel: Domination et liberté politique." *Philosophiques* 30, no. 2 (2003): 321–51.

Najemy, John M. "Audiant Omnes Artes: Corporate Origins of the Ciompi Revolution." In *Il tumulto dei Ciompi: Un momento di storia fiorentina ed europea.* Edited by Istituto Nazionale di Studi sul Rinascimento. Florence: Leo S. Olschki, 1981.

"Machiavelli and the Medici: The Lessons of Florentine History." *Renaissance Quarterly* 35, no. 4 (1982): 551–76.

Between Friends: Discourses of Power and Desire in the Machiavelli-Vettori Letters of 1513–1515. Princeton, NJ: Princeton University Press, 1993.

"Papirius and the Chickens, or Machiavelli on the Necessity of Interpreting Religion." *Journal of the History of Ideas* 60, no. 4 (1999): 659–81.

"Civic Humanism and Florentine Politics." In *Renaissance Civic Humanism: Reappraisals and Reflections.* Edited by James Hankins. Cambridge: Cambridge University Press, 2000.

A History of Florence, 1200–1575. Malden, MA: Blackwell, 2006.

"Society, Class, and State in the *Discourses on Livy.*" In *The Cambridge Companion to Machiavelli.* Edited by John M. Najemy. Cambridge: Cambridge University Press, 2010.

"Machiavelli and Cesare Borgia: A Reconsideration of Chapter 7 of the Prince." *The Review of Politics* 75, no. 4 (2013): 539–56.

Naldi, Naldo. *Bucolica, Volaterrais, Hastiludium, Carmina Varia.* Translated by William Leonard Grant. Florence: Leo S. Olschki, 1974.

Nederman, Cary J. and Martin Morris. "Rhetoric, Violence, and Gender in Machiavelli." In *Feminist Interpretations of Machiavelli*. Edited by Maria J. Falco. University Park: Pennsylvania State University Press, 2004.

Negri, Antonio. *Insurgencies: Constituent Power and the Modern State*. Translated by Maurizia Boscagli. Minneapolis: University of Minnesota Press, 1999.

Nelson, Eric. *The Greek Tradition in Republican Thought*. Cambridge: Cambridge University Press, 2004.

Norsa, Achille. *Il principio della forza nel pensiero politico di Niccolò Machiavelli*. Milan: Ulrico Hoepli, 1936.

Nozick, Robert. "Coercion." In *Philosophy, Science, and Method: Essays in Honor of Ernest Nagel*. Edited by Sidney Morgenbesser, Patrick Suppes, and Morton White. New York: St. Martin's Press, 1969.

Olschki, Leonardo. *Machiavelli the Scientist*. Berkeley, CA: Gillick Press, 1945.

Orwin, Clifford. "Machiavelli's Unchristian Charity." *American Political Science Review* 72, no. 4 (1978): 1217–28.

Owens, Margaret E. *Stages of Dismemberment: The Fragmented Body in Late Medieval and Early Modern Drama*. Newark: University of Delaware Press, 2005.

Paggi, Leonardo. "Machiavelli e Gramsci." *Studi Storici* 10, no. 4 (1969): 833–76.

Pauly, August Friedrich and Georg Wissowa, eds. *Real-Encyclopädie der classischen Altertumswissenschaft*. Stuttgart: Metzler, 1890–1980.

Pedullà, Gabriele. "Il divieto di Platone. Niccolò Machiavelli e il discorso dell' anonimo plebeo." In *Storiografia repubblicana fiorentina: 1494–1570*. Edited by Jean-Jacques Marchand and Jean-Claude Zancarini. Florence: F. Cesati, 2003.

"Disputare con il *Principe*." In *Atlante della letteratura italiana*. Edited by Gabriele Pedullà and Sergio Luzzatto. Vol. 1. Turin: Einaudi, 2010.

Machiavelli in tumulto: Conquista, cittadinanza e conflitto nei 'Discorsi sopra la prima deca di Tito Livio'. Rome: Bulzoni, 2011.

Peil, Dietmar. *Untersuchungen zur Staats- und Herrschaftsmetaphorik in literarischen Zeugnissen von der Antike bis zur Gegenwart*. Munich: Fink, 1983.

Pettit, Philip. *Republicanism: A Theory of Freedom and Government*. Oxford: Oxford University Press, 1997.

Pitkin, Hanna F. *Fortune Is a Woman: Gender and Politics in the Thought of Niccolò Machiavelli*. Berkeley: University of California Press, 1999.

Plutarch. *Lives*. 11 Vols. Translated by Bernadotte Perrin. Cambridge, MA: Harvard University Press, 1914–1921.

Pocock, J. G. A. *The Machiavellian Moment: Florentine Political Thought and the Atlantic Republican Tradition*. Princeton, NJ: Princeton University Press, 1975.

Political Thought and History: Essays on Theory and Method. Cambridge: Cambridge University Press, 2009.

Poliziano, Angelo. "The Pazzi Conspiracy." In *Humanism and Liberty: Writings on Freedom from Fifteenth-Century Florence*. Translated by Renée Neu Watkins and David Marsh. Edited by Renée Neu Watkins. Columbia: Universiy of South Carolina Press, 1978.

Polizotto, Lorenzo. *The Elect Nation: The Savonarolan Movement in Florence, 1494–1545*. Oxford: Clarendon Press, 1994.

Polybius. *Histories*. 6 Vols. Translated by William. R. Paton. Cambridge, MA: Harvard University Press, 1922–1927.

Price, Russell. "Ambizione in Machiavelli's Thought." *History of Political Thought* 3, no. 3 (1982): 383–445.

Rahe, Paul A. "In the Shadow of Lucretius: The Epicurean Foundations of Machiavelli's Political Thought." *History of Political Thought* 28, no. 1 (2007): 30–55.

Raimondi, Ezio. "Machiavelli and the Rhetoric of the Warrior." *MLN* 92, no. 1 (1977): 1–16.

"The Politician and the Centaur." In *Machiavelli and the Discourse of Literature*. Edited by Albert Russell Ascoli and Victoria Kahn. Ithaca, NY: Cornell University Press, 1993.

Rebhorn, Wayne A. *Foxes and Lions: Machiavelli's Confidence Men*. Ithaca, NY: Cornell University Press, 1988.

Reemtsma, Jan Philipp. *Vertrauen und Gewalt: Versuch über eine besondere Konstellation der Moderne*. Hamburg: Hamburger Edition, 2008.

Renaudet, Augustin. *Machiavel: Étude d'histoire des doctrines politiques*. Paris: Gallimard, 1942.

Ricciardelli, Fabrizio. *The Politics of Exclusion in Early Renaissance Florence*. Turnhout: Brepols, 2007.

Ridolfi, Roberto. *The Life of Niccolò Machiavelli*. Translated by Cecil Grayson. London: Routledge & Kegan Paul, 1963.

Ritter, Gerhard. *Die Dämonie der Macht: Betrachtungen über Geschichte und Wesen des Machtproblems im politischen Denken der Neuzeit*. Stuttgart: H.F.C. Hannsmann, 1947.

Robin, Corey. *Fear: The History of a Political Idea*. Oxford: Oxford University Press, 2004.

Rodin, David. *War and Self-Defense*. Oxford: Clarendon Press, 2002.

Rodolico, Niccolò. *I Ciompi: Una pagina di storia del proletariato operaio*. Florence: Sansoni, 1980.

Roecklein, Robert J. *Machiavelli and Epicureanism: An Investigation into the Origins of Early Modern Political Thought*. Lanham, MD: Lexington Books, 2012.

Rorty, Richard. *Contingency, Irony, and Solidarity*. Cambridge: Cambridge University Press, 1989.

Rousseau, Jean-Jacques. *The Social Contract, and other Later Political Writings*. Translated by Victor Gourevitch. Cambridge: Cambridge University Press, 1997.

Rubinstein, Nicolai. "Politics and Constitution in Florence at the End of the Fifteenth Century." In *Italian Renaissance Studies*. Edited by Ernest F. Jacob. London: Faber & Faber, 1960.

The Government of Florence under the Medici (1434–1494). Oxford: Clarendon, 1966.

"Florentine Constitutionalism and Medici Ascendancy in the Fifteenth Century." In *Florentine Studies*. Edited by Nicolai Rubinstein. London: Faber and Faber, 1968.

Russo, Luigi. *Machiavelli*. Bari: Laterza, 1949.

Rutenburg, Victor. *Popolo e movimenti popolari nell'Italia del '300 e '400*. Bologna: Il Mulino, 1971.

Sabia, Daniel R. "Machiavelli's Soderini and the Problem of Necessity." *The Social Science Journal* 38 (2001): 53–67.

Sacerdote, Gustavo. *Cesare Borgia: La sua vita, la sua famiglia, i suoi tempi*. Milan: Rizzoli, 1950.

Salutati, Coluccio. *Political Writings*. Translated by Rolf Bagemihl. Edited by Stefano U. Baldassarri. Cambridge, MA: Harvard University Press, 2014.

Sasso, Gennaro. *Niccolò Machiavelli: Storia del suo pensiero politico*. Naples: Istituto italiano per gli studi storici, 1958.

"Introduzione." In Niccolò Machiavelli, *Il principe e altri scritti*. Florence: La nuova Italia, 1963.

Machiavelli e Cesare Borgia: Storia di un giudizio. Rome: Edizioni dell'Ateneo, 1966.

"Ancora su Machiavelli e Cesare Borgia." *La Cultura* 7, no. 1 (1969): 1–36.

Machiavelli e gli antichi e altri saggi. 4 Vols. Milan and Naples: Ricciardi, 1986–1997.

Niccolo Machiavelli: Vol. 1, Il pensiero politico. Bologna: Il Mulino, 1993.

Savonarola, Girolamo. "Treatise on the Rule and Government of the City of Florence." In *Selected Writings of Girolamo Savonarola: Religion and Politics, 1490–1498*. Edited by Anne Borelli and Maria C. Pastore Passaro. New Haven, CT: Yale University Press, 2006.

Saxonhouse, Arlene W. *Women in the History of Political Thought: Ancient Greece to Machiavelli*. New York: Praeger, 1985.

Schmitt, Carl. *The Concept of the Political*. Translated by George Schwab. Chicago: University of Chicago Press, 1996.

Political Theology: Four Chapters on the Concept of Sovereignty. Translated by George Schwab. Chicago: University of Chicago Press, 2005.

Seneca, Lucius Annaeus. "On Mercy." In *Moral and Political Essays*. Translated by John M. Cooper and J. F. Procopé. Cambridge: Cambridge University Press, 1995.

Shklar, Judith N. *Ordinary Vices*. Cambridge, MA: Harvard University Press, 1984.

Silvano, Giovanni. "Florentine Republicanism in the Early Sixteenth Century." In *Machiavelli and Republicanism*. Edited by Gisela Bock, Quentin Skinner, and Maurizio Viroli. Cambridge: Cambridge University Press, 1990.

Singleton, Charles S. "The Perspective of Art." *The Kenyon Review* 15, no. 2 (1953): 169–89.

Skinner, Quentin. *The Foundations of Modern Political Thought*. 2 Vols. Cambridge: Cambridge University Press, 1978.

Machiavelli: Past Masters. Oxford: Oxford University Press, 1981.

"Introduction." In Niccolò Machiavelli, *The Prince*. Translated by Quentin Skinner and Russell Price. Cambridge: Cambridge University Press, 1988.

Visions of Politics: Renaissance Virtues. Cambridge: Cambridge University Press, 2002.

Sorel, Georges. *Reflections on Violence*. Translated by Jennifer Jennings. Cambridge: Cambridge University Press, 1999.

Spackman, Barbara. "Politics on the Warpath: Machiavelli's Art of War." In *Machiavelli and the Discourse of Literature*. Edited by Albert Russell Ascoli and Victoria Kahn. Ithaca, NY: Cornell University Press, 1993.

Spierenburg, Pieter. "The Body and the State: Early Modern Europe." In *The Oxford History of the Prison*. Edited by Norval Morris and David J. Rothman. Oxford: Oxford University Press, 1995.

Spinoza, Benedictus de. *Political Treatise*. Complete Works. Translated by Samuel Shirley. Edited by Michael L. Morgan. Indianapolis: Hackett, 2002.

Stacey, Peter. *Roman Monarchy and the Renaissance Prince*. Cambridge: Cambridge University Press, 2007.

"Definition, Division, and Difference in Machiavelli's Political Philosophy." *Journal of the History of Ideas* 75, no. 2 (2014): 189–212.

Stella, Alessandro. *La révolte des Ciompi: Les hommes, les lieux, le travail*. Paris: Éditions de l'École des Hautes Études en Sciences Sociales, 1993.

Strauss, Leo. *Thoughts on Machiavelli*. Chicago: University of Chicago Press, 1958.

On Tyranny. London: Glencoe, 1963.

Struever, Nancy S. *Theory as Practice: Ethical Inquiry in the Renaissance*. Chicago: University of Chicago Press, 1992.

Sullivan, Vickie B. *Machiavelli's Three Romes: Religion, Human Liberty and Politics Reformed*. De Kalb: Northern Illinois University Press, 1996.

Tacitus, Cornelius, *Histories*. Translated by Clifford H. Moore. 2 Volumes. Cambridge, MA: Harvard University Press, 1925–1931.

Thompson, Edward P. "The Moral Economy of the English Crowd in the Eighteenth Century." *Past & Present* 50 (1971): 76–136.

"Patrician Society, Plebeian Culture." *Journal of Social History* 7, no. 4 (1974): 382–405.

Tilly, Charles. "War Making and State Making as Organized Crime." In *Bringing the State Back in*. Edited by Peter B. Evans, Dietrich Rueschemeyer, and Theda Skocpol. Cambridge: Cambridge University Press, 1985.

Coercion, Capital, and European States, AD 990–1992. Cambridge, MA: Blackwell, 1992.

Trexler, Richard C. *Public Life in Renaissance Florence*. Ithaca, NY: Cornell University Press, 1991.

Tuck, Richard. *Philosophy and Government, 1572–1651*. Cambridge: Cambridge University Press, 1993.

The Rights of War and Peace: Political Thought and International Order from Grotius to Kant. Oxford: Oxford University Press, 1999.

Turner, Victor. "Sacrifice as Quintessential Process Prophylaxis or Abandonment." *History of Religions* 16, no. 3 (1977): 189–215.

Vasari, Giorgio. *The Lives of the Artists*. Translated by Julia Conaway Bondanella and Peter E. Bondanella. Oxford: Oxford University Press, 1998.

Vatter, Miguel E. *Between Form and Event: Machiavelli's Theory of Political Freedom*. Dordrecht: Kluwer, 2000.

Machiavelli's The Prince: A Reader's Guide. London: Bloomsbury, 2013.

Vázquez-Arroyo, Antonio Y. *Political Responsibility*. New York: Columbia University Press, 2016.

Viroli, Maurizio. "Machiavelli and the Republican Idea of Politics." In *Machiavelli and Republicanism*. Edited by Gisela Bock, Quentin Skinner, and Maurizio Viroli. Cambridge: Cambridge University Press, 1990.

Machiavelli. Oxford: Oxford University Press, 1998.

"Machiavelli's Realism." *Constellations* 14, no. 4 (2007): 466–82.

Machiavelli's God. Princeton, NJ: Princeton University Press, 2010.

Vivanti, Corrado. *Niccolò Machiavelli: An Intellectual Biography*. Translated by Simon MacMichael. Princeton, NJ: Princeton University Press, 2013.

Waltz, Kenneth N. *Theory of International Politics*. Reading, MA: Addison-Wesley, 1979.

Walzer, Michael. "Political Action: The Problem of Dirty Hands." *Philosophy & Public Affairs* 2, no. 2 (1973): 160–80.

Weber, Max. *Economy and Society*. Edited by Guenther Roth and Claus Wittich. Berkeley: University of California Press, 1978.

Wirtschaft und Gesellschaft. Tübingen: Mohr Siebeck, 1980.

Political Writings. Translated by Peter Lassman and Ronald Speirs. Cambridge: Cambridge University Press, 1994.

The Vocation Lectures. Translated by Rodney Livingstone. Edited by David Owen and Tracy B. Strong. Indianapolis: Hackett, 2004.

Wegener, Wendy J. "'That the Practice of Arms Is Most Excellent Declare the Statues of Valiant Men': The Luccan War and Florentine Political Ideology in Paintings by Uccello and Castagno." *Renaissance Studies* 7, no. 2 (1993): 129–67.

Weil, Simone. "A Proletarian Uprising in Florence." In *Selected Essays, 1934–1943*. Edited by Richard Rees. Eugene, OR: Wipf and Stock, 2015.

Weinstein, Donald. "Savonarola, Florence, and the Millenarian Tradition." *Church History* 27, no. 4 (1958): 291–305.

Whitfield, J. H. "On Machiavelli's Use of Ordini." *Italian Studies* 10 (1955): 19–39.

Wilcox, Donald J. *The Development of Florentine Humanist Historiography in the Fifteenth Century*. Cambridge, MA: Harvard University Press, 1969.

Williams, Bernard. *In the Beginning Was the Deed: Realism and Moralism in Political Argument*. Princeton, NJ: Princeton University Press, 2005.

Winter, Yves. "Conquest." *Political Concepts: A Critical Lexicon* 1 (2011).

"Plebeian Politics: Machiavelli and the Ciompi Uprising." *Political Theory* 40, no. 6 (2012): 736–66.

"Violence and Visibility." *New Political Science* 34, no. 2 (2012): 195–202.

"Necessity and Fortune: Machiavelli's Politics of Nature." In *Second Nature: Rethinking the Natural through Politics*. Edited by Crina Archer, Laura Ephraim, and Lida Maxwell. New York: Fordham University Press, 2013.

"The Prince and His Art of War: Machiavelli's Military Populism." *Social Research* 81, no. 1 (2014): 165–91.

Witt, Ronald G. "The *De Tyranno* and Coluccio Salutati's View of Politics and Roman History." In *Italian Humanism and Medieval Rhetoric*. Aldershot: Ashgate, 2001.

Wolfgang, Marvin E. "Political Crimes and Punishments in Renaissance Florence." *The Journal of Criminal Law, Criminology, and Police Science* 44, no. 5 (1954): 555–81.

Wolin, Sheldon. *Politics and Vision*. Princeton, NJ: Princeton University Press, 2004.

"Max Weber: Legitimation, Method, and the Politics of Theory." In *Fugitive Democracy and Other Essays*. Edited by Nicholas Xenos. Princeton, NJ: Princeton University Press, 2016.

Wood, Neal. "Machiavelli's Concept of *virtù* Reconsidered." *Political Studies* 15, no. 2 (1967): 159–72.

"Some Common Aspects of the Thought of Seneca and Machiavelli." *Renaissance Quarterly* 21, no. 1 (1968): 11–23.

Woodward, William Harrison. *Cesare Borgia*. London: Chapman and Hall, 1913.

Xenophon. *The Education of Cyrus*. Translated by Wayne Ambler. Ithaca, NY: Cornell University Press, 2001.

Zancarini, Jean-Claude. "Les humeurs du corps politique." *Laboratoire Italien* 1 (2001): 25–33.

"Une philologie politique. Les temps et les enjeux des mots (Florence, 1494–1530)." *Laboratoire italien. Politique et société* 7 (2007): 61–74.

Zorzi, Andrea. "Le esecuzioni delle condanne a morte a Firenze nel tardo medievo tra repressione penale e ceremoniale pubblico." In *Simbolo e realtà della vita urbana nel tardo medioevo*. Edited by Massimo Miglio and Giuseppe Lombardi. Rome: Vecchiarelli, 1993.

"Rituali e ceremoniali penali nelle città italiane (secc xiii–xvi)." In *Riti e rituali nelle società medievali*. Edited by Jacques Chiffoleau, Lauro Martines, and Agostino Paravicini Bagliani. Spoleto: Centro italiano di studi sull'alto medioevo, 1994.

Zuckert, Catherine. "Fortune Is a Woman – But so Is Prudence." In *Feminist Interpretations of Niccolò Machiavelli*. Edited by Maria J. Falco. University Park: Pennsylvania State University Press, 2004.

"Machiavelli's Democratic Republic." *History of Political Thought* 35, no. 2 (2014): 262–94.

Machiavelli's Politics. Chicago: Chicago University Press, 2017.

Index

accusations, public, 148
Aeneas, 116
Agathocles
  criminality of, 31
  cruelty of, 7, 72, 98–102
  spectacle and, 37
Agrarian Law, 149–51
Alamanni, Lodovico, 72, 75, 77
Alba, 162
Alberti, Leon Battista, 68–69
Alexander VI (pope), 38
Althusser, Louis, 15, 17, 111, 144
Antoninus of Florence, 90
Appius Claudius, 102, 109
Aquinas, Thomas, 89
Arendt, Hannah, 1, 5, 111, 114–16, 134,
  136, 139
Arezzo rebellion, 162
aristocrats. *see* elites
Aristotle, 4, 73, 80, 88
arms, 8, *see also* force (*forza*)
The Art of War (Machiavelli), critical
  readings of, 8
assassinations, 67, 91, 158, *see also*
  executions
Athens, 44
Austin, John, 81, 83
awe, 52

belief, forced, 84–87, 196
Bellamy, Richard, 14
Benedict XII (pope), 43
Benjamin, Walter, 120–21

Berns, Thomas, 115, 119–20
Bible, 54, 76, 126
bloodletting, 129
Bock, Gisela, 19
Borgia, Cesare, Duke Valentino
  admiration of Machiavelli of, 36–38, 44
  called Valentino, 39
  catharsis through Remirro's execution,
    51–58, 65
  as center of *The Prince*, 35, 198
  critical views of, 36
  execution of Remirro, 32, 99, 139, 182
  military conquests of, 38–39
  populism of, 108
  reputation for cruelty, 104–6
  spectacle of Remirro's execution,
    45–51
  state-making, 44–45, 64, 98, 100
  as tyrant, 35
  unification of Romagna, 39–43
Bracciolini, Poggio, 19, 141, 174
Breaugh, Martin, 187
Bruni, Leonardo, 19, 141, 173
Brutus, Lucius Junius, 91, 115, 131–35,
  138–39, 154
Buridan, Jean, 80
Burrill, Alexander M., 83

Calvin, John, 94
Camillus, Lucius Furius, 109, 162
Capitolinus, Manlius, 91
Carr, E. H., 13
cathartic violence, 51–58

Church, Roman. *see also* religion
  papacy, 40, 42–43
  saints, 54
Cicero, 27, 59, 95, 117, 141
Ciompi revolt, 170–91
  demands of, 171–73
  effects on political memory, 173
  historical interpretations of, 173–74
  lessons of, 177, 186–90
  limitations of, 190–91
  motivations of, 190
  politicality of, 175–79, 187, 191
  roots of, 170–71
  strategic use of violence in, 179–86
citizen army, 116, 158, 160
citizen-soldier, 8
city-state model, 159
civil principalities
  cruelty and, 100–2
  nature of, 36
  political structure, 142
  versus republics, 143
civil religion, 55–58
class conflicts, 30. *see also* inequality
  binary vs. ternary confrontation, 167,
    197
  Ciompi revolt, 170–91
  cruelty as anti-oligarchic tactic, 32,
    149–52
  emergence of plebs, 167–70
  plebeian exploitation of elite military
    ambitions, 159–60
  source of republican violence, 142–52
  state-making through populism, 38–43
Clausewitz, Carl von, 22
Clearchus, 182
Cleomenes, 101
coercion
  of belief, 84–87, 196
  contemporary models of, 32
  dissociation from violence, 192–94
  embodied materiality of, 195–96
  force and, 32, 79, 86
  necessity of violence for, 11
  relationship between force and law,
    81–87
coercive instrumentalism, 21–23
common good (*bene comune*), 17
conjuncture, definition of, 14–15
consent, 82, 85–86, 195
Corazzini, Giuseppe O., 173
Corcyra, 108

corruption
  inequality, 19, 130–31, 156
  reformation of, 127–33
  therapeutic violence, 128–30, 157
  violence as result of, 149
  violence as symptom and cause, 127–28
Corvinus, Valerius, 153
criminal justice. *see* laws and legal systems
Croce, Benedetto, 11, 104
cruelty (*crudeltà*), 89–110
  appearances of, 103–7
  coercion and, 193
  definition of, 28–29, 89, 91, 110, 195
  foundation of states and, 32, 111–40
  as inhumanity, 89
  justification of, 98–102, 110
  modern conceptions of, 90
  of the people, 107–9
  reputation of perpetrators, 102–7
  Seneca's notion of, 94–98
  social status and, 32, 107–8
  triadic structure, 23, 196
  unjust, 53
  weapon of weak, 108, 181
  well-used vs. badly used, 38, 99–101,
    108, 110, 120
cultural hegemony, 135
Cyrus, 76, 84–85, 88, 112

David (king of Israel), 115, 123–27
de Grazia, Sebastian, 49
Dean, Trevor, 175
death penalty. *see* executions
Decemvirate, 102
deconstruction, 119–22
defenestration, 93
Del Lucchese, Filippo, 16, 19, 64
democracy
  defense with force, 75–78
  elite opposition to, 70
  governo largo, 76
  marginalization of violence as opposite of, 3
  plebeian, 184–85
demos. *see* people, the (*popolo*)
depoliticization, of violence, 9–12, 193
Derrida, Jacques, 6, 119, 136
dictatorships, 79, 146–47
dignity (*dignità*), 96–98
dirty hands problem, 5, 13–14, 104–5
Discourses on Livy (Machiavelli), 155
  compared to *The Prince*, 100
  corruption, 128

critical readings of, 9–12
cruelty, 107–9, 192
elites in, 40
fear, 167
hope, 59
imperialism, 161
institutional solutions to conflict, 167
institutionalization of violence, 143–47
limits of nonviolent conflicts, 149–51
necessity of force, 66, 76, 124
ontology of force, 78–81
proportion needed for effective force, 84
punishment, 61, 154–58
state foundations, 113, 117, 123
subject cities, 164
vengeance, 63

effectual truth (*verità effettuale*), 15, 63–64, 106
elites. *see also* oligarchy
biases against plebs, 177–78
Ciompi revolt against, 170–91
cruelty against, 94, 96–97, 102, 107–9
embrace of force, 71–75, 77–78, 87
instrumentalization of plebs, 191
populism, 16–20
positive view of force under Medici, 69–73
reformative violence against, 131–33
Remirro's attack on, 52–53
ruinous ambition of, 150–52, 160
strategic use of plebeian violence against, 179–86, 191
terms for, 18–20
empire. *see* imperialism
ends and means. *see* means and ends
enmity, discourse of, 68
Erasmus, 94
evil
cruelty as human, 89
moralistic discourse, 5, 10
tyranny and, 73–74
executions
assassinations, 67, 91, 158
of Brutus's sons, 131–35
as catharsis, 51–58, 65
creation of political memory, 133–36
death penalty in Florentine Republic, 92, 154
as demonstration of centralized state power, 44–51, 93
honor in, 97

as institution, 155–58
modes of, 49
popular or mob, 175–79, 181
as spectacle, 48, 93, 97, 139
as vengeance, 108–9
exile, inadequacy of, 133, 154
Exodus, Book of, 76
extraordinary and ordinary modes, 108–9, 118–19, 140, 155

Falletti-Fossati, Carlo, 173
Fanon, Frantz, 198
fear. *see also* passions
awe and, 52
Borgia's command of, 37–38
of God, 124
of plebs, 168
political role of, 58–61, 63, 82, 142, 153–54
punishment as mnemonic, 107, 157
turning to hatred, 61–63
Feldherr, Andrew, 132
ferocity, 45, 52, 90, *see also* cruelty (*crudeltà*)
feudalism, 40–41
few, the. *see* elites
Ficino, Marsilio, 89
Florence/Florentine Republic
Ciompi Uprising, 170–91
death penalty in, 92, 154
discourse of force, 68–75, 87
emergence of plebs, 167–70
Great Council (*Consiglio Grande*), 70
imperialism, 161–65
oligarchy, 70–71
opposition of nobility to, 70
patronage in, 154
pillory, 50
political character of, 66
potenze di plebi, 170, 182
republicanism in art, 126
Savonarolan movement, 56
Signoria, 38, 70–71, 92, 171–72, 186
Florentine Histories (Machiavelli)
cathartic violence, 51
critical readings of, 9
emergence of plebs, 167–70
hope, 59
imperialism, 161, 163
limits of nonviolent conflicts, 150
Marx on, 174
nature of plebeian violence, 181–83

Florentine Histories (Machiavelli) (cont.)
  popular cruelty, 107–9
  private vs. public force, 145
  state foundation, 123
  Volterran rebellions, 164–65
force (*forza*), 66–88
  on behalf of the people, 104
  coercion and, 32, 79, 86
  defense of democracy with, 75–78
  definition of, 27, 67, 195–96
  economy of violence, 78
  Florentine discourse of, 68–75, 87
  plebeian deployment of, 178–79
  as principle of movement, 78–81, 87–88
  purgative, 128–30
  relationship with law, 81–87, 141
  vocabulary of, 67
fortune (*fortuna*), 137
Foucault, Michel, 47
foundation of states, 111–40
  cruelty of, 32, 122–27
  determination through succession, 144
  empirical perspective on violence, 114, 124
  imperialism, 163
  influence on institutional trajectories,
    113, 197
  necessity of solitary leadership, 116–17
  paradox of founding violence, 118–22
  performative nature of, 125–27, 139–40
  political memory and, 133–36, 140
  political theories of, 111–13
  reformation of corrupt states,
    127–33
  transcendental perspective on violence,
    114
  transitions as giving form to matter,
    113–14
  transitions as transformations, 112
  women, 131, 136–38
Frank, Jason, 121
Frazer, Elizabeth, 21, 28
freedom
  elitist interpretations of, 17
  inequality as barrier to, 18–20, 149–51
  maintenance of, 143–45
French Revolution, 133

Gaille-Nikodimov, Marie, 114
gender
  feminist readings of Machiavelli, 10
  founding violence and, 136–38
  violence against women, 99, 131
  Gewalt, 120–21

Ghiribizzi al Soderino (Machiavelli), 64, 167
Gilbert, Felix, 69, 75
Girard, René, 54
Gorgias, 86
governo largo, 76
governo stretto, 71
Gracchus, Gaius, 148–50
Gracchus, Tiberius, 148–50
Gramsci, Antonio, 15–16, 34, 196
Green, Jeffrey, 184–88
Guha, Ranajit, 179
Guicciardini, Francesco, 19, 28, 42, 68,
    71–72, 92, 178
guilds. *see* Ciompi revolt

Habermas, Jürgen, 4
Hannibal, 109
harmony (*concordia*), 141
harshness, 52, 91, 154, 158, *see also* cruelty
    (*crudeltà*)
Hart, H. L. A., 83
Hartman, Saidiya, 35
hatred, 61–63, *see also* passions
  enmity and, 68–69
  as political resource, 52, 63, 183
  prevention of, 99
historicism, 14–15
Hobbes, Thomas, 58, 196
Honig, Bonnie, 121
hope, 59
Hulliung, Mark, 161
human nature, 12
humors, 129
Hutchings, Kimberly, 21, 28

imagination, 64
  engineering of, 32, 35, 46, 64, 98, 100,
    110, 161
  forced belief, 85
  founding moments and, 136, 140
  indissociable from cruelty, 110
  mercy and, 95
  realism and, 15–16, 103
imperialism, 158–65
  inevitability of, 159
  perils of, 160–61
  spectacle as means of incorporating new
    territories, 161–65
individuals, 144
inequality, 30. *see also* class conflicts
  opposition of Machiavelli to, 19
  plebeian violence as strategic recourse,
    179–87, 191

root of popular violence, 175–79
as determinant of violence, 18–20, 131
Inglese, Giorgio, 102
injustice. *see also* justice
    correction through violence, 51–58,
        65
    nature of, 10
    violence as, 26
institutions (*ordini*), 134, 145
    accusations, 149
    avoidance of violence through, 141,
        148
    Decemvirate, 102
    dictatorship as, 146–47
    harnessing of force by, 145–46
    magistrates, 146, 148–49, 153, 155
    necessity of, 125, 143–45
    plebeian violence as response to
        inequality of, 185–86
    public violence as substitute for private,
        145–46
    Roman Senate, 116, 131, 149–51,
        162
    Signoria, 38, 70–71, 92, 171–72,
        186
    tribunes, 148
instrumentality, 9–10, 22–23, 67, 81, 96,
    125, 140
irony, 57, 92, 101
irrationality, 95–98
Isocrates, 95

James, C. L. R., 190
Jefferson, Thomas, 119
Jurdjevic, Mark, 76
just war theory, 5
justice. *see also* injustice
    definition of, 10
    founding moments, 119
    good government, 42, 60
    as motivation, 177, 182
    punishment mechanisms, 49, 145,
        152–58
    tyranny and, 73
Justinus, Marcus Junianus, 125
Jütte, Daniel, 93

Kafka, Franz, 194
Kahn, Victoria, 85, 148
Kalyvas, Andreas, 21
Kelsen, Hans, 81, 83
Kingston, Rebecca, 61
Kyle, Donald, 96, 156

Lando, Michele di, 172
Landucci, Luca, 91
laws and legal systems
    establishment of, 119–20
    punishment mechanisms, 152–58
    relationship with force, 81–87, 194
Lefort, Claude, 12, 136
Leviticus, Book of, 54
Lintott, Andrew, 27, 96
literacy, political, 16, 25–26, 51, 64, 106,
    175, 197–98
Liverotto of Fermo, 37–38, 72, 98–100, 137
Livy
    Brutus's execution of sons, 134
    Brutus's overthrow of the Tarquins,
        131–33
    history as visual artifact, 132
    on murder of Tatius, 117
    on Nabis of Sparta, 31
    on plebeian violence, 185–86
    Romulus's murder of Remus, 116
    unification through law, 118
Lorqua, Ramiro de. *see* Orco, Remirro de
Louis IV (Holy Roman Emperor), 43
Louis XII (king of France), 67
love, 58–60, 126, 153–54, *see also* passions
Löwith, Karl, 55
Lucretia, 131, 138–39

Machiavelli, Niccolò. *see also* cruelty
        (*crudeltà*); force (*forza*); revolts;
        spectacle (*spettaculo*); violence; *specific
        works by title*
    admiration of Cesare Borgia, 36–38, 44
    critical readings of, 7–12, 17, 100, 161,
        179–80
    on cruelty, 32, 89–110, 195
    feminist readings of, 10
    on force, 32, 66–88, 195–96
    modern readers of, 30–31
    perspective on violence, 2–3, 11–12
    populism of, 75, 180
    realism of, 12–20
    on spectacle, 32, 34–65
    as teacher, 25, 50
    vocabulary of, 26–30, 79
    Weber and, 20–23
magistrates, 146, 148–49, 153, 155
Manuel, Louis-Pierre, 133
Marchand, Jean-Jacques, 78
marginalization, 3–4, 193
Martelli, Mario, 77
martyrological motif, 53–54

Marx, Karl, 174
McCanles, Michael, 48
McCormick, John, 55, 148, 150, 187
means and ends, 11, 43–51
Medici family
  discourse of force during restoration, 68–75, 87
  revenge on Pazzi conspirators, 91–94, 106
Medici, Cosimo de', 71, 93, 154
Medici, Giovanni de', 72
Medici, Giuliano de', 91
Medici, Lorenzo de', 71, 91, 93, 154, 164
Medici, Piero de', 74
Meinecke, Friedrich, 79, 104
memory, political, 133–36
  Ciompi Uprising's effects on, 173
  founding moments as, 140, 197
  punishment as mnemonic, 157
  spectacle intended to create, 194, 196
mercenaries, 39
mercy, 94–95
Merleau-Ponty, Maurice, 7, 89
military studies, 8, *see also* wars and warfare
modes (*modi*), 125, 134, 144, *see also* institutions (*ordini*)
  extraordinary and ordinary, 108–9, 118–19, 140, 155
monarchy, 73, 94–95, 116, 131–33
Moore, Barrington, Jr., 3
moralization
  of enmity, 68
  interpretation of critique of morality as, 104
  means of containing popular violence, 175–76
  problem of justification, 5–6
  of violence, 3–4, 10–11, 193
  as weakness, 77
Morgenthau, Hans, 13
Moses (biblical leader), 76, 84–85, 88, 112, 124–25
Mouffe, Chantal, 12
multitude. *see* plebs (*popolo minuto*)
murder. *see also* executions
  assassinations, 67, 91, 158
  in ancient Rome, 96
  of Remus, 116, 139
  of Tatius, 117
mythmaking, 123

Nabis of Sparta, 31, 98, 100–2
Najemy, John M., 172
natural law, 4, 74, 112
natural philosophy, 78–81, 87–88
necessity (*necessità*), 137
Negri, Antonio, 140, 146
Nifo, Agostino, 47–48, 52
nobility. *see* elites
Nozick, Robert, 192–93, 195

oligarchy. *see also* elites
  cruelty as political tactic against, 32, 102
  embrace of force by, 71–75, 87
  Florence/Florentine Republic, 70–71
  governo stretto, 71
  punishments of, 108–9, 182–84
ontologization, 3, 6, 193
Orco, Remirro de
  as Borgia's deputy, 41, 98, 100
  execution as catharsis, 51–58, 65
  execution as consolidation of state power, 44–51
  execution of, 182
  spectacle of execution of, 32, 48–49, 97, 99, 139
orders (*ordini*), 2, *see also* institutions (*ordini*)
orders, of violence, 1
Oresteia, 44
Orsini family, 38
Orwin, Clifford, 106
ottimati. *see* elites
Owens, Margaret, 47, 54

pain, redemptive power of, 53–54
papacy, 40, 42–43
partisans and partisanship. *see* patronage
passions
  definition, 23
  fear, 58–63
  hatred, 61–63, 99
  love, 59–60
patricians. *see* elites
patronage, 25, 39, 71, 154, 158, 169
Pazzi conspiracy, 91, 106
Pazzi, Jacopo, 92, 97
peace, 41–43, 57, 98, 104, 142, 158–59, 166, 191
pedagogy, 25, 47–51, 197, 199
people, the (*popolo*)
  cruelty of, 107–9
  divisions of, 136
  force on behalf of, 78, 104

long-term interests of, 100
management of passions of, 99
plebs as counterpart, 168–70
support of, as justification of cruelty,
    101–2
Pettit, Philip, 17
Philip of Macedon, 115, 123–26
Phocians, 126
Pistoia, 104
pitture infamanti, 50–51
Plato, 10
plebs (*popolo minuto*)
    cruelty towards, 102
    democracy of, 184–85
    emergence as political force of, 167–70
    exploitation of elite military ambitions,
        160
    limitations of, 189–91
    modern interpretations of, 186–88
    motivations of, 188–90
    politicality of, 175–79, 187, 191,
        197–99
    potenze di plebi, 170, 182
    strategic use of violence by, 179–86, 191
Plutarch, 125, 132, 148
Pocock, J.G.A., 8, 19, 29
poiesis, 114, 139–40
political crimes, 153–58
political literacy, 16, 25–26, 51, 64, 106,
    175, 197–98
political memory, 133
political realism. *see* realism
political status, 96–98, *see also* dignity
    (*dignità*,)
political theology, 53–56, 175
Polybius, 31, 161
Pompilius, Numa, 142, 156
populism
    justifications of cruelty, 98–102
    Machiavellian critique of, 180
    realism of Machiavelli, 16–20
    state-making through violence, 37–43
potenze di plebi, 170
practices (*modi*), 134, 144
praxis, 139
The Prince (Machiavelli)
    allegory of centaur to explain force and
        law, 82–87
    Borgia's unification of Romagna, 37–43
    cathartic violence, 51–58, 65
    centralization of means of violence, 43–51
    compared to *Discourses*, 100
    critical readings of, 7–12

David as example of virtuous prince, 127
elite grip on property, 150
execution of Remirro, 35–65
heredity, 137
justfication of cruelty, 98–102
justification of force, 142
necessity of force, 66, 76, 81
publication of, 47
Roman armies in, 158
state foundations, 113
princes, hereditary, 18, 131, 133–35, 137
private force, 145–46, 158, *see also*
    class conflicts
property, 149–51
prophets, of force, 71–75, 84–85, 88
public accusations, 148
public violence, 145–46
punishment, 152–58, *see also* executions
    extraordinary, 153–55
    of oligarchy, 108–9, 182–84
    pedagogical nature of, 47–51, 197
    of political crimes, 152
    popular control over, 153
    of rebellions, 163–65
    spectacle of, 155–58
purges (*purgare*), 51–58, 128–30, 163

radicalism, 15–16
Rancière, Jacques, 136
rape, 99, 131, 137–39
realism
    historicism, 14
    of Machiavelli, 12–20, 196–97
    populism, 16–20
    radicalism, 15–16
    technicization of violence, 4
reason vs. force, 69
Rebhorn, Wayne, 181
Recht, 120–21
religion
    civil, 55–58
    means of containing popular violence,
        175–76
    papacy, 40, 42–43
    political theology, 53–55, 175
    saints, 54
    supplement not substitute for violence,
        59, 84–86
Remus, 116
republican violence, 32, 141–66
    class conflicts, 147–52
    dictatorships as means of containing,
        146–47

republican violence (cont.)
  imperial, 158–66
  popular cruelty, 107–9
  punishment, 152–58, 166
republicanism
  in art, 126
  elite opposition to, 71–75
  foundation of Rome, 115–22
  Machiavelli on, 8
  political memory and, 133–36
republics
  effects of violence on, 141–42
  maintenance of, 143–46, 166
  social conflict as source of violence,
    142–43
  succession, 144
  versus principalities, 143
restoration (*racconciare*), 51
revenge, 62–63, 91–94, 106, 108–9, 182
revolts, 167–91
  Arezzo rebellion, 162
  elites as cause of, 152
  emergence of plebs, 167–70
  nature of, 33
  nonviolent, 148
  politicality of, 175–79, 187, 191,
    197–99
  strategic use of plebeian violence, 179–86,
    191
rhetoric, 5, 86
Ridolfi, Roberto, 37–43, 75
Rodolico, Niccolò, 172
Rome, ancient
  accusations, 148
  as basis for new states, 115
  corruption, 131–33
  Decemvirate, 102
  dictatorships, 79, 146–47
  foundation of, 115–23
  imperial expansion, 160–61
  political theory of, 4, 26–29
  public vs. private force, 145–46
  second plebeian succession, 185–86
  Senate, 116, 131, 149–51, 162
  Seneca's notion of cruelty, 94–97
  tribunes, 148
Romulus
  conception in rape, 137
  doxopoietic force used by, 84–85, 88
  as founder of Rome, 112, 115–22
  importance to Machiavelli, 76, 116–17
  murder of Remus, 116, 139
Rousseau, Jean-Jacques, 73

Sacerdote, Gustavo, 49
Salutati, Coluccio, 28, 73, 141
Salviati family, 91
Samuel, Books of, 126
Sasso, Gennaro, 10, 37, 45, 100, 116
savagery (*saevitia*), 89
Savonarola, Girolamo, 56, 70, 74–77
Saxoferrato, Bartolus de, 73
Scali, Giorgio, 108, 181
scapegoat motif, 54–55
Schmitt, Carl, 12–13, 55
Scipio, 67, 109
self-interest, 37
Senate, Roman, 116, 131, 149–51, 162
Seneca, Lucius Annaeus, 27, 59, 67, 89, 91,
  94–98, 129
Ser Nuto, execution of, 181
severity (*severità*), 91, 153–58, *see also*
  cruelty (*crudeltà*)
sexual violence, 99, 131, 137–39
Sforza, Caterina, 137
Shklar, Judith, 90
Siculus, Diodorus, 125–26
Signoria, 38, 70–71, 92, 171–72, 186
Silvia, Rhea, 138
Singleton, Charles, 139
Skinner, Quentin, 11, 17
Soderini, Piero, 66, 70–78
Soderini, Tommaso, 164
Sorel, Georges, 198
spectacle (*spettaculo*), 34–65, *see also*
  executions
  catharsis through, 51–58, 65
  centralization of violence, 43–51
  of cruelty for solidification of power, 92
  definition of, 35
  effectiveness, 23–26
  executions as, 32, 48–49, 131–33
  in ancient Rome, 96
  maintenance of status quo, 34–35
  as means of incorporating new territories,
    161–65
  passions of fear, love, hatred,
    58–64
  performative dimensions of cruelty as
    political tool, 96–98
  political memory, 194–95
  of popular vengeance, 182
  populist state-making, 37–43, 64
  of punishment, 155–58
  state formations, 125–27, 139–40
  triadic structure, 23
Stacey, Peter, 26, 67, 114

state-making
  Borgia's, 44–45
  founding violence, 32, 111–40, 175–79
  populist spectacle, 37–43, 64
Stella, Alessandro, 172
Stoics, 95–96
Strauss, Leo, 10, 37, 73, 115, 156
Struever, Nancy S., 50
succession, in republics, 144
Suetonius, 95
suicide, 138

Tacitus, 63, 95
Tarquins, 131, 138
Tatius, Titus, 117
technicization, 3–5, 193
terror, 58, 107, 135, 155, 157, *see also* fear
theology, political, 53–56, 175, *see also* civil
  religion
therapeutic violence, 128–30
Theseus, 76, 84–85, 88, 112
Thompson, E. P., 177, 182, 188
Torquatus, Manlius, 109, 153, 158
tribunes, 148
Tuck, Richard, 4
tumults (*tumulti*), 167–91
  elites as cause of, 152
  emergence of plebs, 167–70
  nature of, 33
  nonviolent, 148
  politicality of, 175–79, 187, 191, 197–99
  strategic use of plebeian violence, 179–86,
    191
tyranny
  Borgia as tyrant, 35
  control of armies, 158
  David as anti-tyrant figure, 126
  definition of, 73
  dictatorships as, 146
  distinction between king and, 73, 95
  injustice and, 73–75
  politicization of plebs, 170
  unity and, 40–44, 147

unity. *see also* class conflicts
  hatred and, 62
  impossibility of, 136
  isolation as political mechanism, 61
  through fear, 58
  tyranny and, 40–44, 147

Valentino. *see* Borgia, Cesare, Duke
  Valentino

Valeriano, Pierio, 129
Valerius Maximus, 95
Vatter, Miguel, 45, 114–15, 117, 119–20
vengeance, 62–63, 91–94, 106, 108–9,
  182
Vettori, Paolo, 72, 75, 77
violence. *see also* cruelty (*crudeltà*); force
  (*forza*); foundation of states; tumults
  (*tumulti*); spectacle (*spettaculo*)
  cruelty, 32, 89–110, 195
  depoliticization of, 193
  effects on republics, 141–42
  force, 32, 66–88, 195–96
  formations of, 2, 32
  foundation of states, 32, 111–40, 197
  inequality and, 18–20
  modern dissociation of coercion from,
    192–94
  modes of, 26–29, 31
  orders of, 1
  pedagogy of, 25, 47–51, 197, 199
  political character of, 21
  as political tactic, 1–7
  realism and, 12–20
  spectacle, 32, 34–65
  structure of political, 20–26, 197
  subsiding over time, 7
  therapeutic/purgative, 128–30
  trajectories of, 7–12
  tumults, 33, 167–91
  unity through, 40–44
  women and, 136–38
violentia/violenza (unjust violence), 26–28,
  121, 195
Viroli, Maurizio, 16, 180
virtue: moral, 104
virtue (*virtù*), 64, 103, 143
  civic, 85, 141
  of leaders, 36, 127
  mercy as, 94–95
  moral, 60
  political, 25, 95
  wealth and, 173
vis (force), 26–28, 121, 195, *see also* force
  (*forza*)
vocabulary
  of force, 67
  marks and signs, 157
  political, 69
  reconstructing political theories through,
    24, 29–30
Volterran rebellion, 163–65
vulgarity, 73, 184

Walter of Brienne, Duke of Athens, 50, 52, 108–9, 170
Walzer, Michael, 5, 105
wars and warfare. *see also* imperialism
  balance of offensive and defensive, 159
  citizen army, 7–12, 116, 160
  distribution of military capacity among people, 158
  driving imperatives, 158
  imperial violence, 158–65
  mercenaries, 39
wealth, 19, 123, 152, 154, 161, 164, 173, 176, *see also* inequality

Weber, Max, 64, 144
  dyadic nature of political violence, 22
  necessity of violence to political organization, 21–23
  political expropriation, 37–38
Wolin, Sheldon, 1, 7, 76, 78, 104, 112, 193
women, 10, 99, 131, 136–38

Xenophon, 95

Zancarini, Jean-Claude, 177
Zuckert, Catherine, 52, 149, 156